W9-ARD-815

Inside Women's Magazines

■ **Janice Winship** completed a degree in Social Anthropology at the University of Sussex before beginning her research into women's magazines at the Centre for Contemporary Cultural Studies, University of Birmingham. She currently lives in Exeter and commutes to Wolverhampton where she teaches part time in the School of Art and Design at the Polytechnic. Janice Winship has written widely on popular culture, sexuality and representation; she is now writing a book on women's sexuality.

PANDORA PRESS POPULAR CULTURE

CRITICAL READERS

Inside Women's Magazines

Janice Winship

PANDORA
London and New York

First published in 1987 by
Pandora Press
(Routledge & Kegan Paul Ltd)
11 New Fetter Lane, London EC4P 4EE

Published in the USA by
Pandora Press
(Routledge & Kegan Paul Inc.)
in association with Methuen Inc.
29 West 35th Street, New York, NY 10001

Set in Ehrhardt 11/12pt
by Columns of Reading
and printed in Great Britain
by Butler & Tanner Ltd
Frome and London

© *Janice Winship 1987*

No part of this book may be reproduced in
any form without permission from the publisher
except for the quotation of brief passages
in criticism

Library of Congress Cataloging in Publication Data
Winship, Janice.
  Inside women's magazines
  (Pandora Press popular culture)
  Bibliography: p.
  Includes index.
  1. Women's periodicals. I. Title. II. Series.
  PN4836.W56   1987   051'.088042   87-13525

British Library CIP Data also available

ISBN 0-86358-166-8 (c)
     0-86358-025-4 (p)

For my mother . . . and myself

Modern capitalism beguiles with flickering lights, it mystifies with a giant kaleidoscope. We lose ourselves and one another in the reflected images of unrealisable desires. We walk into a world of distorting mirrors. We smash the mirrors. Only pain convinces us we are there. But there is still more glass. Your nose is pressing against the glass, the object suddenly finds herself peeping at herself. There is the possibility of a moment of illumination.

Sheila Rowbotham, 1971,
Women's Liberation and the New Politics

Contents

Contents

Illustrations

Preface

On and off I've been doing research on women's magazines since 1969, originally for an undergraduate dissertation and then for a PhD. For about the same number of years I've also thought of myself as a feminist. It was never easy, however, to integrate those two concerns. Admitting within feminist circles that I was doing research on – of all things – women's magazines used to make me feel just as comfortable as when I hastily muttered an explanation of my 'study' to politely inquiring friends of my parents: 'Oh, you're going to work on women's magazines are you dear, when you've finished?', silently voicing, I believed, 'What *is* the education system coming to . . ..' Whether feminist friends voiced it or not I felt they were thinking that if I really had to do research (intellectual work has always been somewhat ambiguously tolerated in the women's movement) I should do it on something more important politically: 'Surely we all know women's magazines demean women and solely benefit capitalist profits. What more is there to say?' I experienced myself as a misfitting renegade who rarely dared to speak up for magazines, however weakly.

Yet I continued to believe that it was as important to understand what women's magazines were about as it was, say, to understand how sex discrimination operated in the workplace. I felt that to simply dismiss women's magazines was also to dismiss the lives of millions of women who read and enjoyed them each week. More than that, *I* still enjoyed them, found them useful and escaped with them. And I knew I couldn't be the only feminist who was a 'closet' reader.

That didn't mean I wasn't critical of them. I was (and am) but it was just that double edge – my simultaneous attraction and rejection – which seemed to me to be a real nub of feminist concern. Many of the guises of femininity in women's magazines contribute to the secondary status from which we still desire to free ourselves. At the same time it is the dress of femininity which is both source of the pleasure of being a woman – and not a man – and in part the raw material for a feminist vision of the future. For example, we don't so much wish to throw off 'motherhood' as demand that it be assigned a worthier place in society's scale of tasks and values and that it be an option for men as well as women. Thus for feminists one important issue women's magazines can raise is how *do* we take over their feminine ground to create new and untrammelled images of and for ourselves?

Perhaps not surprisingly, given the conflicts I experienced, I never did write the PhD. But gradually, as the women's movement itself changed, I felt less heretical, and more certain that my convictions were shared by others. This book is the product of my being able, eventually, to express those convictions. In so doing I also wanted the book to evoke something of the pleasure of women's magazines. There *are* pics but alas none in colour and no glossy ads; I hope also that it at least verges on what I call a good read. However I wasn't really prepared for what this meant I had to do. I was taken aback by the volume of work I had to do *after* I thought I'd finished the book. Obtaining permission to reproduce the illustrations was my idea of a nightmare, and one that went on for a long time at that. Meanwhile there were significant developments afoot in the magazine world. Inevitably some of the detail in the book is already out of date although I hope the general arguments still hold. And I have attempted as far as possible to update the last chapter, which thus reads a bit differently from preceding ones, to take account of the most important changes up until April 1986.

What I owe to the women's movement and a long list of feminist writers will be clear enough in the ensuing pages. What I'd like to acknowledge here is my intellectual debt to the work of the Centre for Contemporary Cultural Studies at Birmingham University and to the teaching and inspiration of Stuart Hall who was its director while I was doing research. It was there that I learnt what marxism meant, intellectually as well as politically, and how to think about popular cultural forms like women's magazines. Though I may not spell it out in so many words, this book is a product of and, I hope, a contribution to that cultural studies perspective – transformed, of course, by feminism!

In the book's more recent history I'm very grateful to Iris Burton, Martin Richardson and Delia Cooke at *Woman's Own*, Malcolm Abraham, IPC's young magazines' publisher, Deirdre McSharry and Brian Braithwaite at *Cosmopolitan* and Sue O'Sullivan at *Spare Rib* for giving me their time and knowledge about magazines and a glimpse into their working environments. I'm indebted too to the BBC – or at least to Marion Allinson and Bernard Adams: if the former had not pushed to do the series *Inside Women's Magazines,* and the latter had not thought a sort-of-related book might be a good idea, and, more importantly, believed I could write it, I would never have written this. I'm only sorry that as it's turned out their programmes are long past but I've got their title.

My thanks too to the women in Wolverhampton who spent so much time discussing women's magazines with me for those programmes: Alison Phillips, Beverly Sand, Beverly Jones, Carole

Cannons, Stella Hurd, Jeannie Millichamp, Jean Woodhall, and Kay Swain. In a slightly different grouping they have become my women's group; a source of great support as well as of restorative good times while writing.

Writing is a difficult, if not agonising business for me and I'd like to thank those over the past years who've encouraged me and given me the confidence to go on, especially Rebecca O'Rourke, Sue McIntosh, Cath Hall, Ros Brunt and the Open University course team who produced 'The Changing Experience of Women' course (for which it seems now I did a pilot for this book). I'm very grateful too to Helen Armitage at Pandora, particularly for her calm tones at the end of the telephone when yet again the typescript was late.

Finally my love and warmest thanks to my friends who put up with my moans, bore me through the bad patches, discussed ideas with me and shared my minor triumphs: Lucy Bland, Chris Hardy, Rae Harrison, Angela Lloyd and Maureen McNeil, and especially Myra Connell, Bob Lumley and Charlotte Brunsdon who bore the biggest brunt of it all.

Acknowledgments

The Author and Publishers would like to thank the following for permission to reprint copyright material: Syndication International, *Woman's Weekly*, *19*, *Woman*, *Woman's Own*, *Options*, *Honey*, *Woman's Realm*, *Woman's World*, D.C. Thompson Ltd, *My Weekly*, *The People's Friend*, The National Magazine Company, *Company*, *Cosmopolitan*, *She*, *Good Housekeeping*, *Over 21*, International Thomson Publishing Ltd, *Family Circle*, *Living*, *Spare Rib*, *Mayfair*, Lever Brothers Ltd for the Vim advertisement in *Woman*, J. Walter Thompson and Co. for the Horlicks advertisement in *Woman*, Berlei (U.K.) Ltd and Sharps Advertising Ltd for the Berlei advertisement in *Cosmopolitan*, Boase Massimi Pollitt Advertising for the Deep Fresh advertisement in *Good Housekeeping*, *The Daily Telegraph* for material in *The Director*, *Mayfair* for the advertisement in *Campaign*, Rex Features Ltd for the photograph of Jane Warner by Richard Fitzgerald in *The Daily Star*, and the Central Office of Information for the 'Report to the Women of Britain'. Thanks also to Roy Peters for photographing the following: Figs. 1.5a; 1.5b; 1.6; 2.3a; 2.3b; 2.3c; 2.3d; 2.7a; 2.7b; 3.1a; 3.1b; 3.2. Every effort has been made to trace the copyright holders of the illustrations reproduced in this book; unfortunately, in some cases this has proved to be impossible. The Author and Publishers would be pleased to hear from any copyright holders they have not been able to contact and to print due acknowledgments in the next edition.

Chapter 1	# Introduction: survival skills and daydreams

'My story . . .'

My earliest memories of women's magazines are of reading about the mild adventures of the Robin family – Roley, Rosemary, Mr and Mrs Robin – a children's spot in *Woman's Weekly*. My father had his *Daily Telegraph*, dropping through the letter box each day, the *Express* on Sundays; my mother had *Woman's Weekly*, once a week, on Mondays. It used to be unopened until she'd done the weekly wash. Eternally youthful, the Robin family is still going strong thirty years on; less so, my mother is still a loyal reader of *Woman's Weekly*.

1.1a   *Woman's Weekly*, 6 August 1955

1.1b   *Woman's Weekly*, 4 June 1983

Towards adolescence I began to read romance comics, like *Roxy* and *Valentine*, at a friend's house. I would never have dared to ask my parents if *I* could take one of these comics – they were much too risqué – and anyway, intellectual aspirant that I was, I wasn't sure they were 'good' for me either. Around this time too

1.2   *Valentine* cover, 2 January
1960

women's magazines became more intriguing as I tried to glean
hints of the mysteries of sex and, perhaps more importantly, seek
reassurance that my sprouting and increasingly alien body was not
in the first stages of some dreadful illness. It was disappointing
that my mother only had *Woman's Weekly*: a bastion of the old
order, Mrs Marryat gave little away on her problem page. But I
used to love the romance and adventure of the serials – all those
ones set in the bush of Australia, like Neville Shute's *A Town Like
Alice*. At the time this was one of my favourite books, mainly I
think because of one (or so I remember it) highly erotic scene in
which the heroine lets her sari robe slip to reveal and offer up all

her nakedness to the man she loves. Decorous to the end as always, with no more than a passionate kiss, *Woman's Weekly*'s stories were just as thrilling to me.

Less appealing was the fashion. Models with prim Marks & Spencers pleated skirts and twin sets, or smart two-pieces, with the occasional jaunty hat, and gloves, even in summer, seemed so old and maternal. It was impossible and horrifying to imagine looking like them, and I clung to being a tomboy, latterly always in ski pants and huge jumpers in sickly colours. Fortunately the 1960s arrived and, to my utter relief, Mary Quant's styles transformed young feminine fashion into something bright and bold that waistless and chestless teenagers like me looked good in; or at least thought and felt that they did. With *Honey* magazine

1.3 *19* cover, March 1968

presenting page after page of fashion for the 'young, gay and get-ahead' and initiating me into the ways and wherefores of Vidal Sassoon haircuts and Julie Christie's 'natural-look' make-up, the tomboy era was over. I particularly remember the first striking yellow and red cover of *19* in 1968. It provided a blueprint for a pair of bright red-strapped shoes, handbag and beret to match, canary yellow tights (or perhaps it was still stockings), which I used to wear with black culottes and a yellow jumper my mother had knitted for me from a pattern modelled by Twiggy.

In adulthood, when I eventually began to learn how to cook, magazines offered further stores of pleasure and use. My mother and I – for once having a common interest – would search patiently through piles of *Family Circle* and the ever-faithful *Woman's Weekly* for the chocolate-profiteroles-with-mandarin-oranges recipe (it had to be that or nothing) which we recalled seeing somewhere. Later on as a feminist I didn't stop reading women's magazines. Rather I kept quiet about it or made the 'habit' legitimate with: 'Well, I'm doing research on them.'

Today magazines continue to punctuate the routines of my life but I no longer feel uneasy about this. My weekly favourites, *Woman's Own* and *Woman*, have to be bought at Birmingham New Street Station before I get on the train every Wednesday morning. Then, before I settle down to work, I can flip through the pages for a quick visual fix, mentally checking out the delights for a later and more absorbing read. (Sometimes, I have to confess, I never really manage the latter.) But however awful the serials (and they often are just that), I always save them for reading when I'm curled up in bed. As for the offers, I'm a real sucker for them, not least because it's such an easy, lazy way to shop. I love the later pleasure of receiving the by then forgotten item through the post.

For a period *Cosmopolitan* was bought by one or other of the women in my household. We'd turn immediately to the horoscope, ceremonially reading each other's out loud. They are long enough to be very satisfying and always seem, disturbingly, appropriate. Generally, of course, we forget them straight away but that's irrelevant. Personally I have firm likes and dislikes in *Cosmo* and sometimes I cannot bear it at all. Its super-jolliness, its presumption that everyone is heterosexual and its commitment to individual success I find saddening, not ennervating. I avoid Tom Crabtree's 'On the couch' as well as many of the sex therapy-type pieces, but I lap up Irma Kurtz's problem page and love many of the tongue-in-cheek fashion pics.

Spare Rib, the women's liberation monthly, arrives at intervals with the mail. As the antidote to other magazines it has a difficult job to fulfil, and provides, I find, a mixed and prickly satisfaction. I'd never dream of throwing away issues of *Spare Rib*; many of the articles I will return to at a later date and use for teaching.

Nevertheless, perhaps because I'm so used to the visual turn-on and more hedonistic values of commercial magazines*, perhaps because I hope for so much more from *Spare Rib* and tolerate less than I do in other magazines, it as often leaves me disappointed as it does encouraged and excited. But committed as I am to the project *Spare Rib* is engaged in – supporting radical change to improve women's lives – I stay with it in a way I wouldn't consider staying with some other magazines.

She, for instance, with its too-large pages I find visually messy and cramped, and its jokey tone has no appeal for me. *Woman's Realm* and *My Weekly*, *Annabel* and *Living* are hardly my style; I have never bought them (except for the purposes of this book!) although in times of desperation I have been known to resort to them – in the doctor's surgery or waiting at the hairdressers. On the other hand *Company* and *Over 21* tempt me with their wet-look sensual covers alone and I will occasionally buy them; similarly, I buy the odd *Good Housekeeping* or *Options*.

For all my magazine reading though, I cannot say that I have found my ideal magazine. But then my desires for reading magazines, like my desires for the kind of woman I want to be, are perversely contrary. They sway between demanding the gloss, the dross and the hype of femininity, with its unlikely dreams, and finding just those qualities of commercial magazines repellent; they sway between hungrily wanting the sharp, informed and angry analyses *Spare Rib* offers and finding it achingly all too much. I don't doubt that I am not alone in feeling these conflicts about my wants, though their manifestations may be peculiarly feminist. Similarly I tell these personal anecdotes of my relation to women's magazines neither for their intrinsic interest nor for their uniqueness, but rather for what I imagine, at least in parts, is their typicality. My story is 'yours'; at heart it is a history of growing up as a woman. And above all, perhaps, becoming a woman is fraught with the pains and the pleasures of all manner of conflicting pulls. Not least women's magazines – as we'll see – bear witness to that. But for the moment . . . .

'. . . a story about men; and women'

Women's magazines, perhaps especially *Woman* and *Woman's Own*, have become as well known nationally in Britain as any of the daily or Sunday newspapers. Yet though a million of *Woman*'s 5 to 6 million readers and around one-third of *Cosmopolitan*'s, for example, are men, magazines are very specifically associated with femininity and *women's* culture. Indeed, it is impossible to think

---

* I use this description throughout, not wholly accurately, to refer to magazines other than the small circulation and alternative magazines like *Spare Rib*. The latter, of course, do have to maintain a commercial viability but are not in the league of big business and big profits like the rest.

about femininity and women without considering, among other things, motherhood and family life, beauty and fashion, love and romance, cooking and knitting – and therefore romantic novels, cookery books and women's magazines. It is difficult to envisage a masculine culture without contemplating work and careers, brawls in the boxing ring or on the 'real' battlefields of war, train spotting and messing around with cars, the pub and pulling girls – and therefore newspapers, hobby journals and 'girlie' magazines. No matter that not all women are mothers or read women's magazines, and that many men loathe boxing and have rarely glanced at a 'girlie' magazine; no matter either that feminism has chipped away at the stereotypes of femininity and masculinity, those versions of two genders are still profoundly influential in our experiences of growing up. Our lives as women and men continue to be culturally defined in markedly different ways, and both what we read and how it is presented to us reflects, and is part of, that difference.

The cultural image of father-reading-newspaper-at-breakfast, mother-busy-on-the-domestic-front may have been starkly present in my family thirty years ago. But it has not yet disappeared, either literally or symbolically (see Figure 1.4).

The same cultural gap can be seen at any local newsstand. There on the rack marked 'Woman's World' are the women's magazines which women are glancing through and buying. A short distance away is another stand marked 'Leisure' or 'Hobbies'. There are all the 'girlie' magazines, the photography, computing and do-it-yourself magazines (crochet, cooking and sewing magazines are, of course, with the women's magazines), and *their* voyeurs and purchasers are almost exclusively men. All this we take for granted as we amble or scurry through the shop for our own purchase. Yet those labels and that separation between a 'woman's world' and 'leisure' or 'hobbies' reveal much about our gendered culture. Men do not have or need magazines for 'A Man's World'; it *is* their world, out there, beyond the shelves: the culture of the workplace, of politics and public life, the world of business, property and technology, there they are all 'boys' together. Women have no culture and world out there other than the one which is controlled and mediated by men. The 'girls' are drawn in to support the masculine quest: 'boys will be boys' whatever the game being played.

Women tend to be isolated from one another, gathering together briefly and in small huddles, stealing their pleasures in the interstices of masculine culture so graciously allowed them: family gatherings, rushed coffee mornings or the children's events, and the occasional night out with the 'girls'. The tasks they immerse themselves in, the priorities they believe in, constantly take second place to the concerns of men. In men's

1.4 *Woman*, 28 February 1981

Everyone said they had the perfect marriage. But she did sometimes wonder if she wasn't expecting just a bit too much

presence women are continually silenced, or they are ridiculed, scolded or humiliatingly ignored. Thus the 'woman's world' which women's magazines represent is created precisely because it does not exist outside their pages. In their isolation on the margins of the men's world, in their uneasiness about their feminine accomplishments, women need support – desperately. As Jane Reed, long-time editor of *Woman's Own* and then editor-in-chief of *Woman*, put it, 'a magazine is like a club. Its first function is to provide readers with a comfortable sense of community and pride in their identity' (Hughes-Hallett 1982, p. 21).

Yet such is the power of masculine wisdom that women's magazines and their millions of readers are perenially belittled – by many women no less than by most men. As TV soap opera is to news and current affairs, so women's magazines are the soaps of journalism, sadly maligned and grossly misunderstood. Over the years critics have disparagingly opined that women's

1.5a   W.H. Smith
1.5b   W.H. Smith

1.6   *Mayfair* ad/*Campaign*, 8 July 1983

magazines are 'a journalism for squaws . . . you find yourself in a cosy twilit world' (1965); it is a world of 'the happy ever after trail' (1976); 'cooking and sewing – the woman's world' (1977); 'kitchen think' (1982). They lament that women's magazines do not present a true and real picture of women's lives: 'Why . . . does the image deny the world?' (1965). Worse, magazines are 'completely schizophrenic' (1958); 'experience and make-believe merge in a manner conducive to the reader's utter bewilderment' (1971).

But if the focus of women's magazines *is* predominantly home and hearth, if the world they present *is* a happy-ever-after one, if they *do* refuse the reality of most women's lives, if they *do* offer a schizophrenic mix – and none of these characteristics is quite accurate – then there are pertinent cultural reasons why this is so. I want in this book to delve beneath this simple and dismissive description in order both to explain the appeal of the magazine formula and to critically consider its limitations and potential for change.

If the profile of women's magazines is partly determined by the state of play between women and men, it is also (as indeed is the 'game' between women and men) shaped by a consumer culture geared to selling and making a profit from commodities, and whose sales are boosted (it's firmly believed) through the medium of advertising. As commodities, women's magazines sell their weekly or monthly wares not only by advertising proper but also by the 'advertisement' of their own covers.

Hidden cover lines: talking to 'you'

On any magazine stand each women's magazine attempts to differentiate itself from others also vying for attention. Each does so by a variety of means: the title and its print type, size and texture of paper, design and lay-out of image and sell-lines (the term the magazine trade aptly uses for the cover captions), and the style of model image – but without paying much attention to *how* a regular reader will quickly be able to pick out her favourite from others nestling competitively by it. Cover images and sell lines, however, also reveal a wealth of knowledge about the cultural place of women's magazines. The woman's face which is their hallmark is usually white, usually young, usually smoothly attractive and immaculately groomed, and usually smiling or seductive. The various magazines inflect the image to convey their respective styles – domestic or girl-about-town, cheeky or staid, upmarket or downmarket – by subtle changes of hairstyle, neckline and facial pose. They waver from it occasionally rather than regularly with royals and male celebrities, mothers-and-babies and couples. Only magazines on the fringes of women's magazines, like *Ideal Home* (concentratedly home-oriented and with a high male readership) never use the female model. It is no profundity to say that as the sign of 'woman' this cover image affirms and sells those qualities of white skin, youth, beauty, charm and sexuality as valuable attributes of femininity. In marked contrast *Spare Rib* covers break sharply with the stereotyped plasticity of the model face, and communicate immediately how far that magazine distances itself from such an evaluation of femininity.

There is one other important and defining characteristic of this cover image: the woman's gaze. It intimately holds the attention of 'you', the reader and viewer. Such an image and gaze also has a wide currency in ads directed at women and men, has a daily venue on page 3 of the *Sun* and *Star*, and appears on the cover of 'girlie' magazines like *Mayfair* and *Fiesta*. The woman's image in these latter is obviously caught up in a provocatively sexual significance. Her partially revealed body speaks the sexuality about which the facial expression often equivocates. Her gaze holds that of the male voyeur; but it is he who has the controlling look: to look or not to bother, to choose to be sexually aroused or

Left:

1.7a *My Weekly* cover,
11 June 1983

1.7b *Company* cover, April 1983

1.7c *Options* cover, July 1983

1.7d *Spare Rib* cover, April 1983

Below:

1.8a Berlei advertisement in
Cosmopolitan, June 1983

1.8b *Daily Star*, 7 June 1983

1.8c *The Director*, November
1983

to turn over the page. She is the object and toy for his sexual play. It would be pushing it to suggest that the covers of women's magazines work in quite this way. For one thing many completely play down the 'come-on' look, for another the covers are primarily addressed to women. Nevertheless, what I would argue is that the gaze between cover model and women readers marks the complicity between women that we see ourselves in the image which a masculine culture has defined. It indicates symbolically, too, the extent to which we relate to each other as women through absent men: it is 'the man' who, in a manner of speaking, occupies the space between model image and woman reader.

In fact few women readers will make an immediate identification with these cover images: they are too polished and perfect, so *un*like us. Paradoxically, though, we do respond to them. Selling us an image to aspire to, they persuade us that we, like the model, can succeed. For the image is a carefully constructed one, albeit that it sometimes apes a 'natural look'. The model is only the cipher, the (often) anonymous face for others' skills and a range of commodities to fill. As *Company* puts it: 'Cover photograph of Joanne Russell by Tony McGee. Vest dress by Sheridan Barnett; necklace by Pellini. Hair by Harry Cole at Trevor Sorbie. Make-up by Philippe at Sessions' (April 1983). Easy then, 'you' too can create the look – given the ready cash. *Company* continues, 'Our cover girl look can be achieved by using Charles of the Ritz signature Collection for spring: complexion, Amboise Ritz Mat Hydro-Protective Make-up; cheeks, Cinnamon Glow Revenescence Cheekglow; eyes, Country Plums Perfect Finish Powder, Eyecolour Trio, Black Ritz Eye Pencil, Black Perfect Lash

Mascara; lips, Pink Carnation Perfect Finish Lip Colour; nails, Champagne Rose Superior Nail Lacquer.' Phew! Etched though the final image is here by the combined talents of men and the myriad make-up offerings of consumer culture, it also offers 'you' hope – of sorts: she is 'successful'; why not 'you'? It is a seductive appeal.

There is however, a counterthread to this image which perhaps provides the stonger attraction for women. Woman is placed first here; she is centre stage and powerful. The gaze is not simply a *sexual* look between woman and man, it is the steady, self-contained, calm look of unruffled temper. She is the woman who can manage her emotions and her life. She is the woman whom 'you' as reader can trust as friend; she looks as one woman to another speaking about what women share: the intimate knowledge of being a woman. Thus the focus on the face and the eyes – aspects which most obviously characterise the person, the woman – suggests that inside the magazine is a world of personal life, of emotions and relationships, clearly involving men and hetero-sexuality, but a world largely shunned by men. This is all women's territory.

More than that, the careful construction of the model's appearance not only points to the purchase of certain commodities but also covertly acknowledges the *creative work* involved in producing it, a work executed in everyday life not by the 'experts' but by women themselves.

The cover image shouts that this woman's world of personal life and feminine expressivity is one worth bothering about, engendering a feel for the reader that such pursuits are successful, and moreover bring happiness: the model smiles. Idealistic as all this is (some would say oppressive), it is less a denial of the 'real world' than an affirmation of how much women and feminine concerns are neglected in that 'real world'.

With the model's gaze on 'you', the magazine invites 'you' into its world. It may address you directly: 'Self-esteem': a little more will take you a long way' declares *Company*; or (You) 'Win a speed boat worth £4000' urges *Options*, the magazine 'For your way of living'. Like the language of advertising, these sell-lines for that issue's inside delights ambiguously address 'you' as an individual. There is the suggestion that the relationship being struck up is the intimate one between the magazine and 'you' – just one reader. The same is implied in the title *My Weekly*. This address to the individual is one I'll be returning to. Suffice it to say for the moment that it heightens the sense of, on the one hand, the magazine speaking to the 'lonely woman', and, on the other, the strength of the support the magazine provides for its readers.

What 'you' are also offered on the cover is a careful balance between practical items linked to daily life and those which draw you, dreamily, into another world. Regarded by some critics as 'conducive to the readers' utter bewilderment', this mixture of entertainment and advice has been consciously promoted by editors since the inception of women's magazines. For example, *The Lady's Magazine* of 1770 aimed to combine 'amusement with instruction'; *The Englishwoman's Domestic Magazine*, published in 1852 by Samuel Beeton (husband of that doyenne of cookery Mrs Isabella Beeton) and one of the forerunners of modern middle-class home magazines, combined 'practical utility, instruction and amusement'. More contemporarily, in 1976 Beatrix Miller, then editor of *Vogue*, remarked, 'We are 60% selling a dream and 40% offering practical advice.' And in the launch issue of *Options* in April 1982 its editor Penny Radford hopefully declared, 'We want *Options* to be a lot of information, a lot of help and a lot of fun. So enjoy it.'

Why should women's magazines offer this mix? Men's magazines seem to settle for one or the other: 'entertainment' ('girlie' magazines) or 'information' (all the hobby journals). But then men's lives tend to be more clearly compartmentalised and – often thanks to women's hidden labour – men are singular about their activities: they are at work *or* at leisure; they are watching TV *or* engaged in their hobby. Many of the activities women carry out – often several at once – cut across categories: at work they can find themselves 'being mother', entertaining visitors or giving the feminine (sensitive) ear to others' work problems; lunch breaks are devoted to the 'work' or 'pleasure' of shopping; running a home can be both 'work' and a 'hobby' – cooking and sewing are tasks which can eat up leisure time, while ironing can be done in front of the TV.

After my father had glanced through the newspaper at breakfast he would go out to work and my brother and I would rush off to school, but my mother would stay put. Working mainly in the house, she often had to take 'time off' there too. When we all came home she had to cater to our needs, switching hats according to our various moods, and moving from one thing to another as we each in turn wanted this – a clean collar (my father rushing out to a meeting) – or that – a hem of a dress pinned up (me) – even as she was baking, tidying up or doing her own sewing.

At odd moments in this many-faceted and disrupted routine she would snatch the time to escape into her *Woman's Weekly*. At other times *Woman's Weekly* would deliver 'the recipe' or the answer to a stubborn stain. Women's magazines provide for these rhythms and routines of women's lives in which private time and space are precious, work and leisure merge, activities overlap, and dreams and escape often feed on a modest vocabulary of everyday possibilities: modest partly because the horizons of women's lives are still limited and partly because women's desires are constantly forestalled. The predominantly masculine world neither welcomes women nor women's ways of doing things. Notwithstanding its (often empty) tributes to mothers and wives and page 3 pin-ups, it will do its damnedest to exclude them from certain domains, frighten them on the streets, hassle them in the pub, or stamp on their hopes and ambitions.

No wonder that women need the 'refuge' of women's magazines.

For their part most women tolerate these harassments because, whatever the costs of being a woman, there are also compensations. The balance sheet of feminine qualities far outweighs that of masculinity. Women do not want to be the kind of people men are and it is difficult to envisage *other* ways of being women (and men). Women's magazines provide a combination of (sometimes wholly inadequate) survival skills to cope with the dilemmas of femininity, and daydreams which offer glimpses that these survival strategies *do* work. They are dreams of a better and different life, but one that remains well within a spectrum of familiar possibilities.

The survival skills offered by feminist magazines like *Spare Rib* and *Everywoman* may be more political, aimed at getting women off the 'desert island' of femininity and encouraging their daydreams of a radical future. Yet the formula is similar. They offer help and, above all, hope. They present a catalogue, both sad and heartening, of women's ability to survive in a world where the odds are stacked against them.

A short guide

What comes next is neither a historical nor a sociological survey of women's magazines, although historical and sociological questions are by no means absent. Nor is it comprehensive. Regrettably, since they reach a more working-class reader than most other magazines, I have omitted romance story magazines from this study for reasons of space. So too teenage girls' magazines and 'the costlies' – like *Vogue* – are only briefly mentioned, in the statistics and tables at the end. What I do offer are some general ways of understanding, first, the place of women's magazines in women's lives since the Second World War, and secondly, the social processes and cultural codes which shape those magazines as a combination of 'survival skills and daydreams'.

The first half of the book explores these concerns, drawing across a range of magazines; the second half is devoted to a close examination of *Woman's Own*, *Cosmopolitan* and *Spare Rib*. I chose these magazines for personal and social reasons. Apart from just happening to be the ones I was regularly reading at the time, *Woman's Own* was the 'best read' weekly in Britain, *Cosmopolitan* one of the most successful monthlies of the 1970s and early 1980s, and *Spare Rib*'s radical journalism and commitment to the women's liberation movement influenced a far greater number of women than its circulation figures would suggest. In different ways *Woman's Own* and *Cosmopolitan*, too, had been concerned (as *Woman's Weekly*, *Woman and Home* and *Family Circle* – all with high sales – had not) with women's changing position and issues around feminism. Thus one of the underlying themes in looking at these three magazines in particular is to understand, on the one hand, the limitations of commercial magazines' feminism and also how and why these magazines have been so popular; on the other hand, what constitutes *Spare Rib*'s comparative radicalism and its relative lack of popularity.

The last chapter picks up where the case studies leave off. The mid-1980s have seen movements afoot in the magazine market which have brought new magazines to compete with *Spare Rib*, as well as with *Woman's Own* and *Cosmopolitan*, and brought fresh definitions of the category 'feminist magazine', no less than of 'women's magazine' more generally. As some commentators might put it, the mid-1980s marks the appearance of post-feminism, or of a social and political context which no longer requires either such clear demarcations between those who are, and those who are not, feminists, or, as a consequence, such disparity between feminist magazines and those more geared to commercialism. But the mid-1980s are also a period of even worsening unemployment and in direct and indirect ways this has exacted response from the magazine market. What I consider in this last chapter is this shifting profile of magazines as we move towards the 1990s.

Finally, in the light of all that I have discussed earlier, I contemplate the possibilities for a magazine which takes on board feminist questions but in a way none of the available magazines yet do.

Chapter 2

Looking back – with thoughts on the present

Women without a history

The history many of us were taught at school in Britain was primarily about European battles and colonial wars, governments and acts of parliament, building canals and roads and factories, and inventing steam engines. It more or less, hid people's everyday lives from view. Consequently this proud national heritage (there never seemed any doubt that it was something 'we British' should be proud of) had a spurious relation to the present. It explained *something* about Britain's place in the world: its imperialism, its agricultural and industrial structure, its monarchy and democratic parliament. It explained all this, however, as if history were some inexorable progress to a munificent present, just occasionally rusted up by the tyrannical hands of dictators. History had little or nothing to say about women.

Women cropped up as queens of England and Henry VIII's many wives, or as those downtrodden and supposedly immoral women who had to be excluded from coal mines, protected from working long hours in the 'satanic mills' of nineteenth-century England, and bludgeoned into caring for their families in a 'proper' manner. We learnt of a few spirited figures, like Joan of Arc, Florence Nightingale and the suffragettes – the Pankhursts and Emily Davidson – whose strident image was hardly one we were encouraged to respect (in spite of our debt to them for winning women The Vote). Perhaps Jane Austen, certainly not the passionate Brontës, was presented as both a woman of achievement and of estimable femininity. It was a motley canon and a fragmented sort of past to look back on from our state of nascent womanhood. We mostly forgot it.

Given such a tradition, or rather lack of, it is not surprising that few readers of women's magazines today have the faintest idea whether they even existed one hundred or two hundred years ago, let alone what they were like, who read them, or their contribution as the ancestors of today's magazines. Such questions have rarely been the stuff of history. When they have, as in Cynthia White's excellent study (White 1970), such books have tended soon to go out of print. Thus on the whole women carry out their daily lives with only personal histories having any meaning: life-time memories, the oral history passed on from generation to generation.

It is this currency of history that commercial magazines

Letters and Pictures

THIS is your page, so if you've something to tell other readers why not put pen to paper at once? You could win a "People's Friend" tea caddy filled with a pound of delicious tea.

There's a special prize for the writer of the Letter Of The Week. Our address is: Letters and Pictures, "People's Friend" Office, 80 Kingsway East, Dundee DD4 8SL. Please enclose a stamped, addressed envelope for the return of snaps and poems. All letters should be original and should not have been sent elsewhere for publication.

More Special Cloths

A RECENT reader's letter in the "Friend" concerning an embroidered cloth reminded me of the one that a friend of mine did.

Each time she had visitors to tea, she asked them to write their name and the date on the cloth and, later, she would embroider over it.

What a lovely keepsake and reminder of friends who have moved away.

— Mrs R. W., Preston.

Stitches In Time

IN 1936 I remember there came into my possession a royal sampler to commemorate Edward VIII's succession to the throne. When he abdicated I lost interest in working it and didn't finish it.

Now that I am handicapped I've found time heavy on my hands. So I unearthed the sampler from a drawer where it had lain all these years.

At last I have completed it and it is really beautiful. It has ER in the centre, with the crown on top surrounded by all the different flags, the Union Jack, Royal Standard and flags of New Zealand, Australia and Canada.

The Army, Navy, Air Force and Sentry Guard are depicted on it and also the rose and thistle. The royal residences, including Buckingham Palace, Holyrood House and Edinburgh Castle, complete the picture.

Fortunately I had all the finer stitches of the flags worked as my failing eyesight would not now have let me finish it. And as there is no date on it, it can apply to our own Queen Elizabeth.

— Miss A. R., Ballymoney.

LETTER OF THE WEEK

MY father was a Presbyterian minister in North London. We had a big Sunday school and I started going there when I was just three years old.

On the first day, we were all given a little card with a text on it which we were to learn. The next Sunday we would be asked to say it.

I rushed home to my father's study. "What does it say?" I asked.

My father took me on his knee and gave me a reading lesson.

"God is love," he said.

All the week I kept on saying it and on the big day I was all ready to say the text, but I wasn't asked.

I was a very young and shy little girl, so Mr James, our infants' teacher, thought he'd better not ask me.

I rushed home to my father, sobbing, and he took me on his knee.

"Did you forget it?" he queried.

"No," I sobbed. "I wasn't asked."

"Do you know it?"

"Yes," I replied. "God is love."

"Well," my father said, "as long as you know it, it doesn't matter whether you were asked or not."

I wasn't sure about that then, but now I do know it!

— Mrs W. MacR., London.

A Mother's Warning

THIS is an experience which happened to me some years ago. I hope it will help somebody somewhere to realise what dangers lie in everyday life.

My son Christopher was 15 months old, just walking, and he was beautiful. I had just made a cup of tea, when he ran into the kitchen and pulled the flex on the electric kettle, which fell on his head.

Christopher was taken to the nearest children's hospital with a burns unit.

The doctor said we could go in and see him and it was terrible. At that point we didn't realise how bad he was. His face was all puffed out. This was caused by the fluid in his body running to the burn area. He had tubes and machines attached all over him and the burns covered one fifth of his body.

We were devastated. I felt it was all my fault. I couldn't bear to look at his picture, just in case he never looked like that again. My husband was a great strength to me at the time.

Christopher needed grafts on his neck and shoulders. His face was saved because my husband had put him under the cold water tap, just after it had happened.

Christopher is five now, his face is perfect and the skin grafts don't bother him, but they are a reminder of what I let happen. He will always be scarred and I hope it doesn't bother him when he's older.

It's a pity people don't realise how easily these things can happen. They seem to be gambling with kettles and cups of tea, all in arm's reach of the little ones. I learned through experience. I think everybody could do with the knowledge, without the actual experience.

— Mrs S. N., Swinton.

Pot Of Many Uses

THE large, three-toed pot in the picture is nearly 100 years old. It was mostly used for boiling water for the pig killing days. A fire was built with stones on the outside and coal and wood was burned in the middle.

This large pot was then set on the fire. Filled with water it took a long time to boil, so the fire was lit early in the morning.

However, for a number of years now the pot has been used for quite a different purpose. It has been mended with cement and painted black and now houses a beautiful display of summer flowers.

— Mrs E. B., Orkney.

Get It Right!

*O*NCE, when I was baby-sitting for my sister, I stayed at her house overnight. The next morning my little nephew woke me and pushed his animal picture book in front of my face. Still half asleep, I pointed to a picture.

"Look, reindeer," I said.

He pottered off, climbed on a chair and peeped out of the window. I nodded off again, but back he came and pulled my arm.

"Not raining, dear!" he replied.

– E. W., Dalkeith.

Oops! My Mistake

DO other people's good deeds go wrong like mine? As I reversed back down the drive from delivering a parcel to a big house, my front bumper caught against the gate and left a large scratch right across it.

Not liking to leave it like that, I went into town and purchased a tin of paint and a brush and returned to repair the damage.

Alas, when I had done so, my painted piece made the rest of the gate dull, so back I went to town for a larger tin of paint.

Two hours later the gate sparkled like new and the lady of the house came out, as I thought, to admire it and thank me.

"I notice you've painted our gate," she said.

So I explained why I did it.

"It will be a surprise for your husband when he gets home, won't it?" I finished.

"It most certainly will," she remarked. "They are oak gates and we do them with linseed oil every two years."

— Mr E. J., Keighley.

Washday Thoughts

I WONDER what my gran would say
   If she could see me here today.
In my garden deck-chair sitting
With my feet up, busy knitting.
This is Monday, she would say,
Surely this is washing day?
But, dear Gran, I am not shirking,
Hear my automatic working.
Washing, rinsing, spinning, drying,
While I'm in the sunshine lying.
No more washday blues for me,
For this is 1983.

– Mrs M. W., Sutton Coldfield.

Do YOU have problems when you buy shoes?

Most people do, and indeed I know that most customers require and rightly expect advice and a good selection of footwear in their correct length, size and width fitting.

ALAN MICKEL
the footwear specialist

CLARKSTON TOLL, GLASGOW.
Branches Bearsden, Glasgow and Crieff.

themselves trade in. History is drawn on to affirm an identity in the present. The readers' letters' page, especially in the more traditional magazines like *People's Friend* (see Figure 2.1), are full of memories intertwining the personal and social – as in 'Stitches In Time' – in which the past is denied and taken over for personal and present purposes. Miss Ballymoney deliberately 'forgets' that her sampler commemorates the succession of the king who abdicated and sees it as applying 'to our own Queen Elizabeth'.

Sometimes bits of the past are recalled and described, but plucked from their context and socially unlocated, as in 'Pot of Many Uses': *Who* used the pot? Where? The result is to romanticise the past, to remember it fondly, selectively leaving out 'bad' memories – perhaps the heavy labour of 'pig-killing days'. And the pot's use in 1983 – to house 'a beautiful display of summer flowers' – only adds to the romanticism.

At other times there is a nostalgia for the past: people enjoyed themselves more, were kinder, more thoughtful and honest then. They had wisdom, too, according to the 'Letter of the Week'. More generally nostalgia can avoid the responsibility of living in the present and shaping the future: harking back is about neither understanding the in-between developments which have made the present, nor feeling implicated or having the power or say to make the present otherwise.

If nostalgia is not to the fore, then a notion of optimistic progress is. 'Washday Thoughts' celebrates just how far women have travelled along the line of history. Moreover it is this view – history as a gradual progression – which is the dominant one adopted in the relatively rare articles about history in magazines and usually occurring at anniversary times. *Woman's Own*'s golden anniversary issue, for example, offered pages from its first issue of October 1932, and commented:

> 'You'll be fascinated, as we were, by the prices – tea 1s (5p) a
> quarter! – the advice – stay beautiful after marriage! – and the way
> this issue clearly mirrors a woman's life in the early Thirties. As you
> see, we've come a long way since!'

History is the spectacle to be looked at from the detachment of an always *better* present.

I don't want to suggest that progress has not been achieved for women. Rather, I want to think again about history, about what it can do and mean for women. First, there is never just one history, but histories. The history lessons at school offered, broadly, a history of those who rule us. It started therefore from an assumption of the political centrality and importance of that group or class. A history which begins from a position of feminism, and is interested in the development of women's lives, is likely to discover other aspects and to view the 'victorious' history of rulers in a very different light.

October 15, 1932   WOMAN'S OWN   15

Looks <u>Do</u> Count After Marriage

Even More than Before ! Mary Carlyle is ready to give you practical beauty advice. Write to her c/o "WOMAN'S OWN," 18 Henrietta Street, London, W.C.2

sing self-pride and a willingness to take pains, need ever look drab or uninteresting. I will not listen to the little housewife who tells me she is so busy looking after the house that she has no time to "bother about herself." That is sheer bunkum and a woman with that point of view deserves all the heartbreak that is coming to her.

Well, let us consider the case of the busy housewife; the great thing is for her to plan her day so that there is a little time reserved at the beginning and at the end of it for personal beautifying.

I presume that you have to rise early, prepare your lord and master's breakfast, and see him off the premises before 8.30 a.m. Well, I suggest that you have a very pretty cretonne overall which you can slip

one word of warning about your hair. Don't get dusty hair, like so many young women who work in the house. With a scrap of gingham to match your overalls, make yourself three little dust caps such as that patterned on page 11. This will ensure your hair remaining immaculately clean despite any amount of dirty work and it will allow you to fix your hair with setting combs or curlers and conceal the fact until you are ready to remove the cap and face the world !

Do *try* not to neglect your daily bath and jump into it *after* all the housework is done. So many women make the mistake of sticking to the habit of bathing before breakfast and get thoroughly grubby afterwards ! It gives one a great feeling of

Don't let yourself "go"— especially in the mornings. Wear a pretty, crisp overall, and leave him with a good impression for the day !

MY DEAR READERS, I am so glad to be able to talk to you each week, through the pages of WOMAN'S OWN, on the all-important

2.2 *Woman's Own*, 15 October 1932, reproduced in *Woman's Own*, 16 October 1982

Over the last ten years or so feminist historians have scoured the archives to reconstruct a knowledge of women's past that we never knew existed. It makes both depressing and encouraging reading – depressing because the exercise has revealed that *other* feminists at *other* times have also had to rescue and re-rescue their past. The history of women is one of perpetual struggle, with the lessons learnt, and the moments of seeming victory, continually being lost for the generation that comes after. It is encouraging nevertheless that the knowledge enables us to understand the elements and processes which have made our culture and which, in particular, allow us to live in certain ways as women but not in others. Such collective knowledge can provide a strength for women to share; it is also an analytical tool with which to prise apart our present lives and begin to carve a different way into the future. It is this kind of historical approach that characterises many of the articles in *Spare Rib*: a history about the past but which has its thoughts on the present and its sights on the future; very much a political history.

A question of politics

For those who do not read or do not like *Spare Rib*, it is generally because of its political reputation: staunchly feminist and, it is supposed, socialist. For some, *Spare Rib*'s politics set it apart, unfavourably, from commercial magazines, which have always insisted on their non-political status. Until the 1970s commercial magazines boasted a non-party political alignment. In 1964 Mary Grieve, the editor of *Woman* from 1939 to 1963, stated that '*Woman*'s strong influence on the readership made the paper very tempting to the political partisans and both right and left wooed our support. My view always was that since the magazine set out to be the trade press of all women it was manifestly wrong for it to show any political bias' (1964, p. 53) She firmly believed that it would be 'a ludicrous exaggeration of feminism that in art, politics, entertainment, ethics or religion there should be a point of view exclusive to women . . . it would seem to me inappropriate to find in *Woman* a serious political article, as to find in the *Economist* a practical guide to weaning' (p. 177). As I'll discuss in a moment, in the light of her editorial role in the 1940s these comments read very strangely.

By the 1980s commercial magazines feature members of parliament in their pages, though it is usually their personal life which is under scrutiny. At most the magazines discuss issues pertinent to women, i.e. non-party issues, editors remaining wary of a party commitment. Yet there are slight signs that with some magazines' increasing involvement in feminist issues this may be changing (though I'm doubtful, as will be clear later, how far, or if, this process will go any further). Before the June 1983 general election, for instance, *Honey* sent out a questionnaire to MPs asking them what they would do for women if they were re-elected. *Honey* carefully asked them only about issues on which they could vote by conscience rather than by party line. Nevertheless the results revealed a stark disparity. As Carol Sarler pointed out in her editorial (July 1983), 'the differences between the parties has been vivid: it has become crystal clear that if you believe in radical reform on women's rights, you won't return the Conservative party to power. Even their female leader wasn't interested enough to offer us her view.'

Cosmopolitan, too, had at least one lead article at this time condemning the Conservative government's policies aimed at keeping mothers at home (May 1983) entitled 'Maggie's family policy. A plot against women?' Melanie Phillips concluded, 'Help to prevent it from being adopted as policy by writing to your MP.'

The dangers before editors who tread any vaguely political path is perhaps best illustrated by the sacking of Carol Sarler in September 1983, ostensibly on the grounds of *Honey*'s falling circulation (but then that decline had been widespread), more likely because of her efforts to introduce feminist arguments and ideas and, generally, a 'more thinking' editorial style alongside *Honey*'s usual fashion and beauty spreads. It is not improbable either that what could be seen as socialist sympathies also compounded her fate.

Whilst some forms of feminism *are* tolerated and supported in commercial women's magazines, the combination of feminism and socialism is not. The consequences of this I shall be returning to in the three case studies in chapters 6, 7 and 8. What I want to point out now is that opting out of the so-called political arena – whether of party politics or feminism or both – does not exempt individuals or magazines from assuming political positions. *Not* accepting a feminist politics is just as political in some senses as being an active feminist. The form the political takes, however, is of a slightly different order; it is about a commitment to certain ideologies.

By ideology – a term I shall use a lot in this book – I am not subscribing to the view of it as propaganda, i.e. what 'they' (often the Russians) inflict on a people who are given no freedom to know otherwise. Nor am I using it to refer simply to a set of doctrines, as it might be used in the phrase 'Conservative party ideology'. Instead I am using it to refer to commonsense knowledges to be found in newspapers and magazines, at the movies and on TV, and in scholarly books, which shape how people think and feel and act in their daily lives. One of the characteristics of ideologies is that from a political position 'outside' them it is possible to see ideologies as partial and selective, favouring the activities of some groups of people but not others. Ideologies tend to render certain aspects of life as natural, sometimes as biologically natural, but also as just what seems normal and proper, rather than as the outcome of social and historical factors. Seen from the 'inside', ideologies appear to be right and appropriate for deciding how to conduct one's life. And they do not seem to be about politics at all.

To give one example, a traditional ideology of femininity (which has by no means wholly disappeared) maintains – among other things – that women are 'weak and passive', and backs it up with sets of 'scientific' data, relating it to women's allegedly biological capacity for nurturing babies, and with empirical instances to demonstrate its objectives occurrence. Many other presuppositions go along with this knowledge: women do not fight in wars; in peacetime women need the protection of men; they do not work on building sites or become managing directors of multinational companies; they are not very good at certain sports, such as rugby and football, and so on. Girls are brought up to believe this of themselves and generally act accordingly. If they do not they tend to suffer for it, being disparagingly labelled as 'the wife who wears the trousers' or 'the iron maiden'. These beliefs and the associated behaviours therefore involve certain attributions of power and choice which are different for men than for women. To that extent questions of politics are implicit in ideology. So, too, are questions about history: How has this division arisen? Why has it shifted ground at various moments with women doing heavy manual jobs during wartime for example?

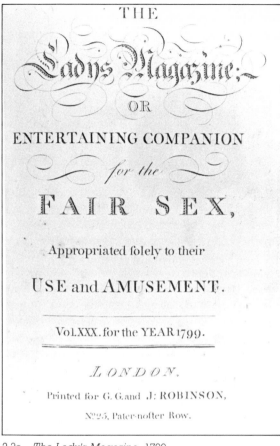

2.3a   *The Lady's Magazine*, 1799

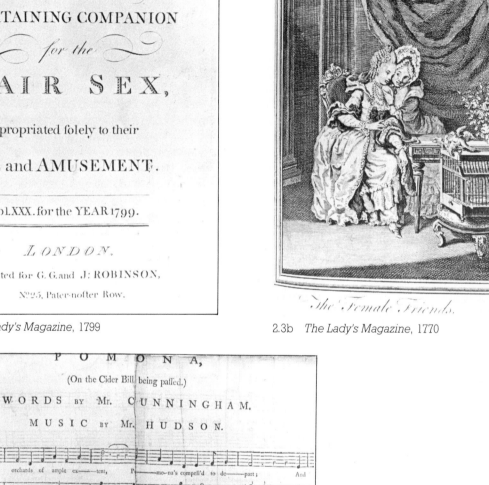

The Female Friends.

2.3b   *The Lady's Magazine*, 1770

P O M O N A,

(On the Cider Bill being paſſed.)

WORDS BY Mr. CUNNINGHAM.

MUSIC BY Mr. HUDSON.

Lively, but not faſt.

From orchards of ample ex——tent, Po——mona's compell'd to de——part; And

thus, as in an—guiſh ſhe went, The goddeſs un—bur-then'd her heart: To flouriſh when

li—ber—ty reigns, Was all my fond wiſhes re—quir'd; And here I agreed with the

2.3c   *The Lady's Magazine*, 1799

Right:
'Frock of bombazeen, the body made low and ornamented with a trimming of black crape . . .'.
The occasion for the dress was the death of the 'Royal Highness the Princess Charlotte Augusta, the daughter of his Royal Highness the Prince Regent, and consort of his Serene Highness the Prince Leopold of Saxe-Coburg . . .'

Women's magazines trade selectively in some ideologies and ignore others. Each magazine has its own ideological pattern offering knowledge, posing problems and providing solutions to capture its readers' hearts and minds. Such patterns have not, however, appeared out of nowhere: they are the product of many historical developments and are constantly being reworked to make sense and deal, as best they can, with the changing experience of women's lives.

In subsequent chapters I will look inside women's magazines of the 1980s to examine why and how they so successfully capture the hearts and minds of readers. I also want to prise apart their ideological patterns, as part of a feminist politics of understanding how inequalities between women and men continue to be reproduced. But first let us take a brief look at some historical developments.

Highlights

2.3d *The Lady's Magazine*, 1817

In her book *Women's Magazines 1693-1968* Cynthia White provides a very detailed and interesting history and sociology of women's magazines, tracing the development of their form and their readership. Irene Dancyger, in *A World of Women*, offers an illustrated history which enthusiastically, but uncritically, captures the feel of magazines. I direct you to both of these books. Here I merely want to highlight some of the key influences up to the Second World War which were relevant to the shape magazines subsequently took after 1945.

Though there were pioneer publications before it (the first was probably *The Ladies' Mercury* published in 1693 by a bookseller, John Dunton), *The Lady's Magazine*, brought out in 1770 and continuing until 1847, introduced the visual elements both pleasurable and practical for which women's magazines were to become noted. Aimed to aid upper-class women fill their lengthy, leisured days – these magazines were no guides to homemaking – the attractive 'embellishments' stood alongside amusing literary contributions, often titillating fiction or 'autobiography', full of virgins who are seduced, wives who take lovers, and heroes who commit suicide, and regular educative (but very tedious) pieces like 'The Moral Zoologist or Natural History of Animals'.

By the middle of the nineteenth century, however, the old class groupings and the position of women in English society had been disrupted and overhauled to form some of the major social divisions still characterising our society today. For our purposes one of the most significant changes to which the development of industrial capitalism gradually gave rise from the 1780s onwards was the establishment of a sizeable middle class – the manufacturers, merchants, professional people and shopkeepers – who worked hard but gained wealth, and stood apart from both the (allegedly lazy) aristocracy and their own often impoverished

23

and usually overworked employees of the new working class.

As the scale of manufacturing expanded, so was production no longer organised around the household where wives shared in the work. The 'workplace' – factory and offices – was separated from home. And whereas the former public world became the domain of men, the private world of the home – now associated solely with domesticity and childcare, and established as the retreat the master came back to each evening – became identified with women. Unlike their aristocratic counterparts, middle-class wives undertook to supervise and manage the running of their homes, and the care and education of their children. To mark that, in 1851, the Census formulated a new occupation: 'the wife, the mother, the mistress of an English family'. This family structure and division of labour between wife and husband was one which gradually became the model (if not the practice) for working class families too. The most respectable wife in Victorian times and for long after was one who did not work outside the home but was financially supported by a breadwinning husband.

Women's magazines documented these changes; they also contributed to them. By fixing a cheap price Samuel Beeton aimed his *English Woman's Domestic Magazine* at the burgeoning middle classes. It contained its share of fiction but much was also practical and domestic: 'How to treat illness: diarrhoea, dysentery and cholerine', 'Gardening' (since the middle classes had moved from town centres to leafy suburbia, like Edgbaston in Birmingham), and 'Good cooking recipes'. To wit (1872):

'Stewed livers'

Ingredients: Two or three chicken's livers, an onion, good gravy, yolks of two eggs, cayenne, mushroom powder or ketchup.

Mode: Stew the livers in the gravy with the onion; take them out, chop them and put them back into the saucepan, stirring in the eggs, etc. Serve it on hot buttered toast.

There were also patterns for the family's clothes, and advice on where a lady might, with propriety, take lunch in town. The magazine was much concerned with the 'cultivation of the morals and the cherishing of domestic virtues'. The 'service' magazine, or what Mary Grieve referred to as the 'trade paper' for women, was on the drawing board.

With *The English Woman's Domestic Magazine*, a blueprint for the modern magazine industry was also laid out. For one thing it marked the beginning of a diversification of the market, that is, the production of magazines for different groups and classes of women. For another, its rapid rise in circulation, from 25,000 after two years of publication to double that in 1860, pre-figured mass publishing achieved by improved technology and

2.4a *The English Woman's Domestic Magazine*, 1852

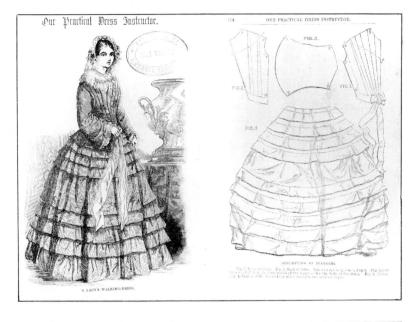

2.5 *The English Woman's Domestic Magazine*, 1853

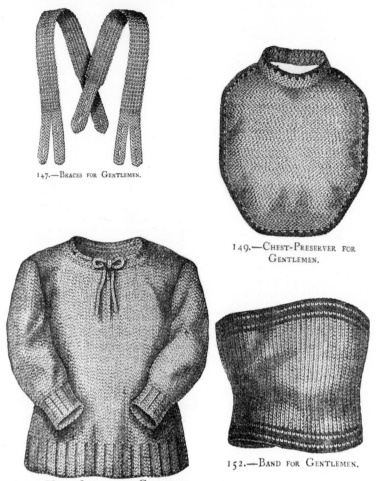

147.—Braces for Gentlemen.

149.—Chest-Preserver for Gentlemen.

152.—Band for Gentlemen.

2.6   *The English Woman's Domestic Magazine*, 1876

151.—Under-Jacket for Gentlemen.

large investments of capital on the one hand, increased literacy and purchasing power of the working class on the other. As circulations rose so did production costs and Beeton's magazine, like others, began to rely for its revenue on what had hitherto hardly been respectable – advertising. It was soon to become their lifeblood.

One notable magazine founded in 1885 was *The Lady*, then as now described as 'A Journal for Gentlewomen'. Though its first cover advertised, among other things, 'Iced savoury moulds (for the dinner or supper table) and carriages combining "elegance of style, with lightness, durability and easy riding"', its steady success began nine years later when Rita Shell, herself once a nanny, introduced a 'where-to-live' column and a 'small-ads' section. In the 1980s *The Lady* is renowned for its holiday accommodation ads and, as Rupert Morris in *The Times* puts it,

2.7a Khiva Corset advertisement in *Home Notes*, 1894

2.7b Bovril advertisement in *Home Notes*, 1894

the magazine 'is perceived among certain sections of the middle class as a sort of *Exchange and Mart* for nannies' (Morris 1985).

By the beginning of the twentieth century the number of magazines available had more than doubled. There was a clear class differentiation too in the market whose characteristics are still discernible in the 1980s: upper-class magazines chronicling 'society', the arts, music, theatre and high fashion; middle-class magazines concentrating on home and fashion, and working-class magazines offering a staple of romantic and melodramatic fiction and featuring aspiring heroines whose impeccable morals always shine through in the end.

Samuel Beeton's magazine was coolly formal and distant in tone, like its title. The cosier titles of *Home Notes* and *Home Chat* for the lower middle class introduced a more relaxed and less intimidating style in the 1890s. But it was *My Weekly* (1910), making a bid for 'an active and intimate relationship' with its readers, (quoted in White 1970, p. 88), and quickly followed by *Woman's Weekly* (1911), which established the personal and friendly address now typical of most magazines. It was *Woman*, however, launched in 1937, which had the added attraction for a weekly of colour pages, and in post-war Britain magazines won or lost the circulation stakes according to whether they could offer such colourful images, connoting glamour, daydreams and pleasure.

At the beginning of the war women's magazines were, in Mary Grieve's view (1964, p. 125), 'the Cinderella of the British pub-

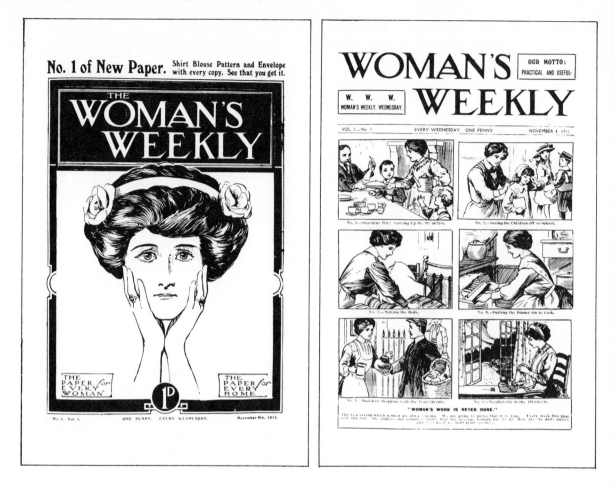

2.8a *Woman's Weekly* cover, 4
November 1911
2.8b *Woman's Weekly*, 4
November 1911, p.1

lishing industry'. By the end their reputation had soared (p. 134):

> There is no doubt that the war stretched the women's magazines and
> tested them as never before. And in this atmosphere of practicality,
> improvisation and strong comradely feeling the magazines throve . . .
> we were so short of paper that circulations were held down. As the
> papers developed more and more strongly their service approach and
> at the same time wisely kept up the entertainment value of their
> fiction, a tremendous unsatisfied demand built up.

'Service and entertainment' was to be the key to the meteoric rise
of magazine sales in the 1950s.

But between the consolidation of the war and the boom of the
1950s were the hard years of austerity when, as the social
historian Arthur Marwick evocatively describes (1982, p. 23), 'the
country lay in a crepuscular zone with the shadows of night firm
upon the landscape as the heartening hints of the rising sun.'
Certainly the dominant feature of many women's lives then was

2.9 *Woman* cover, 5 June 1937

an anxious and uncertain discussion about their future. In the pages of women's magazines – and here I look at just one, 'The National Home Weekly', *Woman* – there are signs of what was probably a more intense public argument about women's new post-war role. How that argument was waged and played out by the early 1950s is important to an understanding not only of the blossoming and wilting of women's magazines throughout the 1950s into the 1960s, but also of the developments in women's lives until the late 1960s when a radical feminism re-emerged.

First, then, *Woman* between 1945 and 1953.

Nation, family and women

Looking back to the immediate post-war years James Drawbell, the editor of *Woman's Own*, portrayed what it felt like for women (1968, p. 45):

> The war was over, peace was here but in 1946 the longed-for era of 'plenty' had not come. The world of women was at its lowest ebb.
>
> It was a drab and dreary let-down after our high expectations. Rationing was still with us, more severe in some things than it had been during the war . . . . There was little scope for gracious living of any sort, except vicariously from a hungry scanning of the colour food ads in the plush American magazines.

Unfortunately the battle of war for Britain only gave way to a 'battle for peace'. As Mary Grieve said in her editorial of 20 October 1945, 'There is a national emergency . . . . To rebuild our own homes and industries requires at least as much effort and discipline as to destroy the might of Germany and Japan.' And the 'effort' was to be demanded more of women than of any other group.

The magazines of the 1940s have been appropriately labelled by Cynthia White 'utility journals' concerned to 'make do and mend'. (The latter was the slogan for one of the government's national campaigns during and after the war.) And *Woman* was no exception: Edith Blair for instance urged women to try their hand at mending their own saucepans (11 January 1947):

> During the war it was found that women could do a wonderfully expert job on these tiny, intricate parts [i.e. bomb fuses]. And who says we in the home can't use this skill on our pots and pans? All that's needed is a stick of solder; a soldering iron; flux – and patience – it may not work out the first time . . . .

The example is illustrative: *Woman* in those years was engaged in keeping open a view of women's role and interest beyond the bounds of domesticity. That is not to say that most of the magazine was not devoted to the traditional concerns of home and hearth, fashion and beauty. It was. But there was something else too: an incipient feminism which insisted on women's equality (of a kind), assumed that some women would be doing a paid job and caring for a family in post-war Britain, encouraged women as citizens to participate in local politics and the concerns of the world – like peace and the nuclear threat – and, recognising how overworked women were, urged the provision of childcare and other social facilities.

Thus, compared to the introverted femininity *Woman* was to offer in the 1950s, the face of womanhood in the late 1940s looked both inwards to the family and outwards to the public world of work and the concerns of the nation. And there was a clear political edge to the magazine, especially in Mary Grieve's editorials judiciously commenting on the nation's uphill struggle

2.10   Horlicks advertisement in
Woman, 18 December 1948

to win its 'economic Dunkirk'. Indeed it was the foregrounding of the nation's needs over those of the individual and the family that licensed, as it had during the war, a limited questioning of traditional femininity. Britain was exhorted to be a nation of families each selflessly doing their bit for king and country – and the dollar drive. And that meant women too.

But a magazine like *Woman*, with its wide and mixed readership, had to step gently around feminist issues; its feminist sentiments were dealt with indirectly, sometimes with flippancy.

They were no less seriously meant. For example, in her editorial on the subject of the New Look fashion, 'It's got a fiery look now', Mary Grieve reported (28 January 1948):

> The firechief of Middlesboro' recently accused it of increasing risks of fire – 'With the knee length skirt,' he said, 'scorched legs were sufficient warning. Now a woman's calves are protected, and flames will reach her dress before she realizes her danger.'

And retorted:

> Come, come. For generations men have been wearing garments that protect their invaluable calves – and men have always been the sex with the privilege of standing with its back to the fire . . . .
> I doubt if the accidents caused by feminine skirts are any more numerous than those created by masculine cigarette ends, dottles of smouldering tobacco tapped from pipes or matches cast aside. (Women have reasonable smoking manners.) No, the root of the trouble is the New Look – something about its swinging bravado is obviously incendiary.
> I'll strike a bargain with Middlesboro'. I'll shorten my skirt when I hear the Middlesboro' firemen – including their chief – are wearing shorts on and off duty.

Similarly an article entitled 'Your smoke gets in his eyes', and described as 'a new outbreak of an old sex war', is used as a medium through which to discuss the double standards of behaviour men impose on women (25 September 1948): 'tobacco is the solace of the working man', but 'the uncomfortable truth is that men don't like us to smoke'. There were stories featuring women doctors (with men patients) and working mothers, while the magazine's resident doctor advised how the latter could successfully continue breastfeeding at work, an idea anathema only a few years on.

In 1947 the economic crisis was compounded by the foulest winter on record, and the demands on women were both onerous and conflicting. Homes were deprived of adequate heating and lighting, the BBC Third Programme, cinema, and their copies of women's magazines and newspapers; rations were at their lowest ever, and the Ministry of Food was persuading housewives of the delights of 'snoek', an unfortunately named, 'large, ferocious and tropical fish' which even the minister had to admit was 'one of the dullest fish I have ever eaten' (Cooper, p. 56). Meanwhile, though the economy was far from booming, the marriage rate had never been higher, and women's 'production' of babies was delivering the nation with its post-war baby bulge. Against that background it is not surprising that when the Ministry of Labour urged married women to return to certain industries (immediately after the war many women had left their wartime jobs) there was heated dispute about it.

Woman found itself caught between two camps. On the one side it acted as the government's mouthpiece, publicising the National Health Service and willingly publishing its propagandist appeals, like the Reports to the Women of Britain. On the other hand it politically intervened on behalf of women and pointedly attacked government and industry for their short-sightedness. And it tried to reconcile these disparate claims of 'we the nation' and 'we women'.

It is clear from Mary Grieve's editorials that many women had no desire at all to return to work: with rations so bad and inadequate housing the work of home was difficult enough without adding to it another job. In those winter months Mary Grieve tirelessly reiterated her arguments: 'If industry expects women to return to its ranks it must give them a better deal than it gave them in wartime.' 'It's no good offering a mother a job which starts, say, at 7.30 in the morning. Children don't start school till 9, and the gap is too long for any mother's peace of mind.' 'Women must be helped back'; 'Do it now'; 'Mothers need help'; and she concluded one editorial only half-jokingly, 'Perhaps what we need is a Mothers Union affiliated to the TUC!'

Women didn't get one. Nor, though by January 1948 70,000 women had responded to the appeals to return to work, did they gain any of the other social facilities, like nurseries and late shopping hours, that the magazine had urged. And by the end of the decade the feminist voice in *Woman*, and more widely, had

2.12   *Report to the Women of Britain*, no.5, 21 February 1948

become quiescent. Its demise probably bore some relation to the collapse of the Labour government, but there were other reasons for it.

In particular, even at its peak, the feminism was limited. Despite the fictional role reversals *Woman* never wholly challenged the traditional division of labour between wife and husband. It was assumed, firstly, that women would bear the chief responsibility for home and childcare, whatever else they might also do. Secondly, it was the awful conditions of home life, exacerbated by the pulls to do paid work, which partly created the feminist demands; and these were aimed at achieving the social conditions under which women could do their job in the home as well as men were able to do theirs in the work place. Feminism and equality were envisaged as about a complementarity between wife and husband.

With the introduction in 1948 of the NHS and social security scheme, and the adoption of a policy of 'full employment' to ease family worries and finances; with the economic crisis diminishing (rationing was gradually phased out and supplies of consumer items improved) to make shopping, feeding a family and furnishing a home less arduous and time-consuming, with the repairs and building of housing stock to relieve overcrowding and strained relationships in the family, at last domestic work and childcare could be tackled 'professionally'. Most women were utterly relieved at the improvement in their lives; many believed they had won their equality: the right to be equal to but different from men. And voicing the prevalent view by the mid-1950s J.W.B. Douglas in *The Economist* declared, 'The feminists mop up'. For feminists in the 1980s it seems almost laughable that anyone could think that; in the 1950s it was faintly ludicrous to think otherwise.

It was however the Festival of Britain on the South Bank of the Thames in 1951 and the lavish coronation of Queen Elizabeth II in 1953 which symbolised the end of one era and heralded in another – a New Elizabethan Age – and, as *Woman* magazine celebrated, it was this special *woman* who as wife and mother, was leading her country into a future of stable family life and – at last – of plenty. In June 1953 *Woman*'s 'Talking about health' slot was devoted to 'Family life'. Joan Williams, SRN, SCM, expertly drew lessons from the example of the royals: 'Here is family life at its best. And the woman and its centre is a wise and understanding person as well as our loved Queen.'

In the pages of magazines after 1953 the nation was left to look after itself. For women the burning concern and proud burden to bear became how best to make marriage, family and home all that had been hoped for during those long years of disruption and deprivation. And perhaps their most vivid dream was of what to buy. It was consumption which was to provide the impetus for a

The Queen and the Duke of Edinburgh pick up their children for the sort of photograph which every family loves to treasure

Family Life

NURSE WILLIAMS stresses the priceless value of a happy home . . . symbolized by the two children whose mother is the Queen

2.13 *Woman*, 30 May 1953

new form of an old ideology of femininity, and it was not until this 'new' ideology of femininity had (literally) delivered its goods that it became apparent that the 'mopping up' had been more of a shoring up – until the new stormy tide. But before feminism broke again consumption and women's 'new' post-war role were also to provide bountiful scope for an unprecedented expansion of the magazine market – and of its profits.

Chapter 3   Selling and buying

Options: a hard sell

The largest publisher of women's magazines in Britain, the International Publishing Corporation (IPC), owns eighteen of the fifty women's magazines on sale in 1983 and owns fifty-one other magazines. It is merely part of the multinational conglomerate Reed International, who own Hamlyn Publishing, lay claim to such well-known brand names as Crown paints and Twyford lavatories, and reckon they produce 1 in 5 of the nation's envelopes. Subsidiary companies also include the North American Paper Group, Reed Inc Canada, and Reed Holdings Inc USA. Reed Publishing publish consumer and specialist magazines and directories, and supply electronic information services, throughout the world. In 1983 the trading profit for Consumer Publishing (of which IPC women's magazines are a substantial part) was 11.5 million, about one-seventh of the total profit (cf Appendix)).

Yet in spite of what appear to be vast sums, IPC's share of copies sold in Britain has gradually diminished since the early 1960s. And for the magazine market as a whole the deep recessions in the 1970s and 1980s, notwithstanding a short-lived expansionist period in 1978-79, have been severe: sales have dropped across the board. Nevertheless one sector has continued to be a growth area: the monthly (and largely middle-class) 'leisure and home' sector including such venerables as *Good Housekeeping* and *Woman and Home*. With a 72 per cent share of this market, and their position buoyant in 1981 due to their successes with *Woman's World* (launched 1977) and a revamped *Woman's Journal*, IPC made another stab at purloining more riches in a crowded but relatively safe sector. The magazine was *Options*.

Its multi-media campaign costing an unprecedented £1 million seduced potential advertisers with the hype that *Options* was for the woman who

> . . . is an entirely new breed of consumer. She sees herself as the kind of woman who should have a calculator in her handbag, a stereo in her car, a note recorder at her office. She is the generation for whom video and telecom were made. Busy women with open minds who will take advantage of every technological advantage to make work more efficient and play more fun. The first generation of women for whom freezers, dishwashers and microwave ovens are not luxuries but essentials. (promotion material)

On TV a slick ad courted readers:

> *Options* is the most exciting new magazine of the 80s .... *Options* is about you and everything about you. It has style and sophistication, innovation and inspiration, choices and creativity, outside interests and inside stories, confidence, charisma, and sometimes it can be – well, just like you – very surprising.

When, at 60p a copy, the first issue hit the newsstands in April 1982 it had achieved (or so vaunted IPC) record ad bookings for a new magazine – three-quarters of a million pounds' worth – and its print order of 395,000 had sold well. A year and one editor later, *Options* cost readers 65p for a much slimmer editorial and advertising package. Nonetheless for the publishers the magazine was a success: it had attained a circulation around 260,000 and sufficient ad revenue for its commercial viability.

The case of *Options* divulges much about the business of magazines. Firstly it is a venture involved in two disparate but intimately linked selling operations: one to women, the other to advertisers. Since no magazine gains any profit at all from its cover price (in a 1983 interview, Brian Braithwaite, the publisher of *Cosmopolitan*, estimated that to break even *Cosmopolitan* would have to double its coverprice), it is the wooing of advertisers which is so pivotal in the competitive search for revenue. *Campaign*, the advertisers' own weekly magazine, is full of ads from publishing houses selling the merits of their magazines. A National Magazine Company ad, stressing the quality of its magazines, makes a 'plea for a better environment for your ads'. IPC's sales pitch convinces advertisers of the circulation

3.1a   National Magazine Company advertisement in *Campaign*, 10 June 1983
3.1b   IPC advertisement in *Campaign*, 1985

successes of their magazines: 'We talk to women and they respond' (*Campaign* 18 February 1983) and 'you can persuade them to be yours for life.' To further ensure sales, however, advertisers want to know what kinds of products a magazine's readers buy. The ad selling space in *Family Circle* and *Living* conveys that knowledge visually and verbally, and also rather cleverly. (The latter was one of a series also featuring the magazines as different wine bottles, and as compact and lipstick.)

In the case of *Options*, readers were sharply defined as 'an entirely *new breed* of consumer'. Such tailoring around certain commodity purchases arguably epitomises IPC's marketing approach to publishing. As Terry Mansfield (the managing director at the rival National Magazine Company) quipped (*Campaign* 19 March 1982), 'They find a marketing idea and slot the editorial in.' Certainly IPC *had* selected a growth area of consumption – and therefore a clientele of eager advertisers – and had roughly hewn both reader and editorial around that. The 'options' the magazine offers are, first and foremost, between one set of goods and another. And its claim to be 'the most exciting new magazine of the 80s' arguably rests or falls on the quality of its 'Better food. Better homes. Better fashion.'

In contrast, the National Magazine Company maintains that the 'editorial product is everything .... We would not start with what we thought was a gap in the market but with what we thought was a good idea.' Their magazines are sold to advertisers not on the basis of potential consumption patterns of readers but on the quality of their 'good ideas': *Harpers & Queen*, *She*, *Company*, *Good Housekeeping* and *Cosmopolitan*.

But for all their creditable editorial singularity National Magazines, like other companies, cannot avoid the dictates of a market in which the need to win ad revenue as well as readers is paramount, and the necessity to yoke readers to what they buy is a constant pressure. Those market pressures have built up from the 1950s and decisively shaped not only the available range of magazines but also, in highly significant ways, the contents of any given magazine. At the same time women reading the ads and consumer features in their magazines have been caught up in defining their own femininity, inextricable, through consumption.

Scoured by more women every month.

Family Circle and Living

3.2 *Family Circle* and *Living* advertisement in *Campaign*, 3 June 1983

'Petticoat battleground': fighting for profits

In the sombre twilight years of late 1940s Britain women's magazines were still commercial small fry. With enforced printing restrictions the sales of magazines were kept low and competition minimised. They had few pages, little colour, and cramped little ads could only promise the arrival of goods *soon*: children gaze wondrously at orange juice: 'Ah! Oh! Solo! Solo means *real* orange juice. You'll see it again soon!' (*Woman*, 21 July 1945)

The first sign of the highly competitive edge that magazines were to adopt appeared in 1950, just as print was derestricted in Britain. James Drawbell at *Woman's Own* achieved a scoop. He outbid Amalgamated Press (who owned the well-established but old-fashioned *Woman's Weekly*) for a royal story called *Little Princesses* – Elizabeth and Margaret – and written by their governess Marion Crawford who, as 'Crawfie', was to become almost as familiar a name in women's magazines as Edith Blair and Evelyn Home. *Woman's Own* paid the outstanding sum of £30,000 for the story (the usual figure was under £5,000) and with its winning combination of 'ordinary' family life and royal glamour it was an editor's dream. Mary Grieve enviously admitted it had 'everything'. And while *Woman's Own* gained 500,000 sales overnight the business world duly noted the burgeoning commercial potential of women's magazines.

As the 1950s progressed magazine sales rose enormously. Ad and editorial pages increased; so did the proportion of colour pages. For example the top-selling weekly *Woman* cost 3d in 1946, had just twenty pages and sold a million copies. In 1951 the number of pages was doubled, the issue size increased and circulation rose to nearly 2¼ million. In 1957 the magazine's 100-page issue cost 4½d and its circulation peaked at a post-war record, not to be repeated by any magazine, at nearly 3½ million. Commensurately ad revenues of women's magazines soared: from £1.1 million in 1950 to £5.3 million in 1958.

This revenue helped to keep the cover price of magazines down but it also shifted the balance, however subtly, between editorial and advertising departments. In 1956, when *Woman* began carrying double-page colour spreads, British Nylon Spinners booked one of these (then) costly insertions for £7,000. (By 1963 *Woman*'s biggest advertising booking was £17,000.) Mary Grieve, believing it to be reasonable given the size of the sum, agreed to refrain from publishing any article which prominently featured natural fibres in the same issue (Grieve 1964). Such silences, conscious or not, were to become commonplace.

Magazines also aided advertisers, as well as readers, by increasingly listing stockists for the goods discussed and colourfully displayed on editorial pages, and the magazines themselves entered the business of selling goods. Offers of high-quality goods at reasonable prices became one of their big attractions. *Woman* in 1962 sold 107,746 of their wool jersey suit offer at a cost to readers of £269,853. In the meantime, against such competition the drabber, old-fashioned weeklies so popular before the war (*Home Chat* and *Home Notes*) ignominiously folded. Only *Woman's Weekly*, renowned for its knitting patterns, inconspicuously held its own.

Yet the expansion of both *Woman* and *Woman's Own* was not without its setbacks. By 1957 they had peaked above their optimum circulation. Generally magazines increase their ad rates according to their circulation success. But there is a cut-off price at which advertisers will no longer continue to buy space, and the extra production costs for a higher circulation begin to outweigh what can be accrued from advertising and sales. To relieve the pressure on *Woman*, the publisher Odhams launched the aptly named magazine in the 'New Elizabethan Age', *Woman's Realm*; Newnes, *Woman's Own*'s publisher, brought out *Women's Day*. Both had lower ad rates than their successful 'sisters'. The *Realm* was a success; *Women's Day*, perhaps because it cost ½d more, was not.

The launch of these magazines indicates a common strategy for publishers. When a magazine is doing very well they expediently bring out their own 'copy-cat' publication rather than run the risk of a competitor rushing in with what Brian Braithwaite and Joan Barrell call a 'me too' publication. *Company* as a sister to *Cosmopolitan* is an example from the 1970s. As Michael Bird of National Magazines explained, 'If you had a craving for, say Bovril, you could buy and consume as many jars as possible, but if you were mad about *Cosmo* the most you could ever buy would be twelve different issues a year. The supply solution to this is to publish a sister publication' (*Campaign*, 5 March 1982).

The success of the *Realm* put Odhams on a strong financial footing, allowing them to weigh in on what an *Economist* article called the 'petticoat battleground' (21 November 1959). The Mirror Group of newspapers had already bought up the 'somnolent' Amalgamated Press and, renaming it Fleetway, had 'swept through its offices with the crusading vigour of a new broom'. In sharp riposte Odhams bought up the Hulton Press (who owned the monthly *Housewife*) and then the much larger Newnes.

With National Magazines (then owning *Vanity Fair*, *Good Housekeeping*, *She* and *Harpers*), D. C. Thomson (publishers of, among others, *My Weekly* and *People's Friend*), and Condé Nast (*Vogue*'s publisher) only on the sidelines, Odhams and Fleetway played for the kill. By 1961 the strains of promotion expenditure were showing and finally, outbidding the Thomson Organisation, the Mirror Group won. Despite concern voiced by the Royal Commission on the Press a near monopoly (of the weekly market at least) was formed: the International Publishing Corporation. Ironically, as IPC was majestically being constituted women's magazines were beginning a slow decline – of circulations if not of profits. Their rise and fall, however, was not entirely the outcome of the magazine trade's business acumen, or otherwise.

Consumption: new work for women

The circulation climb of magazines in the 1950s was consequent on an expansion of a wider commodity market, primarily that of domestic goods (and to a lesser extent fashion and beauty items). Moreover for the first time such goods were being produced relatively cheaply and were available across social classes. The particular form this expansion took was specific to the period; the expansion itself was not. Without embarking on complex details, suffice it to say that one of the characteristic tendencies of capitalist industry is its particular sort of competitiveness. New goods are constantly being produced, first as luxury items then, as technology is improved and less costly labour ensues, more cheaply and on a larger scale: the goods become part of what ordinary people expect to be able to buy too. Profits – a *sine qua non* of capitalist industry – are partly made by firms gaining the edge over rivals in this process. As the latter catch up the whole cycle of innovation, cutting labour costs and prices begins again.

Thus items designed for the middle classes in the 1930s – fridges, hoovers and washing machines – were by the 1950s beginning to appear in working-class homes too. And as the 1950s marched on into the 1960s, 1970s and 1980s there has been a gradual but spectacular introduction of an enormous array of goods into the home: from Kleenex and polythene bags and Flash in the 1950s, to automatic washing machines and non-stick frying pans in the 1960s, to cling film and deep freezers in the 1970s, to food processors and home computers (as yet still middle-class items) in the 1980s. We could record similar, seemingly inexorable, proliferations of goods, whether for care of the family pet or tending the suburban garden.

For the 1950s several factors contributed to the particularly domestic expansion in Britain. The long years of austerity had nurtured an enormous thirst for such goods. In addition the post-war reconstruction, especially under the Conservative administration from 1951, took place literally on the home front. Industry was geared to the production of goods for the home market and domestic and personal use, *not* primarily for export and *not* to build up and modernise industrial production itself. Part of the reconstruction too was to replace bomb-damaged housing stock and nineteenth-century slums. Mobility, moving from one sort of housing to another, and especially into home ownership, which ensued in the 1950s was high and tended to stimulate the need for domestic items, from lavatory brushes and curtain hooks to three-piece suites and dining room furniture.

A combination of the welfare state facilities, 'full employment' and the greater trade union bargaining power which followed, together with increasing availability of part-time work for women, gave many working-class people more money in their pockets. Easier buying on the 'never-never' (hire purchase) and the spur of R. A. Butler's 1953 'New Look' budget (the economic copy of

Dior's fashion look) cutting income tax and purchase tax swung the consumer boom into the High Streets. If it was not the leveller of class differences it has sometimes been made out to be, still the standard of living rose by over 30 per cent between 1951 and 1964. Between 1955 and 1965 the proportion of families owning cars, TVs, vacuum cleaners and washing machines doubled. The rise in food consumption showed a shift towards frozen vegetables, processed foods and instant coffee. In 1959 the then prime minister Harold Macmillan exultantly declared, 'You've never had it so good.'

Perhaps. But the gains for women who, of course, were the ones who mainly chose and bought all these goods were very double-edged. Even as commodities physically lightened much housework for women the tasks of their domestic role were both transformed *and* increased. Occupation Housewife was regarded nevertheless as indisputably upgraded. The influential market researcher Mark Abrams described it succinctly: 'Since now home has become the centre of his activity and most of his earnings are spent on or in the home his wife becomes the *chooser* and *spender* and gains a *new status* and *control* – her tastes form his life' (1959, my emphasis).

The job of women's magazines in the 1950s was therefore to educate and reassure women in this work. Mary Grieve explained (1964, p. 138), 'An immense amount of her personality is engaged in her function as the selector of goods, and in this she endures many anxieties, many fears. Success in this function is as cheering and vitalising to her as it is to a man in his chosen career, failure as humiliating.' There was a new knowledge to be learnt about what commodities were available, how to judge and choose them in the shops and, finally, having made the purchase, how to arrange it to conform to the tasteful (or tasteless?) 'contemporary' style. Offering advice on all these aspects, and presenting it in a colourful, desirable and entertaining way, the magazines could not fail to be popular. Mary Grieve again (p. 135):

> the professional man's wife struggling to manage her money so that her children could get a better education was just as glad of the practical recipes, the well-designed clothes, the hints on value-for-money as was the welder's wife . . . . Furnishing schemes and attitudes of mind which were hopelessly out of her reach and experience before the war were within her ken now.

By the 1960s the magazine formula seemed to be less appealing to women. Perhaps the novelty and pleasure of its 'consumer education' function had worn a bit thin. More importantly, it's easy to see retrospectively that TV, especially commercial TV, must have played a considerable part in offering alternative entertainment and relaxation for women, and with its soap operas and situation comedies provided 'stories' on those moral themes much loved by magazines: family, marriage and romance. Not to be thwarted the magazine industry endeavoured to improve its competitive position in two ways. Firstly the mass market appeal across age and class and to all 'women's interests' was fragmented. The market was 'rationalised' with more specialised publications emphasising particular buying habits by women. Secondly the publishers sought to modernise magazines both in terms of design and the package offered to readers. They attempted to address a 'New Woman' with interests other than those of home and hearth. The first strategy was successful commercially; the second, with a few exceptional moments (which I'll look at in the next section), stumbled badly until the 1970s and the launch of *Cosmopolitan*.

The year Harold Macmillan told his electorate they'd never had it so good, Mark Abrams was highlighting the increasing affluence of *young* people: the 'teenage consumer' market – records, clothes and beauty products – was a potential gold field still to be mined (Abrams 1959). Although the fashion and beauty market had already expanded in the 1950s – the modern frontages of Marks & Spencers, C & A and British Home Stores, and the pages of women's magazines, were witness to that – it was in the 1960s that the beauty and fashion trades mushroomed with products aimed at young and largely unmarried women across the class spectrum. While the boutiques, selling ever shorter skirts, set the fashion scene for the local High Street, the cosmetic industry was filling the branch stores with a colourful and sometimes bewildering array of items. Rimmell, Woolworth's 'Baby Doll' range, Outdoor Girl and Miners produced infinite shades of fibre mascara, waterproof mascara, block mascara, mascara for sensitive eyes, eye shadow as cream or as powder, in tube or palette, shiny, dull or sparkly, cleaners, toners, moisturisers for oily, dry, allergic, spot-prone skins, false eyelashes and nails, hairpieces and hair removers, and so on, at very cheap prices. Between 1966 and 1972 the retail sales of cosmetics had grown at a rate of 4.5 per cent per annum; the clothing sector had increased by one quarter.

Taking advantage of this market potential IPC published *Honey* in 1960 as a direct response to Abram's research. With its ads and editorial increasingly similar in presentation it provided a glossy shop window for the latest in fashion and beauty products. It pushed its links with consumption further than most magazines by establishing its own boutiques and hairdressing salons carrying the *Honey* sign and standards, and it launched the *Honey* Club offering free gifts, special buys and the chance to be invited for a beauty treatment in London. *Honey* was followed by *Petticoat* (in 1966), *19* (in 1968) and *Look Now* (in 1972), all from IPC and all for the fashion-conscious and fashion-buying young woman.

3.3   *Chic* cover, January 1985

Petticoat (a weekly) and *Look Now* were aimed, as *Honey* grew up with its readers, at their younger sisters.

The other most notable tailor-made magazines of the 1960s were *Family Circle* (1964) and *Living* (1966). As the Thomson Organisation's bid to break IPC's stronghold they were clear examples of attempts to capture a very specific readership: the young and domestically oriented housewife. These magazines had (and still have) the unique advantage of being displayed at supermarket check-outs. *Annabel* (1966) from D. C. Thomson was designed to appeal to young mums interested in reading about parenthood and buying maternity and baby clothes, toys and prams. *Slimming* was initially a small independent enterprise started by Audrey and Tom Eyton which proved to be one of the gilded lilies of the 1970s. It was soon followed by a rash of copy publications. It also owed its success to a specialisation advertisers and readers could both 'enjoy' and to the astute decision, made on the basis of the limited supply of that advertising, to be a bimonthly. In the 1980s not only *Options* but also *Fitness* (1984, see chapter 9), *Black beauty and hair* (1982) and *Chic* (1984) have launched themselves on particular consumer-cum-interest bandwagons. *Black beauty and hair*, a fairly specialised publication endorsed by hair salons, and the more general magazine *Chic* are, significantly, the first British publications specifically to address black women. Winsome Cornish, *Chic*'s editor, described the magazine's editorial before publication as covering 'the whole spectrum of hair care and beauty, as well as fitness, fashion and all the other facts which contribute to the total look of a sophisticated contemporary black person'. *Chic* is also circulated in the USA, Nigeria and Zimbabwe.

Consumption patterns are, undoubtedly, an important factor in the profile of individual magazines and of the magazine market as a whole. But they are not by any means all that magazines are about. In the 1960s, as in the 1970s and 1980s, the industry adopted a second strategy, on top of 'rationalisation', to stave off decline. It first discovered and then addressed the 'New Woman'.

'The New Woman': a case of mistaken identity

In 1955, when the magazine trade was gloating over the steady climb of circulation figures, the National Magazine Company launched *She*. As the first editor, Joan Werner-Laurie, explained, 'The women's magazines of the time just didn't reflect women as I knew them. Of course women have softness, but they are also funny, vulgar and tough. They are in touch with the harsh realities of life' (cited in White 1970, p. 166). Unlike other magazines *She* made no attempt to appeal to a particular market of women based either on women's role or age or socioeconomic background. It did not therefore offer advertisers a group of women with obvious consumption 'needs'. Instead it appealed to what Cynthia White describes as an attitude group. The editors produced a magazine largely to please themselves and hoped that their viewpoint and the ideological assumptions they held would be shared by readers. *She* represented both the approach and the kind of audacious experiment National Magazines were to risk again with *Cosmopolitan*.

She allowed space for a highly individualistic voice, like 'Kenneth Horne criticises *She*'. It almost engaged in topical social and political issues of the day, with a discussion of the television programme *That Was The Week That Was* and its satire on the church, and cartoons about CND ('It really is the e-N-D!') in

3.4 *She* first issue cover, March 1955

1963. It ventured into adventurous fields of women's pursuits like mountaineering and sailing. But *She* then retreated into eccentricity with 'Stuff your pet' (to keep for posterity) and flip punning: 'Weight lifting for bust lifting'. And it had a prurience much in the vein of the 'family' periodicals like *Tit-bits*, being at heart upright but with a veneer of breaking moral codes and discussing the social unmentionables. Not at all out of character, the romantic novelist (as well as mother and grandmother) Denise Robins was its agony aunt. Visually it plumped for a packed, busy, newsprint look using cheap paper rather than the spaciousness and colour favoured by other magazines of the 1950s. It was (and is) the one magazine women love or loathe. Taking five years to establish itself, *She* was the first post-war magazine to successfully break from the domestic or fashion mould. Yet it knew less *what* kind of a woman it was creating than that it was addressing women whose interests (in light reading at least) did not centre on the housewife role. One suspects, however, that that was what their readers were (and are).

By 1963 IPC's four main weeklies had lost about 700,000 readers since 1957. Concerned, they looked to the USA where a similar but earlier collapse in the magazine market seemed to have been arrested, and invited Ernest Dichter, president of the Institute of Motivational Research in New York, to assess the prognosis, healthy or otherwise, of just one magazine – *Woman's Own*. The decision was to have far-reaching effects. Dichter had largely worked for advertisers. With simplistic Freudian theory he had, for example, come up with the now classic (masculine-defined) 'sexuality' of cars. As one particularly odious ad has put it, 'It was one expensive affair after another. Then I met the wife.' Or a sports car is a man's mistress, a saloon his wife. Some of Dichter's other sexual characterisations have been even less credible, for instance that the Parker Pen Company were selling not pens but penises. The psychological principle here was as much to shock and be bold with the selling imagery as to imply sexuality *per se*. For *Woman's Own* too he recommended a bold editorial sweep.

He pointed out that women's horizons had widened – the result of education, TV, the growth of married women's employment – and the magazine needed, firstly, to reflect that: to adopt a more realistic approach in fiction and articles, dealing with, rather than skating over, marital and familial problems, and introducing a broader range of social issues. Secondly, it was necessary to visually update the magazine with sharper illustrations and a crisper style of typography. Thirdly, he stressed the need to cater to readers in terms of their attitudes and interests, much in the mould *She* had adopted.

Whether Dichter's ideas were copied directly or whether his views confirmed changes that budding young executives and editors at IPC were already bursting to try, these strategies were adopted as blanket solutions to the sinking market. The most dramatic face lift was of *Woman's Mirror*, renamed with a modern logo *WM*. Its first new cover in September 1965 broke all protocols with an image of a human foetus; the issue was a sell-out. But over the months *WM*'s radicalism did not recruit long-term readers, and within eighteen months it had merged with *Woman*. Similarly *Everywoman*, *'E'* in its new regime, and *Housewife*, both sadly ailing, recouped none of their losses when visually and editorially transformed to address the knowledgeable woman interested in new opinions and contemporary social trends. *Woman's Own* too had to backtrack when its new abrasive edge lost readers, though it retained a smarter visual presentation.

But it was *Nova*, published in 1965 as 'the new magazine for the new kind of woman', which was the true Dichterian baby. The 'New Woman' (White 1970, p. 223):

> could be 28 or 38, single with a job, or married with children (and perhaps a job too), a girl with a university degree, or a girl who never took school seriously . . . our new kind of woman has a wide range of interests, an inquiring mind and an independent outlook – not to mention that her numbers are multiplying.

Nova aimed to shock, to intellectually provoke and to be witty. A large magazine, in contrast to *She* it luxuriated in empty space, bold print and experimental photography and copy. *Nova* was for the design gourmet and chic progressive middle classes. At least something in its tone too leant on the 1960s penchant for satire.

If the other Dichterian experiments abysmally collapsed, *Nova* did not so much fail as bloom exotically and briefly. Do these failures mean therefore that Dichter's analyses and remedies were wrong? Or did IPC simply mishandle the cures? It was probably a bit of both. There were several misjudgments. Firstly, that the sales of magazines were falling because they had not 'kept up with the times'; secondly, that the strategies to update existing magazines should be to transform their design *and* ideological message; and thirdly, that the 'New Woman' was well-off, usually married, living in the posh but trendy areas of London and having best friends in the world of theatre, design and advertising.

With the power and influence of TV it may not have mattered *what* the publishers did to revamp magazines: overall circulations would still have dropped. Without acceding to fatalism, however, another mistake IPC made was to underestimate the perverse conservatism of readers. That is, readers may have been bored and fed-up with their magazines without quite knowing what was unsatisfying. On the other hand magazines do become long-time friends whose every quirk and fancy becomes a familiar and reassuring pleasure. To change well-tried, even if failing, formulas, especially by introducing 'realism' (commonly seen as

NOVA

Yes, we're living in sin
No, we're not getting married
Why? It's out of date

3.5 *Nova* cover, March 1967

anathema to entertainment and pleasure), is a risky business indeed. And to simultaneously modernise design, as IPC did with *WM*, is to court the deepest trouble. The case of *Family Circle*, which showed a rapid rise, indicates that it was not so much new ideas and socially updated magazines that some groups of women were eager for but more practical and colourful recipes for the same traditional pursuits.

Nova was new and had none of the disadvantages of contending with reader loyalty. Still it sank. *Nova* was expensive (3/6d compared to *Honey*'s 2/6d in 1968) and had high ad rates to attract quality advertising. It was in league with *Queen*, *Vogue* and *Harpers*, and initially led that field. The problem was that there was a mismatch between the kinds of articles *Nova* carried and their message, and *who* they and the advertising were aimed at. The article shown in Figure 3.7, expressing the first stirrings of (an as yet unnamed) feminism in Britain, by virtue of both its title, 'Mrs John Bull . . .', and the 'county lady' references within, speaks to middle-class and established family women in the 'best' British tradition. Yet on the whole that was not the group who were anything like being the 'New Woman', let alone the feminist one. If the 'New Woman' existed at all in the 1960s she was still at the chrysalis stage: young, single, or possibly just married,

MRS JOHN BULL, YOU STAND HERE TODAY ACCUSED OF COWARDICE IN THE FACE OF EMANCIPATION.

HOW DO YOU PLEAD?

3.6 *Nova*, February 1968

definitely finding her feet. She might occasionally read *Nova* but she read, or had read, *Honey. Honey* offered a mixed diet of fun and provocative fashion and editorially tackled, though rather tentatively, the topical controversies that concerned young women: questions around men and sexuality, leaving the parental home, home and work. Neither conventional marriage nor eternal spinsterhood for the 'career woman' looked attractive options for young honeys. But *Nova*'s upmarket alternatives were just too aloof to be convincing either. It remained for *Cosmopolitan* in the 1970s to begin to flesh out a 'New Woman' who was more popularly appealing.

Significantly, with the launch of *Cosmopolitan* in 1972 *Nova*'s coffin was sealed (though it lingered to die ingloriously in 1975). *Cosmopolitan* was cheaper and by a combination of cheaper ad rates and higher circulation encroached extensively into *Nova*'s ad market – and beyond. It was also more wisely middle-of-the-road than elite, and clearly single and under 25 in spirit if not in fact, and that appealed to readers.

IPC were slow to understand the lesson of *Nova*. In 1972 they attempted to launch a weekly *Candida*. It was intended (again) to be 'progressive' and 'upmarket'. It was a resounding flop,

...I'm always at home... it's such a bore going out when there are such fabulous slink-at-home clothes... well, I mean... who wants to get oyster-satin wet? I'll just cuddle up in a clutch-close wrap in front of the fire... and sling on a few jewels, and how's about it, pal-sie? See you soon...

come up and see me sometime

3.7   *Honey* cover, March 1967
3.8   *Honey*, November 1968

disappearing within a year. That they have succeeded ten years on with *Options* (having liberal chat around its Habitat-style dinner tables) has much to do with the social changes that have occurred for that group of middle-class women. *Nova*'s 'New Woman' did not really exist; the *Options* woman, who is not really 'new' at all, does. In between lie the 1970s, feminism and the influence of *Spare Rib* on the magazine market. With the three magazine case studies I'll return to that formative period. Next, however, I want to look more closely at the inside pages of magazines, especially at their visuals.

Chapter 4

Work and leisure: feminine pleasures

Enjoying 'fictions'

For the publishers of women's magazines the maintenance of healthy finances is the key concern; for their editors the aim is to produce a magazine both entertaining and useful for women. The distinction is a fine one, with 'entertainment' and 'use' slipping one into the other to give a prominent tone of magazines geared to pleasing their readers.

It might be thought that pleasure is subjective: one woman's pleasure is another woman's pain. Yet like all our experiences, though pleasure feels like an individual and spontaneous expression, it has had to be learnt: no event, much less a magazine, can of itself provide pleasure. It depends on being familiar with the cultural codes of what is meant to be pleasurable, and on occupying the appropriate social spaces. Women's magazines provide little pleasure for most men and 'Match of the Day' is not most women's choice for enjoyable television viewing.

What pleasure we derive from a magazine will also depend on the context in which we are reading it. We escape with them in nervous moments at the doctor's or during tedious commuting hours. We read them as relaxation at the end of a long day when children have at last been put to bed, or to brighten up the odd coffee break and lunch hour when life is getting a bit tough, or simply dreary. Pretending to immerse yourself in a magazine because your husband/boyfriend/father is making signs he wants you to make his cup of coffee is a very different experience from choosing to read one on an unexpected day off.

There are formal qualities to a magazine to be enjoyed – the feel of its paper, its size, the quality of its colour, design and visuals. Reading can engross readers in different ways. It can be the voyeurism of peeping at the lives and loves of the rich and famous or at the disasters of the less fortunate; it can be the pleasurable 'conversation with a friend', or the identification with heroines whose problems satisfyingly unfold and are resolved. The contents can mentally stimulate or excite creativity, but magazines are bought, as Jane Reed once commented, 'primarily . . . for relaxation'. Her aim with *Woman's Own*, she maintained, was to offer 'a selfish purchase for women who have only 10 pence to spend' (cited in White 1977, p. 51). Selfish because women, especially as wives and mothers, tend not to have much money or goods which they can justly say is theirs alone, nor private space and private time for self-indulgences. If we firmly shut the bathroom door on an uncooked supper in order to sink into a deep and – children permitting – peaceful bath, or splash out with the housekeeping money on perfume and undies, guilt tends to sneak in like a chill November fog. Traditionally it is men ('the breadwinners') who graciously bestow treats on women; unfortunately, in somewhat sporadic if bountiful gestures.

Women's magazines, on the other hand, afford a reliable and not-too-extravagant treat women can justifiably give themselves; after all, they're useful as well as enjoyable. The regular weekly or monthly purchase is a pleasure that can be anticipated and guaranteed; the occasional and exceptional purchase is more like choosing the favourite box of chocolates which regrettably, no one ever seems to give you. As a *Company* article said of chocolate, it is 'one of life's sensuous pleasures'. Just as sensuous are the 'goodies' to be savoured beneath the cover of a favourite magazine. According to Helen Chappell, a regular contributor to *Company* but writing here in *New Society*, readers consume magazines 'quite deliberately as mental chocolate – give or take a few hard nuts' (Chappell 1983). Providing that 'mental chocolates' are the magazines' naughty indulgences – romance and the exotic experience of their larger-than-life dreams or fictions.

The *Concise Oxford Dictionary* defines a 'fiction' as a 'thing feigned or imagined, invented statement or narrative'. Women's magazines offer, I'd argue, imaginative story lines in which women achieve the successes and satisfactions everyday life cannot be depended on to deliver. In this chapter I look at the (mainly) visual fictions: ads and fashion, cookery and home features. In the following chapter I look at stories about celebrities and 'ordinary' people, and what magazines themselves label as fiction.

When I was discussing commodities and their expansion in the 1950s, I stressed their use rather than the pleasures they might bring into the home. I underemphasised too the degree to which our culture has become one in which pleasures – the magazines we read, the TV we watch, the lager and wine we drink – are primarily, if not exclusively, bought. Moreover changing social and economic conditions have reshaped that pleasure as much as they have altered domestic life for women. For example, even though the wine some of us buy may taste the same as it did ten years ago, it now comes in handy picnic sizes, in cans or, conveniently, 'on tap'; the scope of instances when it can provide the middle classes with pleasure have considerably widened.

Similarly the enjoyment of any magazine in the 1980s is poles apart from that provided by *The Lady's Magazine* of the nineteenth century or even by pre-war magazines. The 'embelishments' the former introduced tuned readers' senses to simple forms of visual pleasure. By the 1980s sophisticated colour photography and graphics have arguably become the most important sources of pleasure in most magazines. Their contribution declines only as the proportion of the magazine devoted to romantic fiction increases. Interestingly, it was mainly fiction on which the early nineteenth-century periodicals depended for their amusement.

The pleasure of colour pages, including ads, is not peculiar to women or women's magazines. Rather women enjoy them differently to men. Colour photography in the printed media has come to be associated in our culture with leisure and pleasure for both sexes. We are likely to assume that a magazine with a high proportion of colour is one intended for relaxation, like the Sunday colour supplements, men's 'girlie' magazines, and women's magazines, and unlike the 'serious' periodicals and newspapers such as *The Economist, Spectator, Marxism Today*. These are predominantly 'black and white', clearly connoting 'news', 'documentary', 'social and political comment' and the harsh 'realities' of life.

Unlike men, however, women occupy an uneasy space in the work/leisure divide and it is the characteristics of the latter which partly give rise to the different meaning of those two visual forms. Symbolically women are men's leisure, to which the 'girlie' magazines are a sad witness. Women personify eroticism, leisure and pleasure. They are, in most men's imagination, the ultimate commodity to be 'enjoyed', the 'commodity' which is so often sold in ads. Woman has only become that symbol of leisure and pleasure since the nineteenth century on account of her association with the coveted private sphere of home and personal life: the restorative from the rigours of capitalism's public and productive domain. Yet for women themselves that private sphere has always meant domestic *work* – to say nothing of many women's additional public and paid work.

Women's own sense of what they do is caught between these two definitions of themselves: as objects of leisure and pleasure who don't really work, and as doing a work that is appreciated amongst women but largely unrecognised by men. The feminine activities of cooking, creating and looking after a home, and making oneself attractive have an uncertain status. In male terms these tasks do not constitute work because they are unpaid and done 'for love', and moreover are often done while men are at work. They are not work because they are about being a woman. In John Berger's telling phrase, 'Men act and women appear' (1972, p. 47). 'Actions' are associated with work; 'appearing' is to be at the disposal of others, on display, with any work to achieve that well hidden. Women (and their homes) just *are* for men: women know 'naturally' how to make a home, how to look attractive and so on.

That these feminine activities can be pleasurable and creative to do, that the finished product may be intended to provide aesthetic and other pleasures for self as well as others, also contribute to their uncertain status. Women themselves experience that merging – of work and leisure, of work and pleasure; and the tensions of that are embodied in women's magazines. 'Useful' articles are 'entertainment' and 'entertainment' is 'useful'. Their visual fictions weave stories around what is demarcated as a feminine work (closely bound up with the purchase and use of commodities) but the feelings those stories engender are pleasurable ones associated with leisure.

Airy routes to dreamland

If consumer patterns have partly determined the range of magazines available in Britain, consumption also visually dominates in any magazine. Most glossy colour pages, apart from illustrations accompanying stories, are devoted to advertising, beauty and fashion, and cookery and home, in varying combinations depending on the magazine. What is significant is that visual imagery, in colour especially, overshadows the written word. It has an immediate and rich impact the latter cannot inspire, while the associations of these colour images tend to stamp the firmest trace on magazine and readers' memory alike.

Such visuals tend to highlight a finished product – the delights of consumption – with the labour necessary to produce it indicated discreetly, often over-the-page, and in black and white. As in this *Options* cookery feature: 'Field Days . . . a picnic that's fun to make and to eat' (July 1983). The pleasure lies in the delights of both the finished product – 'pretty enough to please Grandma' – and what it represents: the joys of the classic English family summer picnic when the sun shines forth and the insects stay away from that idyllic spot by a stream. Women's work – preparing the picnic – has become by virtue of the remembered, or promised future treat in store, the enticing moment arrested in the *Options*-style family snapshot. The pleasure of this kind of visual borrows from advertising. As 'a propaganda for consumption', advertising tends to minimise the labour attached to the use of many of the goods we buy. Whatever the item, however dull and bare, advertising weaves in and around it colourful leisure dreams that feed the senses and the imagination. Through consumption – hey presto! – we have access to 'the good life'. And by consuming such images advertisers hope we are stimulated to consume the product – our key to dreamland. Doubtless sometimes we are.

Yet we frequently luxuriate in the advertisement without ever a thought of the product. Sitting at my typewriter in the overwhelming heat of a freak English July and many miles, unfortunately, from the sea, I've gained enormous pleasure from the ad shown in Figure 4.2. I have no intention of buying the

4.1 *Options*, July 1983

product. Indeed I am hard put even to remember what it is the image is advertising. We recognise and relish the vocabulary of dreams in which ads deal; we become involved in the fictions they create; but we know full well that those commodities will not elicit the promised fictions. It doesn't matter. Without bothering to buy the product we can vicariously indulge in the good life through the image alone. This is the compensation for the experience you do not and cannot have.

Ads allow the reader/viewer to dream; they assume nevertheless the mundane position in which she is placed daily, and play to the unfulfilled desires that generates. The editorial in women's magazines work similarly. Whatever practical activity they might be encouraging – and they usually are – they present pleasurable dreams to revel in (see Figure 4.3). They would not offer quite the same pleasure, however, if it were not expected of women that they perform the various labours around fashion and beauty, food and furnishing. These visuals acknowledge those labours while simultaneously enabling the reader to avoid doing them. In everday life 'pleasure' for women can only be achieved by accomplishing these tasks; here the image offers a temporary

4.2 Deep Fresh advertisement in *Good Housekeeping*, July 1983

The 'Deep Fresh' ad is typical of many. It addresses 'you' – the one and many viewers and readers – and draws 'you' into the visual image. 'You' are the woman diver. 'You' experience the refreshing splash into the ocean-as-bath. The surreal image is framed, the ad making no pretences at representing a 'reality'. Rather it constructs something other than 'your' bath, offering an aesthetic image of coolness – the blue/green shades – and of a 'natural' freshness – the sea, the sponge, the naked woman. The framing device shifts the experience into one of dreams and romance: perhaps the dream from your bath, of the setting sun; perhaps the woman bather whose taut body glows, as 'yourself'. The feel is sensual. What the ad relies on for its meaning and its pleasure is 'you' understanding the gap between your usual daily bath and what the ad evokes.

The most refreshing way to keep you and your family clean.

substitute, as well as providing an (allegedly) easy, often enjoyable pathway to their accomplishment.

A special 6-page feature in *Family Circle*, 'And all because . . . the Lady loves a Prince' was one of hundreds organised by July 1983 around Princess Diana. But it was particularly cleverly contrived. One of *Family Circle*'s regular slots is 'Master class' cookery, in which an expert chef (often male) takes readers through the necessary and skilled stages to produce the perfect and to-be-admired cake or soufflé or crown of lamb; here the esoteric recipe was for chocolate liqueurs. The intensive and fiddly labour involved in this culinary feat, shown on the last pages of the feature, was ideologically transformed by the romantic (and aristocratic) story that went before.

4.3   *Woman's World*, June 1983

'Hot Stuff', from *Woman's World*, is hedged in by ads for suntan creams and the following article revolves around this double page visual spread. The bizarre pose is excessive, playing around the caption 'hot stuff': the climate, sexuality, suggested by the arrangement of their two bodies. She, with her arched body and glistening sunlit leg, resting on him, is the sexual centre. It's the ultimate romantic setting which 'you' are invited to dream about, and to find: 'Jackie Robb shows you the way to a beautiful tan for you and your man . . .'

The opening gambit and end lines make explicit references to this fiction: 'You wander down to the surf, slim and tanned, lithe and lovely, with skin fresh and glowing – and you're followed by a lean, nut-brown man, muscle rippling as he moves towards you . . . All right, cut! End of dream.'

It is worth asking whether *Family Circle* would have been able to sell their moulds (assuming that they *did* sell them) for the 'Diana' liqueurs, and whether women would have attempted to make the liqueurs (assuming that they *did* make them), if the magazine had not used the powerful appeal of the royal romance. The feature perfectly illustrates the double-edge of the fiction these visuals construct: they fulfill women's desires for something other than their everyday lives but what is presented is the ultimate in class and feminine success. The visuals hold out the optimistic hope of what the daily labours of femininity can (and should) deliver, and offer practical routes to those dreams, whether these be via liqueur moulds or beauty advice. They also show living examples of feminine success – like Diana – her royal privilege minimised by the romantic memories all women can share. *Options* carries a slot called 'Lifestyle' (other magazines have the one-off article), full of wondrous fashion, food and furnishings, so creatively produced, and exceedingly happy families. These glowing accounts indicate how one woman's dream (the reader's) can blossom into another woman's reality. 'Lifestyle' women are superwomen lauded for their 'individuality': perfect wives and mothers, attractive, with successful careers. And there it is to see. She's done it; so can 'you' achieve that accolade of 'individuality'. But can you?

4.4a *Family Circle*, 13 July 1983
4.4b *Family Circle*, 13 July 1983
4.4c *Family Circle*, 13 July 1983

This feature pivots around its title, 'And all because the Lady loves a Prince'. 'And because we love a happy ending!' added *Family Circle*. Diana's second wedding anniversary affords the excuse of giving her a present: 'the first ever home-made chocolates in the Prince of Wales feather shape' packaged in 'an elaborate reminder of "that" wedding dress'. The fiction created here exploits the well-known selling line: 'And all because the Lady loves Milk Tray', in which a suitor risks life and limb to fetch the chocolates for his loved one. In a highly pertinent reversal 'he' is replaced by a collectivity of women – *Family Circle* and its readers. It is an implicit (though probably unconscious) recognition of what men do not do for women: only women would go to such creative bother in giving a present – notwithstanding Cadburys' persuasive copy.

Overleaf is another dream: 'Have you ever sighed at the price of liqueur chocolates and wished you could make them yourself?' 'Actual size, the chocolates *YOU* can make – to fill with the liqueurs of your choice, or even with "Princess Diana's fudge" – see opposite!'

And then finally, over the page again: 'How a Master Chocolate Maker has perfected the Home-Made Chocolate Liqueur' (in eleven easy steps). By this time by sleight of copy, visuals and imagination, the act of creatively producing liqueurs (described as an 'art') has become a key to the class pleasures and romance enjoyed by Diana.

'And all because...
the Lady
loves a Prince'

59

Consumer help: finding 'class', 'femininity' and 'yourself'

In the 1950s, when magazines discussed the new consumer work expected of women, women were being educated about a work which reflected not only on their femininity, but on their class status and the kind of individuals they were. As long ago as the nineteenth century when Samuel Beeton was publishing *The Englishwoman's Domestic Magazine* the clothes a woman wore and the contents and arrangement of her home were, on the one hand, signs of her husband's wealth and class position, on the other, signs of her own feminine accomplishments. In the 1950s, with the proliferation of goods and brands and varieties of each item, buying increasingly became a process of decision-making: 'Make your choice from this rich array of *Batchelor's* Wonderful Soups' (ad in *Woman*, 9 February 1957).

Making the right choice, according to the ads, brought you success as housewife and mother: household chores could be performed more easily and quickly; children and husband would be full of love and praise: 'Mum you're wonderful' (for providing Bisto, *Woman*, 9 February 1957). The right choice also improved your class status: 'New Zealand butter and good living go together' (*Woman*, 9 February 1957). And the infinite possibilities of choice spawned the individual effort which could make your home so different from everyone else's.

Ads may have revealed ideologies more clearly; they were not qualitatively different from many editorial features. If men's success and individuality was to be sought in a paid job, women's was to be achieved on the home front through consumption. As one *Woman* article, 'New home makers', began, 'All over the country couples are coming back from Honeymoon to a house that's one of a row. Edith Blair visits *three clever brides* who show how *beautifully individual* a room, same size, same shape as the neighbours can be' (10 May 1958, my emphasis). In 'Traditional furniture in colourful settings' Edith Blair this time guides on how 'to choose wisely' to make 'the most interesting home'. The codes of taste – the carefully placed cyclamen, bowl of fruit, and arrangement of plates on the dresser – have the ring of middle-class styles.

In 'Accent on your waist' Veronica Scott implies that the clever feminine woman needs to know her fabrics and the latest fashion look: 'Waists are in full focus again, for the most feminine line of all.' The look she is to strive for has pretensions to class – 'all-round elegance', the notion of a 'dress for every occasion', the snooty air of the models. And a presentation of choice offers the possibility of individual expression – 'Choose from this selection the clothes you need for work and play, to suit your individual background and way of life.' But this choice is within a tight conformity; literally, 'the belted look'.

By the 1960s fashion (for the young at least) had broken its strict and silly protocols, like 'never wear blue with green', and

Opposite page:
4.5 Vim advertisement in *Woman*, 3 September 1955
4.6 Worcester Ware advertisement in *Woman*, 10 September 1955

It's quicker and easier with VIM

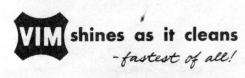

...that's why she's smiling!

Full marks, Mum! Two minutes ago that bath was a *sight*. Young Jimmy left it ringed with half the playground's grime. Look now! Beaming with that never-been-used look that *Sudsy* Vim gives everything it touches. Yes, everything brightens up when you and *Sudsy* Vim get going.

There's time to spare for a well-earned break when *Sudsy* Vim is your daily help. And when you tackle the midday meal there's a shining stove and a row of happy, Vim-trim saucepans ready and waiting. Vim's quick sudsing action deals thoroughly with the stickiest grease, the toughest dirt. Does it so safely, so quickly. *Sudsy* Vim is made to make you feel bright about *all* your cleaning.

VIM shines as it cleans
- fastest of all!

Hudson & Knight Limited

" Why Mary .. it looks a different kitchen. However did you do it ?"

" Just a lick of paint .. and this gay, coloured Worcester Ware "

These three illustrations are examples of the Worcester Ware Plantation range of kitchen equipment. They are also examples of Worcester Ware value.

(TOP) *Canisters in Rack, size complete* 18¾" x 6½" x 4⅛" *deep. Price* 11/6.
(LEFT) *Bread Bin* 17½" x 7" x 10" *deep. Price* 15/-.
(RIGHT) *Hinged-Lid Cake-Box* 8½" x 6¼" *high. Price* 5/6.

Paint up your kitchen, certainly!—but then bring *extra* colour on to tables and shelves with kitchen equipment from the Worcester Ware range! Made in metal, these trays, canisters and bread bins will remain bright and colourful for many years. Their gay decoration is protected from stains and deterioration by a hard, clear, oven-baked varnish. For further details of the wide range of Worcester Ware household articles and kitchen equipment write for illustrated catalogue to The Metal Box Company Ltd., Hardware Sales Office, Providence Works, Worcester.

WORCESTER WARE

brings such *Colour* into your home !

From leading Ironmongers, House Furnishers and Hardware Stores

4.7 *Woman*, 19 September 1959

the 1965 *Honey* girl was one who 'thinks fashion is fun, not a dictator. She'll mess about experimenting but she'll carve her own way through the maze of what's new so that she makes everybody wish they'd thought of the precise way of wearing that.' In May 1966 the magazine proclaimed,

> Next month we're stepping out of line. We're tired of being told what *not* to do . . . . Who says you can't do anything about the face you were born with . . . . Beauty for the individualist . . . and fashion too. Who says you've got to look like the girl at the next desk?

It was fashion, particularly in *Honey*, which most symbolised an individuality young women were searching for beyond the confines of their looks. Audrey Slaughter, *Honey's* editor until the end of the 1960s, asked, 'What is fashion?' and answered (January 1967),

> It's an expression of mood, of our age, of political climate, of economic pressures . . . we're hanging on to the shreds of our individuality . . . . We've discovered a new confidence, a kind of derring-do . . . the current dolly strides in, supremely unconcerned that her outfit is a combination of attic finds, boutique gimmick,

Sellotape creation and tin-foil glitter. She'll take on a big job in a faraway place with little to go on except a terrific optimism and faith in her own ability to make out . . . . Fashion isn't frivolous, though it's fun (or should be); it's a creative expression of our age.

In 'Yellow and black and white and fabulous' the copy constructs fashion as exciting, fun, daring and an individual signature: 'No peas-in-a-pod look this! Free enterprise colours depend on your recipe for fabulous.' Part of the 'excitement' and 'daring' leans on the play of words around fashion colours as racial colours, a connotation strengthened by the use of a (discreetly) black model: 'Get-ups with go-power. Integration of black and white and a spontaneous dash of mustard tin yellow.' At this time, 1969, the issue of race was indeed 'hot', stirred up by Enoch Powell's scaremongering speeches. Paradoxically, perhaps, it was he who in this same issue of *Honey* was overwhelmingly voted the person *Honey* readers would most like to see as prime minister – presumably on account of his individualistic, if highly racist stance!

Yet at the same time as fashion was being presented as a vehicle through which women could assert individuality, it also trapped them. What sort of 'freedom' was the Berlei ad luring women into? There was a pressure from glossy ads and editorial pages to achieve the right look, whether of a wide-eyed, childlike Twiggy, or just 'the *honey* look'. By the end of the 1960s images of women's near-naked erotically highlighted bodies, together with exaggerated sexual symbols (as if addressing a male audience?) confronted women at every turn of the page.

Since the 1960s social and political changes have occurred to allow women more routes to 'individuality' than those following the dictates of the latest fads and fashions in clothes, decor and cookery. And yet that contradictory and often doubtful 'individulity' still haunts us. Women's magazines still herald the consumer options: 'Fashion freestyle – all the options' (*Options* April 1982. In 'Living colour' *Options* sells the feminine standards of the season: 'What's important now is cut, to show off fabrics, textures, colour harmonies . . .'; and the standards of a certain class style: 'Take time and trouble when buying a sofa – it must appeal visually, suit the style of the room, be comfortable and, of course, be in line with your budget. This one, at £595, is excellent value . . . .' And the feature homes in on the need and desire to express 'your' individual taste: 'Creating the right atmosphere and mood to suit your personality is the essence of style – it depends both on your choice of furniture and clever use of colour. To illustrate the point, Andrea Spencer has designed three, individual rooms, each with an elegance of its own' (*Options*, April 1983).

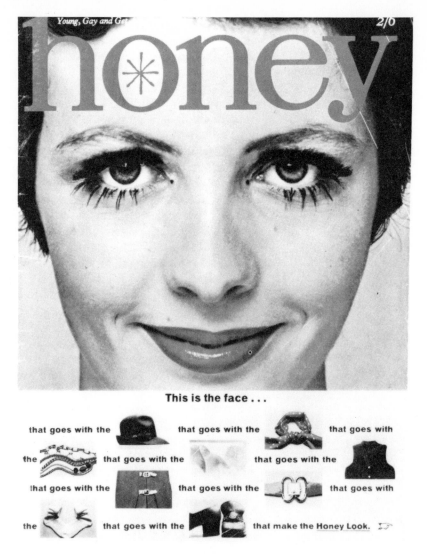

Young, Gay and Get

2/6

This is the face . . .

that goes with the · · · that goes with the · · · that goes with

the · · · that goes with the · · · that goes with the · · ·

that goes with the · · · that goes with the · · · that goes with

the · · · that goes with the · · · that make the **Honey Look.** ☞

4.8a *Honey* cover, September 1968

We do indeed live in a consumer culture and perhaps it would be more appropriate to propose that we might as well make the best of it. Moreover the tasks of femininity do permit some individual creative expression, so why gripe about it? Without denying the real pleasures of consumption and the (sometimes) creative feminine work associated with it, there are two things I want to say here. Firstly, these visual fictions around consumption are peculiarly addressed to women. As a result, any achievement of 'individuality' has a somewhat hollow ring, barely registering on a 'higher' masculine scale of values. Secondly, the terms these visual fictions set for an ideology of individuality – about individual choice, work and creativity – and its aura of success resonate through magazines as a whole. The outcome in many

4.8b Berlei advertisement in *Honey*, May 1969
4.8c English Rose advertisement in *Honey*, May 1969

articles tends to be an unwarranted optimism about the position of women and what it is possible for individual women to accomplish; the spectre of superwoman looms (see chapter 9).

In the next chapter I take up the theme of individuality again, this time in the context of 'the world of we women' magazines construct for their readers. Who, I want to ask, are 'we'? And who does this collectivity leave out?

Chapter 5

Between women

'Our world'

The titles of women's magazines are revealing. *Cosmopolitan* and *Options* have a definite outward-sounding ring; *She* ('Who's she? The cat's mother?') offers a bold and cheeky front; *Spare Rib* indicates a wry cynicism. More usually they fall into one of two camps. Either they offer variations on an introverted world of women: *Woman's World* (not by mere chance the fourth such-named magazine for women), *Family Circle*, *Woman's Realm*. Or they suggest themselves as a hybrid of the life-long friend and most favoured possession, to be clutched warmly to the bosom: 'The magazine is my friend, is mine': *People's Friend*, *Company*, *My Weekly*, *Honey*. If the latter indicates the style of women's magazines – they speak as 'friend' in chatty conversation with their readers – the former indicates exactly what it is the friends share: a woman's world.

In newspapers it is traditionally the editorial that represents 'the voice' of the paper. It makes a public statement about where the newspaper stands on certain issues and about its style of address and relationship to readers. Where editorials exist in women's magazines (some, like *Woman's Weekly*, do not have one), they adopt the personal address of 'I' and 'we – magazine and readers'. Newspaper editors do not call themselves 'I' when addressing their readers. Their names are often unknown and certainly their smiling faces do not head their daily comments. Only rarely, and only in the popular press, do they attach a signature.

In women's magazines the variously named editorials adopt the style of a friendly letter. For instance, Audrey Slaughter in *Honey* in the 1960s used to begin 'Dear Honeys' and finish 'Yours sincerely'. Establishing a personal relationship – which magazines begin to do with their covers – is one of the major purposes of the editorials. And both in and beyond the editorials the personal tone allows women to feel they are being individually addressed: '*Living*, *your* magazine for today' (my emphasis). It brings individual women together in a world they can share. As Carol Sarler commented in a *Honey* editorial, 'at best, a magazine functions like a good friendship. There's contact, there's communication *both* ways, there's mutual exchange of ideas and experiences and interests' (September 1983). In this spirit magazines encourage readers to participate in the magazine's activities, whether to become 'an *Over 21* star for a day' as a

My Weekly, in accord with other D.C. Thomson magazines, does not name the editor let alone offer either a photo or personal signature. The editorial looks nevertheless like a letter and is signed, in somewhat dated style, 'Your Editress'.

In 'Speak-Easy' the editor is ostensibly expressing her views on accents and dialects, saying firmly: 'Local dialects are our heritage, part of our identity and should never be allowed to disappear, but making the effort to communicate fluently is increasingly important now it's so easy to move from place to place.' In no uncertain terms she speaks to the reader from a position of editorial power – suggesting what should be – in a manner similar to newspapers. At the same time she draws readers into a common world she assumes they share: 'It's a thing most of *us* do, *I'm* sure, though *we* laugh when *we* hear others doing it,' that is, altering telephone voices to suit the caller (my emphasis). She assumes that readers have a knowledge and experience of marital intimacy and recognise and identify with those conversational exchanges.

5.1   *My Weekly*, 11 June 1983

Speak-Easy

'That was Colonel Jones on the phone, wasn't it?' I remarked to the Man Of The House the other day when he replaced the receiver.

'How on earth did you know that?' he asked, looking surprised. 'I was only on a couple of minutes and I didn't even mention his name.'

'Ah,' I said, smiling, 'but you used your *posh* voice. You only put it on for the Colonel and your boss.'

It's a thing most of us do, I'm sure, though we laugh when we hear others doing it – using different telephone 'voices' depending on who we're chatting to.

A broad dialect tends to evoke an accent in return, yet if we want to impress someone we become very 'proper.'

Funny how we only do it on the phone – though perhaps it's just as well. Imagine what it would be like in the company of Cockney friends and others with 'up-market' accents. You'd end up tongue-tied, if you tried to match them all!

There is a place for a dual accent or dialect, though. It often seems such a shame when children at school are forced to drop their native words and accents to conform to a standard way of speaking.

Yet, unless you intend staying in the one area all of your life, it's important to be able to communicate with anyone, from anywhere in Britain, or abroad.

Local dialects are our heritage, part of our identity and should never be allowed to disappear, but making the effort to communicate fluently is increasingly important now it's so easy to move from place to place.

Oops, must dash, there's the phone ringing . . .

'That was Marjory Elder, wasn't it?' The Man Of The House says when I've finished talking.

Now, how does he know I was speaking to the president of the Woman's Circle?

But, before I even ask, I see him grinning at me – wryly . . .

My best wishes to you all,

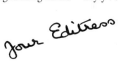

---

fashion model (July 1983), or to sample 'the delights of Paris with *Living*' (July 1983).

The editorials from *My Weekly*, *Over 21* and *Woman* (see Figures 5.1, 5.2, 5.3) demonstrate distinct styles of establishing this personal and friendly rapport with readers. Each engages and embraces readers in a world of 'we women' but assumes and constructs different definitions of who 'we' are – as do all magazines. What I want to explore in this chapter is the tenuousness of those shared worlds. On the one hand the various 'we's of magazines are fictional collectivities only some women are invited into; others are excluded or left on the margins: black women, lesbian women, women who are not able-bodied, older women. On the other hand it is the magazines who set the terms of friendship. When the covers of a magazine are closed women

EDITOR'S LETTER

'Why don't you photograph men for the front cover of the magazine?' is a question many ask. Their reasoning is that women are attracted to men, and if we wish to attract women to the magazine it would seem a good idea to have a male face on the front.

However since we primarily produce OVER21 for the information and entertainment of women, it somehow seems inappropriate that we should feature a man. A good looking man with a good looking woman is the compromise we have decided on for this month's issue. Our fashion pages reflect looks for men too this month and it's certainly encouraging to see the degree of interest they are showing in their appearance nowadays instead of sticking with the unflattering conventions and constraints of the menswear of yesteryear.

If men's clothes have changed, so have their priorities when it comes to finding a wife. Andrew French outlines the new requirements and there's no doubt that there will be a few letters coming to him in the postbag which entirely disagree with his views.

Despite all the liberation that exists today it's amazing how many women still feel at a loss without a man on tow, Wendy Leigh discusses the problem.

Marilyn Pettman advises on all sorts of problems as you know but this month we asked her to focus some attention specifically on male problems as it seems unfair that there should be so few opportunities for them to air their troubles.   PAT ROBERTS

5.2   *Over 21*, August 1983

Above:
In *Over 21* the 'Editor's Letter' is accompanied by a photo of Pat Roberts but not 'personally signed'. (Nor does Pat Roberts offer personal snippets of her own life.) In her photo she gazes frankly at 'you' the reader, and the 'letter' itself displays an honest engagement with readers' questions in order to explain *Over 21*'s editorial line. As with many magazine editorials, part of its intention is to point forwards to the contents – a more reflective expansion of the cover sell-lines (the main one here: 'Man Power').

'awake' from this shared world, alone: a 'friend' has gone. Paradoxically it is because women are 'alone' that they need to enter that world of magazines in the first place: a confirming circle.

Editorials are often part of a page to which readers also contribute. Whereas in many of the monthlies readers' letters take issue with articles in previous numbers, in the more traditional monthlies like *Annabel* and the weeklies, the letters are of a more perennial kind. I discussed some of them in chapter 2 where I emphasised how readers drew on 'history' to affirm an identity in the present. Self-affirmation of a woman's world is the primary characteristic of all these letters; appearing in print, being rewarded – as the lead letter usually is – attests to that. They are from women to women. They are concerned with those aspects of life women can only say with anger, or more often with pleasure, to women: laughing at, as well as praising their 'better halves'; homilies about everyday life or practical advice in living it; humorous acts and sayings of children; and one's own or other's feminine *faux pas*.

The rhythm of the world in these letters is cyclical, organised around the routines of a day, the natural seasons and established annual traditions. Further into the magazines this is more obvious: marmalade recipes at the end of January, romances for St Valentine's week, ice cream and 'Sundae best' fashion for July, roast goose or turkey at Christmas. Everyday life is offered as fulfilling, as having moments of drama and extraordinariness to disrupt and enliven it. It is never the same, from one day to the next (from one magazine issue to the next). Yet despite references to 'history' or obvious signs of 'modernity' – as in 'Pegged' in Figure 5.4a – there is a timelessness about it. 'Mum's the word' or 'The little words' (perhaps with other captions) could as well have been in *Woman* 1983 as *Woman* in the 1950s.

WE THINK

5.3   *Woman*, 16 July 1983

By 1990, say people who mastermind our futures, eight out of 10 of the workforce will need technical skills or qualifications. And who dares to predict what percentage of the population will make up that workforce?

So it isn't only academic education that we're going to need, it's education for life – the 'whole person' approach. Many countries – notably Japan – have planned their adult education accordingly. But have we? It seems that compared to our competitors we are undertrained, resistant to change and ill-prepared for rewarding leisure-time activities. There is a distinct lack of effort too, on the part of industry to train the existing workforce for the changing patterns of technology, work practices and lifestyles; lots of fine words, but not much action. While money for adult education is available, there is no co-ordination of resources to get things moving. The Manpower Services Commission is pressing for a co-ordinated campaign, yet fighting against apathy.

Women's careers could so easily lose out in the education race, but elastic schedules can give us time to follow courses. What we need to know is where and how we can plug in to this great well of self-improvement. Is it through evening classes in computer programming, day release courses in new manufacturing processes, an Open University qualification, or by using an Information Technology Centre? And should we be hiring 'learning tapes' for that video?

Above all, we kneed to know that our communities and companies are committed to the principle of continuing education throughout life, for that's the key to improving a family's changing future.

Editor

Mum's the word

I delivered some shopping to my neighbour and arrived just as her small boy was eating his boiled egg. Of course, he immediately jumped down from the table.

His mother and I chatted for a few minutes and then, with a faraway look in her eyes, she took a spoonful of egg and popped it into my mouth.
– Mrs. A.P. (Greenford Middx).

Your story reminds us of a colleague who came in one day to apologize, shamefacedly, for not sending us a birthday card on time.

The evening before, thinking of the meal she had to prepare when she got home, clutching our card firmly, she had proceeded to post it in the 'used tickets' box as she got off the bus.

5.4a   *Woman*, 17 January 1953

PEGGED!

Taking off a duvet cover and replacing it with a clean one can be a very frustrating business.

I find the best way is to push in the corners and retain each in turn from the outside with a spring clothes peg.

Fasten the press studs, shake the duvet to even out the filling and then remove the pegs.

– Mrs M.C., Leeds

5.4b   *My Weekly*, 11 June 1983

Above:
When Jane Reed took on the job of Editor-in-chief of *Woman* (August 1981) its editorials – 'We Think' – adopted a style which has a lot in common with popular newspaper leaders. They were explicitly set up as hard-hitting 'think' pieces on topical issues with a special relevance to women. Here the focus is adult education in a world where the required skills for jobs are rapidly changing: 'Women's careers could so easily lose out in the education race, but elastic schedules can give us time to follow courses. What *we* need to know . . .' (my emphasis). 'We' includes not just the magazine but *Woman*'s readers too.

The little words

Do other girls find that the male members of their family forget to say 'Please' and 'Thank you'?

Tonight I have been told to switch on the radio, let the cat in, pass the scissors, find an india-rubber, put coal on the fire and get supper ready – and not *once* have they said 'Please', or 'Thank you.' Men! –
Miss M.T. (Sheffield, Yorks).

We suggest that next time you sit tight, and look inquiring when asked to do something or other.

'Put some coal on the fire,' a brother will demand.
'Did you say anything else?' you can ask politely.
'No, I didn't,' he will say. 'What did you think I said?'
'Oh, I thought you said, please' you can murmur, as you ply the tongs.

5.4c   *Woman*, 2 March 1957

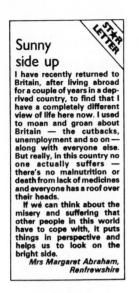

Sunny side up

I have recently returned to Britain, after living abroad for a couple of years in a deprived country, to find that I have a completely different view of life here now. I used to moan and groan about Britain — the cutbacks, unemployment and so on — along with everyone else. But really, in this country no one actually suffers — there's no malnutrition or death from lack of medicines and everyone has a roof over their heads.

If we can think about the misery and suffering that other people in this world have to cope with, it puts things in perspective and helps us to look on the bright side.

*Mrs Margaret Abraham,
Renfrewshire*

5.5 *Woman's Realm*, 16 July 1983

These cheerful and often constructive letters read as antidotes to the gloom and doom and revelling in tragedy and criticism that newspapers wheel and deal in. And women know that. Their letters disclose them trying to define a world other than that, a world in which everyday matters (the fodder of many a day for top executives as well as mums at home) are important, and happiness the aim, not sideline of life. *Woman's Realm*'s 'Star Letter', 'Sunny side up' (Figure 5.5), is a classic example. The letter is at once fatalistic and hopeful. For women ideologically bound to the personal terrain and in a position of relative powerlessness about public events, this tension recurs in their views. Many believe, 'If only individuals would ... the world would be a much better place.' They are caught in an ideology which regards self-help and self-transformation as the key to both a personal and a social happiness.

Against the wall: fictions of triumph

It is what are known in the trade as the 'triumph over tragedy' (TOT) stories in women's magazines that most poignantly epitomise what Marjorie Ferguson has described as the 'recurrent melody of helping oneself to overcome' (1983, p. 51). In these stories – more common in the traditional weeklies than in *Cosmopolitan*, say – 'ordinary' women recount their struggles with diverse personal misfortune, from losing a baby by cot death to holding on to the baby experts predicted would die; from becoming an unmarried teenage mum to living as an already sterilised teenager like Susan Carter in Figure 5.6 – and winning through. Set up as 'real-life' and personal stories, they are recognisable by their visual code of black and white, family-type (if professional) snapshots. Many read somewhat hollowly; perhaps it doesn't matter. As 'religious parables' or a latter-day version of *Pilgrim's Progress* these stories 'teach' that faith in oneself (if not in God), hope (that there *is* a bright light at the end of the tunnel), and individual effort will get 'you' there as well as the 'heroine' of the story. In seeing these women's emotional strength and courage to come through or just go on, whatever the trials sent to test them, 'you' as reader either feel that, well, at least you haven't got that tragedy to contend with – fed-up as you might well be – or that if you are up against some other wall you might just leap it yet.

Recourse to personal testimony in these stories tends to manifest the same mix of fatalism and hope expressed in readers' letters. It is about individual resourcefulness in tackling problems, about making decisions. Yet it also blocks possibilities for women.

This story tells how Susan Carter, aged 17, has a '50-50 chance of developing an incurable paralysing brain disease – the disease from which her mother is slowly dying'. Since Susan could also pass on the disease she and her father had decided she should be sterilised. The story *is* heartbreaking and Dee Remington's pen works very hard to create a mood of brightness to endorse 'happy' family life (it's clearly very strained) and a hopeful future. The story concludes:

> Mum used to tap a lot with her foot. Tap . . . tap . . . tap . . . it drove me mad before we knew what was causing it. When I'm listening to records I start tapping my foot and I think: 'My God, what am I doing that for?' She laughs. She is facing the future with great courage. The same kind of courage with which her father is facing the end of his past.

And the reader gulps.

Exciting, courageous, even heartbreaking. People tell how they faced DECISIONS *that changed their lives*

"I cry when I see children playing in the park"

5.6 *Woman*, 5 February 1983

Personal revelation is used as validation of the experiences: it speaks the unalterable 'truth' of women's lives. Readers are not invited to analyse and understand *why* these experiences have occurred or to see them as deriving from a social as well as personal history. Thus the contemplated future problems of marriage and children for Susan Carter can only arise in a culture placing such primacy on women marrying and bearing their own children.

Short stories, as opposed to serials in women's magazines, have much in common both with the Triumph Over Tragedy stories and the visual fictions I discussed in the last chapter. Like the former, their subject is 'ordinary' women and the problems of personal life. Like the latter, the license of a fictional form allows magical leaps and interventions and 'resolutions' which are profoundly satisfying because they don't happen in real life. If these stories con women, as critics often suppose, women know full well what that con is.

It would be a gross and unjust generalisation to lump all women's magazine stories together. *People's Friend* and *Woman's Weekly* still carry traditional romances. *Woman's Own* and *Woman* have less rejected the romantic genre than played with its codes, with endings, for example, not always the traditional 'happy ever after' as in the story below. With *Honey* and *Cosmopolitan* fiction moves, with more venturesome authors, on to bolder thematic fronts. Rather than skim across this range of fiction I have opted to try to grasp the detailed flavour and pleasure and pertinence for women, of just one story.

He'll be here on Saturday

By Margaret A Robinson

He seemed to be everything she could want in a man. He was sensitive, witty, sophisticated. He liked children. He had a wonderful sense of humour. He was married

Gina met him in the launderette in the High Street early one Saturday morning when it was empty. She was listening to her machine fill when a man touched her on the shoulder.

'Excuse me,' he said. 'The change machine's broken. I wondered if you had any 10 pence pieces.'

He was a completely ordinary man, with dark brown hair and grey-blue eyes. He wore running shoes and jeans and a faded denim jacket. Gina gave him change. He thanked her, started his wash, then came back and leaned on the machine next to hers. His bottom seemed firm and muscled against the taut blue denim.

'Rotten day,' he said, looking at the cold March rain, through the steamy windows.

'Dreadful,' Gina agreed.

Their two machines swished and gurgled. He was using one of the big ones. She saw a pink pair of child's pyjamas, with feet, plastered against its sudsy window.

'Like a cup of coffee?' he asked. 'There's that place across the street.'

Gina glanced again at the pink pyjamas. 'Okay.' she said. 'They've got good Danish pastries too.'

He was forty-two, an engineer, and his name was Jack. His children were four and six, and a girl and a boy. The marriage 'wasn't very good'. He spent his spare time playing squash.

Because he was older, she found him comfortable to be with. She didn't worry about her messy hair or her scruffy Saturday morning outfit. He told her a funny story about his little boy. Clearly he adored his children. Gina liked him.

At the office on Monday morning the editorial assistants were gossiping in the loo. Today's topic was that one of the secretaries, Harriet, had been frequently seen having drinks with one of the senior editors, Bob Hodges.

'Is he married?' one girl asked.

'Of course,' said another. 'All the good ones are married.'

Gina found herself suddenly speaking with some force. 'I would never get involved with a married man.'

'Oh, I don't know,' said Judy, who wore a shaggy blonde perm with a great many gold rings. 'Hodges is awfully attractive. He can leave his shoes under my bed anytime.'

Everyone laughed and went back to work. Gina's words echoed in her own ears and her vehemence surprised her.

She had never even considered having an affair with a married man.

Jack was there the next Saturday, too, this time choosing a small machine like hers. Gina took the one next to his and they exchanged greetings while she emptied her laundry bag and tipped in some soap powder. Then he pushed in his money at the exact same moment she did, which made her smile.

'Coffee?' he asked.

'Fine.'

His ordinariness attracted her.

Owen, the only man she had been seriously involved with had been all dash and fire, out to make his mark in the world by the time he was thirty. They had often gone out when she wanted to stay at home reading, but she had felt Owen was a good influence on her, had liked warming herself at his energetic flame. It had hurt when he left her.

One of the first things she noticed about Jack was that, on Saturday, at least, he didn't wear a watch. He hadn't seen every current film and play and was not apologetic about having missed them. What he was excited about was an old jazz recording he'd just got hold of.

'I heard it for the first time last night,' he said. 'Billie Holiday. I love her.'

'Does your wife like jazz?' she asked, awkward, curious.

'She hates it. We had one of our typical evenings. I listened to Billie Holiday and she fell asleep.'

Gina said, 'I don't know the first thing about jazz.'

'It's the best music there is. It's what people's souls would say to each other if they could talk. I have a stereo in the attic where I keep my records. Soundproofed. I listened to Billie Holiday six times.'

'I'd like to hear it.'

Jack toyed with his spoon. 'I ca[n] invite you over. Marie would [n't] understand. I can't even ask you [over]. Isn't that ridiculous?'

Gina spoke with the same sw[eet]deness she had felt at work during [the] discussion of Harriet. 'We could p[lay] the record at my place,' she said.

His face lit up. 'I can't, not t[his] weekend. Next Saturday morning?'

Gina gave him her address a[nd] phone number. He didn't give her h[is.]

'I have to tell you,' he said, as t[hey] left the corner booth of the café. 'C[ur] washing machine is being repaired [on] Monday.'

That week she went to the launder[ette] on Friday night and then tidied up [her] flat. She did some cleaning out [of]

5.7 'He'll be here on Saturday' by Margaret A. Robinson in *Woman*, 6 July 1983

The illustration, graphic not photographic, signals immediately to the reader: 'fiction' not 'real life'. Together title, visual and blurb hook her into a narrative she can already guess at. The image of a couple tells of a love story – the odd waviness and concentric circles framing them pose the enigma (and the probable

thwarted love) to be unfolded.

Wasting no words the opening paragraph introduces 'the lovers' shown by the visual image and quickly sets an easily identifiable scene. The story is written in the third person – 'she' – but it is as if Gina herself were rehearsing her thoughts: 'I . . .'. Gina, and reader, knowing such situations, dissolve one into the other. From this familiar beginning, and having established that Gina and Jack like each other, the scene shifts to

another commonplace scene: 'the office on Monday' where the gossip in the washroom concerns a secretary's married lover, also her senior at work. Interested, 'Gina found herself suddenly speaking with some force. "I would never get involved with a married man."' With superior knowledge – as always – the reader knows she will. This outburst introduces a tension to drive the narrative along: how will Gina deal with becoming involved despite her

dn't been able to do before, throwing
ay Owen's aftershave, sports maga-
es, the shirt he'd left behind and
ich, for a time, she'd been sleeping

When Jack arrived the next morning,
e flat looked better than it had for
eks. He was wearing what he wore
the launderette and carried a bag of
nish pastries and a small potted
nt.

Gina made coffee and they listened
Billie Holiday, with Jack comment-
g and explaining. Then they had
me more coffee and he asked her
out her family and her job. He
nted to know her favourite colour
d favourite food and when her
rthday was.

'Next week,' she said. 'I'll be
twenty-five on Saturday.'

'A quarter of a century! We'll have
to celebrate. Maybe I can see you on
Friday night, if you're free. Could we
make a tentative date for then? If I can
get away, for Friday at about nine
o'clock? I'll bring a cake and champagne. Do you like champagne?'

'Lovely.'

'Then I'll see you then, most
probably.' He kissed her goodbye,
which made her happy. She was
relieved that he had made no other
move towards her. Perhaps Jack could
be just a friend. He seemed to be
everything she could want in a man.
He was sensitive, witty, sophisticated,
relaxed. He liked children. He had a
wonderful sense of humour.

All day Monday she thought
about him and the way he had
kissed her, cursing herself for
her foolishness. On Tuesday
he was on her mind, the look of him
and the sound of his voice when he
talked about the music he loved.

On Wednesday she received
through the mail a box of detergent
and a poem:

Roses are red.
Violets are blue.
If it weren't for the launderette
I'd never have met you.
Happy Brithday!

On Thursday, on her doormat, she
found a box of gold-wrapped,
chocolate-covered raspberries,
strawberries and cherries. Their
taste was extraordinary, sinfully
fruity, wickedly rich.

On Friday, when she had just
trudged home from work in another
cold March drizzle, the florist round
the corner delivered a dozen pink
and white carnations.

By eight-thirty, Gina was waiting
for Jack. Too excited to think about
dinner, she had tidied up the flat,
bathed and changed. Now she

strolled around her two small rooms,
pressing her nose into a carnation,
nibbling a chocolate. She felt like a
schoolgirl waiting for her first date.
But at nine he didn't come, or nine-
thirty or ten.

At quarter to eleven, he arrived,
saying 'I'm sorry, one of the children
was sick.'

'You didn't phone,' said Gina
miserably.

He took both her hands, then
dropped them, and stepped back.
'Listen,' he said, 'I've been thinking a
lot about whether this whole thing is
fair to you. I can never phone. You'll
never be able to phone me, though I
can give you my office number in
case of an emergency. But just to
talk – no. We'll never be able to go
out, because even London, big as it
is, is too small. But I want to be with
you and to know you and I want you
to know me. I think I can give you a
lot, but those are the terms.'

'I don't do this sort of thing,' said
Gina.

'Neither do I. I've never done it
before. I know its dishonest, sneaky.
But it also feels alive. I've been
thinking about you every day. I
loved sending you presents. It's
been a wonderful week.'

Gina said, 'I had a wonderful
week too. But now I don't know what
to do.'

'We could have some cake and
champagne, if you want to. Life is
short. Everything takes so long to
work out. It's taken me forty years to
realise that people should have
what they want. When we've had
our cake and champagne, we'll talk.
Then I'll go home. Or we'll go to
bed. It's up to you.'

She woke on Saturday morning later
than usual, feeling weightless. The
other side of the bed was empty. The
love-making had not been wonderful.
What she had liked was the holding

and stroking, the feel of skin on skin.
And now Jack was at home pouring
milk on his children's cornflakes. The
carnations breathed, pink and white,
on her table, surrounded by crumbs.

He rang her bell again a week later
and he made love to her right away,
barely speaking first. It was too quick
for her, but she wanted to be with him
and did not insist that he slow down.

She had been in a state of terribly
mixed feelings – joy at having found
him, guilt, anger that her time with
him was so short.

'I know I won't be enough for you,'
he said, afterwards, running his hand
over his hair. 'I hope you'll go out with
other people. Single people.'

She looked at him aghast that he
could make such a suggestion when
she was still feeling the imprint of his
body.

'How can you say that? How can I
do that? I don't want to do that.'

'I don't want you to either,' he said
desperately. 'But I know this isn't fair
to you. Please don't be hurt.'

For breakfast they ate slices of the
left-over birthday cake. They talked
and listened to the new record he had
brought. They made love again, more
slowly, but Gina did not have enough
of being held before it was time for
Jack to go. It hurt her to see how
carefully he washed, so there would be
no trace of sex for his dog or child or
wife to detect.

The secrecy was exciting. The secrecy
made her wince with guilt. She longed
to introduce him to Judy, talk about
him at work. When she could contain
herself no longer, she did.

'Marvellous!' Judy said. 'A sugar
daddy!'

'Not really. He's not supporting
me.'

But all those presents – the plant
and the chocolates and the flowers.

---

*better wisdom of its folly? The
narrative then spirals upwards
(sometimes stories slump initially but
an up and down combined narrative
and emotional movement is always
present in them). Gina's spirits rise as
she becomes acquainted with Jack.
Boldly she invites him to her flat. He
comes bearing what are soon to be
recognised by the reader as symbolic
gifts, 'a bag of Danish pastries and a
small potted plant', and they enjoy
cakes and coffee together. So far, as*

*friends, so good. End of Act 1.
Act 2 cultivates a heightening
sexual frisson: 'on her doormat, she
found a box of gold-wrapped,
chocolate-covered raspberries,
strawberries and cherries. Their
taste was extraordinary, sinfully
fruity, wickedly rich.' Expectantly
Gina awaits Jack for a romantic
soirée; only he's late: 'I'm sorry, one
of the children was sick.' Gina is
miserable and a first cold dawn of
realisation nips their ardour. While*

*the reader detects signs of the
beginning of the end for Gina, Jack
is persuasive. Stating his terms
(contradictory but they clear his
conscience) he magnanimously (?)
leaves the 'choice' to Gina. She
chooses.
Their now sexual encounters
continue but their 'secrecy made her
wince with guilt'. She becomes
obsessed with his wife, caught up in
the fantasy that he will leave her.
Meanwhile he, at one and the same*

It's so romantic.' Judy lowered her voice conspiratorily. 'Have you seen his wife?' she whispered.

Gina glanced away. Soon after the affair had begun, she had been overwhelmed with remorse and curiosity. She had looked up Jack's address in the phone book and walked to his road. Eventually a woman had come out of the house with a small child in tow. Gina watched how carefully Marie lifted her daughter into the stroller and buckled her in. She was short and dark with deep set eyes and curly hair. Oh, God, Gina had thought: She looks just like me.

'I saw her once,' Gina replied.

'Supposing she finds out?'

'She probably knows.'

'It's too much, Gina! You see him Saturday mornings and the rest of the time he's a faithful hubby, taking out the rubbish and reading to the kiddies. How can you stand it? Isn't it driving you bats?'

Gina smiled and shook her head.

'Listen. In ten years you'll be a senior editor, thirty-five years old and somebody's once-a-week girlfriend. What kind of a life is that?'

'Maybe his wife will leave him.'

'Maybe cows will learn to tap dance.'

'His kids will grow up. Once they're out of the nest, he'll be free to leave the marriage.'

'That's like waiting for a mountain to erode. You started seeing him in March and it's May already. You have no idea what you're doing. You're nuts. Absolutely nuts.'

Gina looked at Jack's potted plant sitting on the window sill over her kitchen table. It had put out several new leaves and was a tiny bit taller. She got up now, felt the soil, which was dry, and gave it a drink. The water sank quickly into the thirsty earth.

Summer warmed the parks and pavements. Sometimes late on Friday night they went out for a walk, a drink, a snack, staying out of her neighbourhood and his, not going to the same place twice. Her cherished fantasy was that he would leave his wife.

'But you know I never will. I made that clear from the start. I can't leave my children. If we were divorced, or even separated, she'd remarry fast or she'd take the kids and go back to Wales. She's very attractive, I know her. I'd never see the kids and some other man would become their stepfather. I can't do that.'

He won't do it, Gina thought. He could, but he won't. He has it both ways. Why should he?

'I wish you'd go out with other men. Men your own age. Single ones.'

'I would,' she said, and tossed her head, 'if the right one came along.' But she knew the right one wouldn't come along as long as her emotional life was tied up with him. Every week he sent her some silly present, and whenever he arrived, he brought French roast coffee or croissants.

'I suppose a person could get tired of this,' she said when she opened the door to find him with another load of paper bags, 'but I don't.'

They put on some music, danced, made jokes, made love. He had encouraged her to tell him what pleased her, and the love-making had become good for Gina in an entirely new way, a totally different experience from Owen's marathons. What she still wanted most was to find Jack in her bed in the morning. But it was a point of pride with her not to whine. She didn't complain. Let Marie be the one to nag him.

Jack kept urging her to go out with other people, though she knew she was inviting no advances. She did spend the evening with a new editor at

work. It was a tedious date, the long process of getting to know him, asking questions and having to reply to questions, whereas with Jack everything was in an easy shorthand. She regaled Jack with a comic account of that tiresome evening and they laughed about it until they ached. During the week that followed, she felt smug and content, convinced that she had the best of all possible lives.

It was September when Gina came back to her flat one evening with shopping to see a shadowy form through the frosted glass in the hall of her building. She thought it might be Jack. Perhaps he was surprising her with one of his whimsical presents or had by some miracle come to see her, though it was only Wednesday night. She opened the door and went in, fumbling in her bag for the key to her own front door. She barely realised that the man was standing in a dark corner, before he had snatched her bag with one hand and thrown her violently to the floor with the other. Her head thudded against the wall on the far side of the hall and for a moment she lay helpless, gasping for breath, her head aching and spinning.

A door banged open on the second floor. Footsteps hurried down the stairs. Her neighbour was bending over her.

'Are you all right?' She was asking.

After a few moments, Gina was able to nod weakly and get to her feet. Her door key lay on the floor. Her handbag had gone. One of her shoes had come off and was lying in the corner of the hall. Her groceries lay scattered. A broken bottle of tomato sauce oozed wetly on to the floor.

'Shall I phone someone for you? Your friend, that one who comes on Saturday?'

'No, no. I'm okay.'

The neighbour helped to collect Gina's things, wiped up the sauce, and accompanied her upstairs. Gina thanked her, locked the door, the bolt, the chain. Then she began to cry.

She couldn't phone Jack. She had his office number, in case of emergency, but he would have left by now. The person she wanted most in the world at the moment, to comfort her and reassure her, to hold her while she shook with fear, then to help her repair the damage and laugh crazily because she was still alive and almost unhurt – that person could not be called on.

When he came on Saturday morning and stood on her doormat with a bouquet of yellow crysanths, ignorant of her ordeal, freshly shaved and smiling, a tidal wave of anger rose up in her.

'I was mugged on Wednesday night,' she said.

'No! How?'

'In the hall downstairs.' She remembered how she had imagined that the indistinct figure was he and she became even more furious. 'I needed you and you weren't with me and you're never going to be with me. This whole business has got to end.'

'Did he hurt you?'

'Not as much as he could have done.'

'It must have been terrible. I can see your cheek's bruised. Poor love.' He held out his arms and she went to him.

'Maybe we can work something out,' he said softly, stroking her hair. 'So I can be here more often.'

'No, you can't. We've been through that before. I know how it is. Your children come first. Then work. Then Marie.'

'That's in order of time, not importance.'

'Don't split hairs. It comes to the

---

time (near enough) makes love to her, too quickly, and says somewhat unconvincingly, that he hopes she'll go out with single men. Not surprisingly Gina's feelings are 'terribly mixed': 'What she still wanted most was to find Jack in her bed in the morning.' At other times 'she felt smug and content.' With the problem and pleasures all confusingly to the fore Act 2 ends.

Act 3 introduces the fateful, 'unreal' event stories rely on to pivot the narrative towards a 'resolution'. Gina is mugged. And: 'The person

she wanted most in the world at that moment, to comfort and reassure her, to hold her while she shook with fear, then to help her repair the damage and laugh crazily because she was still alive and almost unhurt – that person could not be called on.' The crunch has come; the moment of truth – he is not and will not be there when she wants him – hits her. She (and the story) have reached their lowest ebb. The reader and she now know that the threads of the relationship must be undone.

When he appears on Saturday

morning armed with a bunch of chrysanths (autumnal if not funereal in association), 'A tidal wave of anger rose up in her.' For once they eat mere toast and drink instant coffee: '"The honeymoon seems to be over," Jack said . . . . Gina nodded.' Each however, sees the situation differently. He seems content to continue offering the impossible – more of his time. She 'can't stand it any more . . . . She was exhausted.' It is Gina who recognises that it is 'time for it to end. His nurturing, ironically, had made her strong enough to realise that. She

Worlds apart: and lonely women

Gina and Jack in 'She'll be here on Saturday' seem to be situated somewhere amongst the hazy middle classes of British culture. The signs are subtle: French roast coffee and croissant, she's an editorial assistant, he an engineer. 'Heroines' and 'heroes' never work on the factory floor or live in council houses. Many magazine readers and their men probably do. In a class-divided society, however, the classes in authority are continually affirmed culturally, whereas working-class culture is always represented as something 'to be improved upon', and it as often seems that way to those who live it as to those who do not. The 'best, proper and normal', and the 'model' magazines spur women to emulate, to aspire to or simply to admire, is white, middle-class (sometimes aristocratic) culture.

Class differences are accepted in magazines as inevitable; it is never questioned why there should be rich and poor, royalty and commoners, executives and lavatory attendants. It's just life. In the more traditional magazines a deferential class respect is expressed. In *Woman's Weekly* we see inside 'Hagley Hall, a working stately home' and are told (4 June 1983),

> Maintaining a stately home involves hard work, and there is certainly no sitting down on the job for the Viscountess, who married at 19 and three years later found herself responsible for turning Hagley Hall into a successful business venture . . . . The whole adds up to what must seem a daunting prospect for any ordinary wife, but on being asked what she felt about it, the reply was unhesitatingly, 'I simply love it.'

The 'ordinary' wife is definitively set apart from the viscountess; she knows her place, somewhere near the servants to whom 'the mistress of Hagley is affectionately known as "the dragon"'.

More often class divisions are covertly made irrelevant: women are daughters, wives and mothers whatever their class. The colourful keyhole views of the lives of the rich and famous

---

same thing. I can't stand it any more.'

'Let's have breakfast,' he said, 'and talk.'

She made instant coffee. Jack made toast.

'The honeymoon seems to be over,' Jack said, indicating the ordinary fare.

Gina nodded. Though she had never felt like this before, had clung to their few hours together, she almost wanted him to go away. She didn't want to 'talk'. She was exhausted.

'What do you want me to do for you, Gina?' Jack asked. 'Not long-range future stuff. Now – in this time we can spend together. Tell me what you need *now*.'

He'd said things like that to her before and she'd thought it was like an exercise in meditation, where you block out the past and future and stay right in the present moment. 'Rub my back,' she had said on other occasions, or 'Put on some Art Blakey.'

Today, looking at him across the breakfast table, she was no longer angry, only sad to find she couldn't think of anything he could do for her, only sad to be discovering that it was time for it to end. His nurturing, ironically, had made her strong enough to realise that. She would have to do it, because he never would. And she would have to start soon, before she lost her courage. She glanced away from him to the potted plant on her window-sill, taller now, green and sturdy.

'You've done so much for me,' she began. 'I've loved every minute of it. You couldn't have done more.'

---

would have to do it, because he never would.'

And she does: 'She glanced away from him to the potted plant on her window-sill, taller, green and sturdy' – the symbol of her growth – and says, lying through her teeth if we're to take seriously what has gone before: 'You've done so much for me . . . . I've loved every minute of it. You couldn't have done more.'

Paradoxically, breaking the relationship is fictionally represented as a sewing up. Improbable in real *life the romance and story 'succeeds' and satisfies: in leaving her sad but not angry, strengthened and not weakened; it leaves him wholly irreproachable. As in the* Triumph Over Tragedy *stories there is a moral: not that you shouldn't have a relationship with a married man but that if you do be warned, you may 'grow' through it but you will have to end it. It is Gina who has to bear that personal responsibility: after all he gave her a 'choice', didn't he? He never backtracked on his family* *commitment, did he? Ironically the latter is what Gina wants and the reason she ends the relationship. Marriage, family, women's and men's different sexualities are totteringly acclaimed. With the knowledge women have of themselves and men and relationships there is an acute pleasure and pain in this fragile end: woman alone; she's lost, but convinces herself she has won. It will be left to her friends, those women who play only bit parts ideologically, to pick her up – after 'The End'.*

unfailingly strive to present them experiencing exactly the daily ups and downs of readers. Brought down from a celebrity pedestal, they meet readers on the latters' terrain: marriage and relationships, children and home, and work.

In this vein *Woman's Realm*, relaunched in September 1982 for the 'young married woman with children', carried 'What motherhood means to Esther Rantzen' (16 July 1983). Its introductory blurb ran, 'For ten years now Esther Rantzen has been battling for your consumer rights on 'That's Life!' In the same action-packed decade she has also married and become a mum - three times over. And her new family has changed her life completely, as Jay Nelson discovered . . . .' Further on, and on cue it seems, she remarks, 'The most important thing that's happened in the past ten years . . . is my marriage and my children.'

Doubtless. But her problems of being the harassed working mum cannot be quite the same as those of most of *Woman's Realm*'s less well-off and less middle-class readers, in spite of Esther Rantzen and the magazine trying to convince otherwise: 'The truth is the children don't like my work much, but I'm in a cleft stick: I impress on them that I'd rather be with them – that theirs is the company I treasure – but on the other hand, I *don't* want to convey the impression that work is boring.' Esther Rantzen may have in common with readers the responsibility she (and not Desmond Wilcox, her husband) has for the children. (I presume the children do not whine about Daddy's work.) But whereas she is publicly valued in her job, readers are unlikely to experience that confidence. Nor are they likely to have the ample financial means to manage and ease worries about childcare arrangements. Therefore in stressing the importance of personal life for Esther Rantzen, and hence supporting the reader in her own familial role, the immense gulf between the two women in terms of status, wealth, class and lifestyle is minimised.

If it is middle-class culture which magazines and readers alike see as ideologically desirable, it is not surprising that (more working-class) readers tend to appear as in need of help or 'education' on the femininity front. Or they are the 'victims' of the Triumph Over Tragedy stories. What is so significant about these stories is that the human triumphs they detail are emotional and not material ones. They are not even modest 'rags to riches' stories. There are two things to infer. Firstly, notwithstanding the weighty visual evidence to the contrary, there is an ideological insistence in magazines (and probably half-shared by readers) which places personal life, emotions and relationships above wealth and possessions, career success and celebrity lifestyle. Any class 'advantage' is deemed superfluous here. Secondly, and more controversially, these human triumphs of the emotions represent the 'success' readers would in fact like to have on other fronts, but which is more difficult to achieve. The presence and enjoyment of these articles perhaps indicates that magazines and readers indirectly acknowledge that class *is* a limiting factor in people's lives. Indeed it is highly significant that according to *Woman's Own*'s editorial staff it is these 'success' stories which have refound popularity with readers in the 1980s; just as unemployment and financial cutbacks makes material success increasingly impossible for many people.

Thus the 'we women' feeling magazines construct is actually comprised of different cultural groups; the very notion of 'we' and 'our world', however, constantly undercuts those divisions to give the semblance of a unity – inside magazines. Outside, when the reader closes her magazine, she is no longer 'friends' with Esther Rantzen and her ilk; but while it lasted it has been a pleasant and reassuring dream.

Certainly from the evidence of the problem pages many women are not only not 'friends' with Esther Rantzen but lack any friends to be intimate with. The voices speaking in these letters are sad or angry, anxious or guilty, but they are always alone with their problems. The letters on the pages themselves are a mere tip of the iceberg of letters that magazine aunties and their teams answer (though some, like Irma Kurtz, do not offer a private service). The kinds of problems and the styles of answers on any page are congruent with the profiles of respective magazines. 'Incest' *Woman's Own* will answer privately but not publish; *Honey* tackles it publicly. Mary Marryat's answers are smotheringly maternal, Irma Kurtz's brusque or witty. Without exception letters are edited, 'the problem' pruned down to a few simple paragraphs, always in standard English. In part the reasons are eminently practical: space is limited, readers need to grasp the problems easily. It also means a heavy-handed obliteration of cultural differences between readers. Despite being tucked away in the 'hinterland' of magazines (as Evelyn Home, that most renowned of aunties, put it), the problem page is perhaps the most read of all pages. The 'enjoyment' is either that 'you' identify with the problem, or it is a more voyeuristic pleasure (much like that of the Triumph Over Tragedy stories), observing problems which are blessedly not yours. Either way you are reassured: that you are not alone with your problem, that really you're all right.

Unlike their predecessors modern-day aunties support rather than blame women, encouraging them to be self-assertive about their own needs rather than place marital or familial stability above all else. Nevertheless, as Mary Louise Ho has pointed out, their advice tends to assume a 'bionic woman' who can succeed against the social odds (1981, p. 33). Virginia Ironside's (self-admitted) heartless reply to 'Did I go wrong?' does just that (*Woman* 12 December 1981). She ignores completely the social and economic pressures on women in the 1950s, and continuing to a lesser extent in the 1980s, to keep them in failed and miserable marriages. Indirectly, Virginia Ironside *is* blaming all those women who haven't got the guts to get out.

This self-assertive advice also tends to assume an equality between women and men. Irma Kurtz's advice below seems a tough but reasonable tit for tat (*Cosmopolitan*, July 1983). But it would be the rare ex-wife who could manage it without guilty feelings. Irma Kurtz neither discusses the problem as one women and not men are likely to experience, nor, though she acts as 'friend', does she advise recruiting real friends as back-up in meting out the Kleenex treatment. The writer is left to do it by herself.

When the differences are recognised they are not challenged. In 'I can't forget her past' a man is worried that he cannot come to terms with his about-to-be wife's previous sex life although he's had 'various flings' and realises he is caught in believing in a double standard of sexuality (*Woman*, 20 August 1983). Virginia Ironside is heartening: 'to be honest it's a common problem with men', the 'commoness' pre-empting an explanation of why this should be an inevitable part of manhood. 'Time will put your girlfriend's past into perspective for you.' But time alone cannot wipe out the double standard he (and other men) hold on to of the woman as the sexual possession of one man. And the double standard – at the woman's expense – could quite easily manifest itself in other forms in their marriage.

More generally, the problem page reassures women that they are not alone with their personal problems. It simultaneously

---

The other half
I can't forget her past
I'm about to marry my girlfriend, who I love very much. And I know she is totally dedicated to me. My only problem is that I can't come to terms with her past sex life. I've had one-night stands and various flings with other women before I met her, but I can't accept that she's done the same thing and I've behaved very immaturely and sulkily, constantly bringing up her past. I think I still believe that women shouldn't sleep around before marriage and men should, which I know sounds very old-fashioned.

It sounds as if you are very insecure sexually, and to be honest it's a common problem with men. I suspect that when you've been married some time and it's quite clear that you're both faithful and happy sexually, these memories will simply fade away. Just before you get married, a lot of fears can get exaggerated and anxieties can blow up out of all proportion. Sometimes it's worth paying attention to them; but in your case I feel that time will put your girlfriend's past into perspective for you.

Q My husband left me for another woman over two years ago. Last week he rang me late at night in tears, pleading for my forgiveness, and asking to see me. I have been through a great deal because of his behaviour; he was very cruel to me when he left, telling me I was boring and dull, that I didn't know what good sex was, and how exciting his new girlfriend was by comparison.

He said in his phone call that he couldn't leave her as he had caused her so much trouble, but that he had to see me at least once in a while, and would I let him come and stay sometimes. I didn't ask how he planned to explain that to her, but he does travel and I suppose he could add an extra night or two to his visits if he wanted to. I was very upset at hearing him cry as he is not that sort of man. I do love him, but I can't forget the things he said. I'm in turmoil. Please help.

A On top of all else, now he wants to turn you into a henchman as he practises deceit on his new woman! Didn't you cry when he left? Well, now it's his turn. Send him a box of Kleenex.

Did I go wrong?

I'm 60 and so unhappy. When I was 21, I married and it was a shock when, six weeks later my husband started giving me notes of what I was doing wrong. However, I tried to please him, and eventually I had a child. My husband was brutal to the child, and wouldn't allow me to go to him at night if he cried. However, I tried my best, and then my next baby was born. My husband completely ignored this one, who became nervous and terrified. He never allowed the children the smallest treat. I tried so hard to give them a happy childhood, scrimping and saving to make do. Finally, after 26 years, I went to a marriage guidance counsellor and agreed to leave as my husband's behaviour was now terrible. I was suffering with arthritis and on anti-depressants. Anyway, the long and short of all this is that I have been quite abandoned by my family, they never come to see me though they see their father. Is there any justice in this world?

I hate to sound heartless when you are in this sad state of mind, especially as you tried so hard, but why didn't you leave this man long before things got so bad? I wonder if you weren't misguided in your view that to stay with your husband would bring happiness to your children? No one has to stand for behaviour of the kind he dished out to you and the children over the years and you, as their mother, were the only one who could have made a move. If I sound a bit hard, it's only because I hope some will take your letter as a sad example of what happens when you bury your head in the sand. However, it's never too late. Send your children gifts and cheerful letters and I'm sure they'll soon reply. Be very strong and positive now and you will reap rewards.

undermines that support. It's all very well to answer personal problems with personal answers – that is after all what the letter writers want and need – but unless women have access to a knowledge which explains personal lives in social terms, that is, as women's problems, problems of age and class and race, and of who has more money and muscle, public space and private time than others, then the onus on 'you' to solve 'your' problem is likely to be either intimidating or can only lead to repeatedly frustrated 'solutions'. Individuals cannot, for example, solve the problems around the double standard of sexuality; the problem goes well beyond one couple.

Agony aunties (and magazines) act as 'friends' to women – they bring women together in their pages – and yet by not providing the knowledge to allow women to see the history of their common social condition, sadly and ironically, they come between women, expecting, and encouraging, them to do alone what they can only do together.

Polemical interlude

What aunties (and magazines) rarely aid is women coming together independently of the magazine. Commercial magazines are not and do not wish to be part of the women's movement. If I am, like many a modern auntie, being tough, not to say unreasonable, in making that kind of criticism, it is with concerned intent. I am not suggesting that aunties or magazines more generally are doing a lousy job. On the contrary I'd speculate on how much more lonely and difficult life would be for many women without the support of magazines. What I do take issue with is an ideological commitment to 'the individual', more far-reaching than the pages of magazines but with a particular inflection there.

The problems this ideology raises are sticky ones. We undoubtedly are individuals. But what we ignore most of the time, or simply do not see, is the scope of the limitations, especially for women, on what 'individuals' we are allowed to be. It is those limitations on our 'freedom' which a feminist and socialist politics takes issue with. Yet in arguing that, such a politics is always seen by those opposing, or not understanding, it as a curtailment of individuality in favour of something on the lines of the much maligned and feared state socialism – a restrictive uniformity of thought and permitted behaviours.

Nothing could be further from any imagined feminist and socialist utopia. Feminism holds stalwartly to the importance of women's individual experiences and voices, but its slogan 'the personal is the political' is an attempt to indicate that individuality and personal life – 'I' – do not exist as an island unto myself, but

I am caught up in a web of social structures I do not, and cannot, control, and in which only certain paths are open to me, a woman. Feminism insists that for women and men to have the 'freedom' to be individuals – and that ultimately is the aim of its politics – those manifold structures, and not just individuals, must be radically changed.

Commercial women's magazines, however, constantly hold out something that is possible for individual women to achieve. As one *Woman's Own* article put it, 'I am my own woman' (25 April 1981). If only 'I' and 'you' were; but the shadow of masculinity (to say nothing of class and racial ideologies) is persistently at our feet. We're not sad and sorry victims always at men's mercy but we do daily have to deal with the effects of masculinity in our lives. We are 'their' woman even as we try to be 'our own'. And it is on that unspoken assumption that magazines are premised; it is a knowledge intimately shared between women.

Woman's Own, *Cosmopolitan* and *Spare Rib* are all magazines concerned that as women we should be 'our own woman'. They tackle the problem in very different ways. Whereas *Woman's Own* and *Cosmopolitan* sway towards the liberal and overly optimistic approach to what as individuals we can do, and to the neglect of social relations, *Spare Rib* adopts a radicalism which stresses the need for social as well as personal change, but can sometimes appear to forget its own premise of starting out from (all) women's individual experiences.

It is against this background of 'the individual' especially that I want now to go on to explore those three magazines.

Chapter 6

Woman's Own: 'Britain's best read magazine'

'Look what we've got for you this week'

The women's weeklies, in contrast to the monthlies, are perhaps peculiarly British. Other countries, like the USA and France, neither support such mass circulation weeklies nor make the same appeals to nationhood. In Britain, however, the weeklies are familiarly known even by those who don't read them and their insistence on a national heritage has always been strong. In the 1940s *Woman* was 'The National Home Weekly'; *Woman's Own* in the 1980s has variously hailed itself as 'First in Britain for women', 'Britain's best seller' and, most recently, 'Britain's best read magazine'. Britishness is pivotal, an ideology the weeklies mobilise around and create. For, faced with the enormity of producing magazines that readers divided by class and age and race can all enjoy, a national culture – most often symbolised by the royal family – is one around which, whatever their differences, all can patriotically unite – Britishness as (royal) familiness.

Thus in one week, as *Woman's Own* began a serialisation by their resident royal writer Douglas Keay, *Royal Pursuit: The Palace, The Press and The People* (first episode 'Princess pursued'), *Woman* was selling 'Royal special: what now for the Windsor boys?' (1 October 1983). Periodically all 'the family' feature, but it is Princess Di who has become the big-time circulation puller, conveniently just when the weeklies had been struggling through a rough patch. For *Woman's Own* Diana's relaxed style, her apparent friendliness towards the 'ordinary' people she meets, together with her youth, freshness and stylish glamour have proved just right for the casual but also respectful style it has been quietly evolving for the 1980s. At the same time Diana as loving wife and mum well affirms the traditional values of marriage and family life *Woman's Own* still likes to endorse and which, it is assumed, readers as much share with Diana as they do with one another, albeit that marriage and family life in *Woman's Own*'s pages are not quite what they were when Princess Elizabeth as young wife and mother was crowned.

In the 1950s *Woman's Own* may have landed a scoop with Crawfie's *Little Princesses* story but it was *Woman* which led the field until the mid-1970s when under Jane Reed's deft editorship *Woman's Own* edged its way to the fore. Having been stuck in traditional backwoods in the 'swinging sixties', *Woman's Own* emerged with vigour to voice ideas about women's secondary place: lack of equality at work, the double standard of sexuality, problems of childcare. It aired the hitherto unspoken in women's magazines: women's particular and often feared health problems, like cervical and breast cancer, vaginal infections and cystitis. Gently nudging women, *Woman's Own* trod a careful line, encouraging women to take on a world beyond home and hearth, but without undermining their commitment to marriage and family. In the 1980s Iris Burton still balanced on this editorial tightrope. (Iris Burton resigned as editor in Spring 1986.)

Slower to update itself in the 1970s, *Woman*, on the other hand, has vacillated editorially. When Jo Foley took on the editorship (early in 1983) *Woman* adopted a style of sexual sauciness and 'plain speaking' foreign to *Woman's Own* but showing signs of the *Sun*'s taint (whence came Jo Foley). By early 1985, however, Richard Barber had become editor of *Woman* and the magazine was once again being remoulded.

6.1a *Woman's Own*, 20 November 1982
6.1b *Woman's Own*, 1 September 1984

ME & MINE A refreshing, sometimes humorous, look at life from Polly Graham

If I can't sleep late, why should anyone else?

DISAPPROVAL is a word I don't much like. It implies superior judgment on behalf of those who disapprove and I feel that there are few of us who can afford the luxury. Disapproval is a word one associates with sniffy, prudish, narrow-minded people who secretly envy those of us who live outside the narrow boundaries they have set for themselves.

Miss C., for example, disapproves of fun, but I'm quite sure that fun is what she has missed most in her life. Alison Prate disapproves of working mothers, yet she is a bitterly frustrated, bored housewife who clearly resents her housebound life. The awful B. disapproves of pretty clothes and make-up but I'm certain she'd love to be pretty herself.

I disapprove of lying in bed late in the morning, though there are times when I would love to lie there all day reading novels and being served my meals on trays. I can't help the way I feel—I'm just so resentful as I buzz around the house clearing up yesterday's mess when I know there are three lunks dozing carelessly upstairs. When they were younger and just a little frightened of me, I used to storm into

when I call on them and find them eati
when I have just finished my lunch.

ME AND MINE A refreshing, sometimes humorous, look at life from Polly Graham

Not a great demand for croupiers in this part of the woods

Something is beginning to worry me. It's really none of my business and, short of being absolutely blunt and disgracefully interfering, there is nothing I can do about it.

Cassy Capes came bustling in the other morning. "I want to thank you, Polly," she said briskly, "for looking after Tabby and little Joe on Monday afternoons." Divorcee Cassy, you may remember, is doing a full-time social-work course at the village Poly and the ladies of the village have been taking it in turns to collect her two youngest from school and feed them. "But," she continued, "it won't be necessary any more...

looking for a job at the moment, therefore he's not unemployed."

"Anyway," she continued sniffily, "he is employed, I'm paying him to look after Tabby and Joe." She glared at me defiantly.

"Training to be a mother's-help, is he?" I know that was below the belt, but Cassy irritates me to the point of recklessness.

"If I may say so, I think your sexism is showing," Cassy's eyes flashed dangerously. "Why shouldn't a boy learn to keep house and look after children?"

The person who'll benefit most is Cassy, but she won't admit it

6.2a *Woman's Own*, 20 November 1982
6.2b *Woman's Own*, 24 September 1983

Yet it is with seeming disregard for the distinctive profiles of these two magazines that 60 per cent of each of their readerships continue to read both magazines. Such a statistic provides excellent fodder for those who disparagingly declare that they are one and the same magazine, or scoff like John Cunningham in the *Guardian* that 'the surprise of their pages is how little has changed in two decades' (14 September 1983). To a discerning eye, however, that is simply not true. Just at the level of design *Woman's Own* is constantly revamping its look (see Figures 6.1a, 6.1b, 6.2a and 6.2b). In part this kind of change reflects the repeated updating of a product so integral to capitalist competition and production-for-obsolescence, as though no commodity would sell without the semblance of newness or novelty. But *Woman's Own*'s modernisation also represents a shift in editorial tone from a mildly paternalistic address, authoritative if also caring, to one striving to be on a more equal and friendly footing with readers. Fine adjustments in the tone of address may not be consciously recognised by readers, yet they subtly keep the magazine abreast of what its readers increasingly expect, with notions of women's independence rippling through their lives. Such chameleon-like but self-conscious transformation is one key to *Woman's Own*'s commercial success; another is achieving what Iris Burton refers to as 'getting the balance right' (interview, 1982). And *Woman's Own*'s tone of address is only one of the many balancing acts the magazine is engaged in: serious articles are balanced against more lightweight ones; busy, highly informative visuals are set against simple and bold illustrations;

the very occasional romance takes its turn alongside abrasive 'modern' fiction. However, at the heart of *Woman's Own* is an adroit ideological juggling act, in particular concerning marriage. Only some of its problems are focused on and they are solved in some ways rather than in others to skilfully maintain marriage on an even, if illusory keel.

Marriage: 'till problems do us part'

Our audience, all of you, is vast. And, boy, is it varied! Unlike many other magazines, our readers don't fall into one age and income group. You could be 17 or 70, a single working mum or a housewife who has never had, or wanted, an outside job. You could be a high-powered career woman, or practising self-sufficiency in the Welsh hills . . . .

What unites you is *Woman's Own* – the desire to have a magazine that reports entertainingly and accurately, and helps you through the social, emotional and physical quagmire of being a woman. (Iris Burton, 8 January 1983)

If *Woman's Own* unites this vast audience and if it 'helps you through the social, emotional and physical quagmire of being a woman', the recurring reference point 'you' all share is the institution of marriage – no matter that 'you' are not all married.

Given that recent statistics suggest 96 per cent of women marry and only 10 per cent remain childless, this emphasis in a mass weekly is predictable (*Guardian*, 16 September 1983). However, the figures also show a divorce rate of one in three marriages and *Woman's Own* only ambiguously confronts that. *Woman's Own* is neither complacent about marriage, presenting it as the inevitably happy norm of adult life, like *Woman's Weekly*, nor is it equivocal about it like *Cosmopolitan*. Rather it opens up the problems marriage entails, repeatedly; but for every marital conflict broached there is the calming and more regular voice giving a boost to marital bliss: Claire Rayner, 'In praise of marriage' (7 August 1982) or 'Double beds' (5 March 1983); Cilla Black proclaiming, 'Why I've never had an affair' and *Woman's Own* cooing, 'They're living happily ever after in a huge house in Buckinghamshire' (28 May 1983). Moreover the institution of marriage is not questioned; individual's behaviour within it is.

Problems between 'ordinary' couples like readers themselves are less often tackled head-on than in displaced ways. It is David Soul or Burt Reynolds who beat up their wives and whose marriages flounder on jealousy, anger and alcohol; it is Linda Lewis or Judy Carne who recount the personal destruction ensuing when a marriage breaks up. *Woman's Own* thereby deals with conflicts without threatening readers' own marriages: celebrities' marital failures can always be blamed on their exceptional and not-like-us lifestyles.

In one not untypical issue there were three interviews centring on marriage, plus a short story about the relationship between a single woman and a married man – yet again! – and a serial set around the court of Henry VIII telling a tale of marital and extramarital gambolling (23 April 1983).

Iris Burton clearly introduced and orchestrated this marital theme (see Figure 6.3). Suggesting of women that 'conditioning makes us feel happier and safer being *half* a relationship rather than one whole person in it', she is partly critical of wives who are living only half their potential. At the same time Iris Burton admires but distances herself from the unusually adventurous route Anne Browne pursued, so revealing her own hesitancies (and conditioning?), just like a reader's. Thus are readers encouraged to contemplate their own more modest paths to 'independence' within marriage.

In the article itself *Woman's Own* recognises that Anne Browne is no ordinary suburban, or rural, housewife, frequently going on 'weekend shoots where fellow guests often include Princess Alexander's husband, Angus Ogilvy'. Not only is her class lifestyle a long way from that of most readers, so is her marriage (her third but there is no inkling about the first two . . .): 'It looked as if her desire was going to break up her marriage but, after blistering rows, she and her husband Mike are closer in spirit than ever before. How did she manage to succeed in doing

6.3   *Woman's Own*, 23 April 1983

'Why I feel really close to this saga'

An acquaintance commenting on the break-up of her 20-year-old marriage, told me bitterly: 'The trouble was he wanted to lead his own life and I hardly ever saw him. What's the point in being married if you don't have companionship?' It's a very common complaint, of course, heard from newly-weds and pensioners alike. I'd say women – and most men – firmly believe marriage means being together, doing things together, just as much as it means sharing a home and family.

The sheer emptiness you're left with after a break-up, the awful weight of loneliness, is often the hardest thing to bear. Especially for women. Conditioning makes us feel happier and safer being *half* of relationship rather than one whole person in it. All

those jokes about being the other half! Nothing wrong in that, of course. Unless you suddenly find yourself on your own, not knowing how to cope. Unless, even in the happiest marriage, you feel you're living only half your potential.

Anne Browne is just one woman who determined to be a complete person, though part of a marriage that has brought her much joy and happiness. For years she nursed an ambition of going off to India to work with the Tibetan refugees and last year she announced to her husband **Mike** that she'd be leaving him for a few months. Not as baldly and as selfishly as that – there was much soul-searching, discussion, even arguments, before Anne finally took off. We tell how Mike and

Anne came to terms with her journey on page 28. I think the story will give many wives food for thought.

I personally feel close to the whole saga because Anne has been a friend for many years. I've always admired her sense of self, her belief that anything is possible if you're determined enough – and more than that, the way she has made her life one long adventure. 'Come to India, Iris, *do*,' she said before setting off. Just as, in the past, she has said: 'Come to South Africa, Iris, *do*. Come to Morocco, Iris, *do*. Come to . . .' Well, almost anywhere; not to holiday, of course, but to live, do and accomplish, I never did and I guess I'll be waving her off for many more years to come . . .
. . .

Real life story

'JUST PACK UP AND LEAVE, FORGET OUR MARRIAGE!'

The normal irritations in Anne Browne's life tended to be things like a shortage of good cheese in the village shops. Her marriage was happy, her background loving and secure—until she confessed her over-riding desire to help refugees in the mountains of Northern India. It looked as if her desire was going to break up her marriage but, after blistering rows, she and her husband Mike are closer in spirit than ever before. How did she manage to succeed in doing something other adventure-loving wives would envy but dare not attempt?

> **'I'm not the kind of lady who sits round doing tapestry'**

> **'I like to think marriages work because of love and trust'**

6.4 *Woman's Own*, 23 April 1983

something other adventure-loving wives would envy but dare not attempt?'

The answer: by believing marriage to be about 'love and trust' and in this spirit exhaustively talking (and crying) over the dilemma with her husband. The notion of communication between them, and of husband's support for her independence bid, constructs their marriage as between two equals, despite definite signs of a 1950s style complementarity: he is the main breadwinner, she above all the provider of domestic comforts. Before setting off she has to line up 'a veritable army of Marys', including her 75-year-old mother, to cook and iron for a husband who 'doesn't even know where the salt is kept in the kitchen'.

Angela Willans's afterword also implicitly stresses equality in marriage: 'remember you're a team as well as separate people – you have no absolute right to make any independent move that would endanger your home and family, any more than he does.' And she only covertly concedes that the 'team' – *Woman's Own*'s much-favoured description of marriage – is an unevenly matched one. Advising the wife embarking on her 'independent move' she urges, 'Be practical and work out how the home can be successfully run in the new circumstances. If you don't do this *you'll* feel anxious and guilty and that would spoil the whole deal' (my emphasis). But if marriage really is about being equals why is the home 'your' responsibility? Why will 'you' feel guilty? If Anne Browne's relationship really had been an equal one would such rows have been necessary? The cold truth is that, as the feminist sociologist Ann Oakley puts it, 'complementarity ... is a euphemism for uncomfortable division and difference' (1981, pp. 245-6). Unable quite to tolerate that, *Woman's Own* adopts, maybe not consciously, two strategies. Firstly, it produces personal testimonies of couples, like the Brownes, succeeding at marriage. In an article discussing how 'the deadly weight of boredom' can plague marriage three couples give their accounts of happily keeping the yawns at bay (19 March 1983: 'Has your marriage become one big yawn?').

Secondly, the practical lesson of their success is that 'you' can achieve it too – if you work at it. And *Woman's Own*, like all commercial magazines, is nothing if not pragmatic in the help it offers you. That is, the problems of marriage are thought of in terms of their causes and their practical solutions. Claire Rayner and Angela Willans both offer helpful checklists for readers on what-is-to-be-done about the problem (of boredom or dependency). These practical and promising solutions are undoubtedly appealing. But such an approach, always knowing both 'causes' and 'answers', allows no space for questioning the institution of marriage or for seeing it as a relationship scored by conflicts which may not be resolvable. And by default, if its solutions don't work then the error lies not in the solutions but in the individual's practical execution of them.

Even when Claire Rayner discusses unhappy marriages, as in 'Why on earth does she stay with him?' (7 May 1983), and comes up with the answer that women are trapped financially and by ties of children, marriage and its conventions remain unculpable; wives do not. Other 'practical reasons for staying' include 'self-punishment', 'martyrdom', 'complacency' and 'hope'. By no means innocent words, Claire Rayner is implicitly conferring weakness or stupidity on those unable to leave. There is no suggestion that since ideologically marriage rules the roost, opting out bears the awful slight of failure and that alternative ways of living necessarily appear as second-best. There's no hint either of the conflicting and impossible demands that marriage, once set in motion, is meant to meet, and which women as dependants are sucked into needing: economic and emotional support, sexuality, love and friendship from husbands, home as the place for day-to-day living and relaxation, the care of children, but also the place where one wants to express the child in one's self. Is it any wonder leaving is so difficult even for the strongest-minded?

In 'Divorce: how you can make it alone' Angela Willans concedes its trauma: 'Divorce rates second only to bereavement

6.5   *Woman's Own*, 10 July 1983

on the scale of life-events that produce stress' (20 August 1983). But in dealing with how to get through the trauma, the article never contemplates that if its ending is generally so catastrophic, might something be deeply amiss in how marriage is generally lived?

Paradoxically, *Woman's Own*'s one (?) attempt at lauding single life, pointedly called 'Single and living happily ever after', indicates best how marriage is represented as the norm to readers (10 July 1983): '*We* used to be slightly sorry for single people. Of course, all *they* really wanted was a husband or wife to cosset and care for. But it's time to think again ... Joyce Robins spoke to three single people who are living alone – and liking it' (my emphasis). 'We' – the majority – are married (or wanting to be); 'they' – the exceptions – are single, and in a common ideological slide assumed to be also heterosexual and living alone.

Medical evidence that single patients with depression recover more quickly than married ones, and that 'marriage certainly isn't an all-round protection, as psychologists used to think' is regarded as 'good news for the growing numbers of single people'. It is not, however, quite 'bad news' that 'marrieds take the strain'. There is a strong undertow that marriage offers the challenge of surmounting these stresses and responsibilities, whereas being single is about selfishly avoiding that and being 'independent and ambitious'. Whatever the intention, such a representation of single status affirms marriage – warts and all – as the more humane (and maturely feminine) condition.

In other slots in *Woman's Own*, especially in serials, the romantic myth of marriage as the 'fairy story come true' prevails as one of the chief hopes offered to women. *Winners* ends with Lee deciding not to pursue his career without Tammy, his skating partner. He turns his back on the flight at the airport, and then:

> 'What's the matter champ?' she said. 'Forgot something?'
> Slowly, he smiled. 'Almost.'
> Lastly, he dropped his skates.
> And she was in his arms, whirling around and around, their heads thrown back in laughter, arms embracing joy. It was pushing limits; it was breaking barriers; it was reaching out. It was living.

It is the stirring stuff of daydreams and the experience of moments. But as the hidden hope of marriage, romance sets up expectations which are rarely satisfied. On the problem page is divulged the prosaicness of marriage, and the worst of women's disappointments. Yet Angela Willans's advice is often as rosily optimistic as romance itself: that 'you' can change entrenched patterns of marital living, and his masculinity. It is doubtful, however, that 'you' can.

6.6 *Woman's Own*, 5 March 1983

Why shouldn't he help with the housework so I can relax as well?

We've been married nearly two years, both have full-time jobs and lots of outside interests and are very happy. But the one thing we can't agree on is housework. I hate it and do the least I can to keep the house bearable to live in. But this still means rushing round most evenings when we're not out. My husband washes up three times a week and sometimes loads the washing-machine – and that's all. I've tried asking him to help with the vacuuming and cleaning but he doesn't want to know – it's really not that important to him. But he makes as much mess as I do so why should I have to do everything? And why can't I ever sit down and watch TV all evening without thinking 'I should be doing some cleaning'?

There are several reasons for your frustration – all of them alterable. First, you have to recognise that his priorities are different from yours. A dust-free, shining house is 'not all that important to him,' but other things are – like, perhaps, relaxing in the evenings. You can't alter his priorities, only your own. So it's up to you to decide if a spick and span home rates higher than an occasional evening's relaxation. Second, you need to get rid of the element of competition on the subject of housework. The importance of proving you're always on the go and he just doesn't care has overridden the real point, which is that you're on the same side in making your home a haven of comfort and peace of mind for both of you. You both obviously work hard and play hard. It would be madness to make your house an area of all-out effort and pressure as well. Third, no one likes acting as second mate. Instead of delegating jobs to him, see if he'd be more willing to take complete charge of some particular area.

He's a sexual bully

From the very first year we were married I knew I'd made a mistake. But how could I have known that my husband would turn overnight from a charming suitor to a sexual bully? Now, 20 years on, he still expects sex on demand, with no foreplay and never mind if I want it or not. It's too late for me but I'd advise any young bride-to-be to make sure she knows how her man behaves in bed before she finds herself tied to a brute like my husband.

Well, I think the mistake you made was not in marrying your husband, but in failing to do anything about the sexual conflict except just soldier on with all this anger and resentment. After all, he must be very unhappy about it too. And it's not too late to put it right if you really want to – ask him for his thoughts on the subject. As for your advice to others, I think today's young women are much more perceptive about a partner's sexual attitudes – and that's without necessarily making love before marriage.

Feminism . . . and the liberal hope

If optimism is to the fore in the discussion of marriage and relationships, there is also a harder edge to *Woman's Own*. Since the 1970s the magazine has engaged in a series of surveys and campaigns opening up and confronting issues about being a woman. In spite of a relative inattention to paid work in the magazine's pages, some of the major campaigning efforts have been in that area.

In 1979 a survey to find out about women's paid work led to its most extensive campaign, 'Fair care for children and a fair deal for Mum'. On behalf of its readers the magazine tried to pressure government and local authorities to provide flexible childcare facilities after school hours and during holidays, both to ease the difficulties of childcare for those already working and to make it possible for thousands of others to work if they wished or needed to. Sadly, the massive cuts in social service expenditure and continuing rising unemployment under the Conservative government damply extinguished its fire.

Yet whether effective or not, these agitational endeavours have also been consciousness-raising exercises. Readers have been emboldened to think about their position as women and to consider channels for taking action to improve it. During 1983 issues to the fore in the women's movement and in the public eye – rape, pornography, and the nuclear threat, as the most newsworthy of those – were all aired in *Woman's Own*. The rhetoric of these articles – and not to be underestimated – was in the style of feminist slogans: 'Time to take a stand. Stop the trade in filth – now', 'Rape – the time to fight back.' The arguments were also partly feminist in substance, for example, that porn is not just 'dirty' sex but a representation of a sexuality which is abusive to women. At the same time, in order not to disturb readers' lives too radically, *Woman's Own* slides into compromises the women's movement would not make: 'By porn, no one seriously includes the pin-up girls and page 3 "beauties" commonly seen in newspapers and advertising. These are generally accepted as a harmless form of titillation, though they do portray women as "commodities".' Feminists may debate fiercely exactly what the links between so-called page 3 'beauties' and porn are. Few, if any, would accept that there are none. The magazine also slips into arguments of the 'moral right' (Mary Whitehouse, Lord Longford *et al.*) that porn corrupts children and undermines familial values: women are addressed more as mothers in this article than as women who are themselves violated.

As in the discussions on marriage, a pragmatic approach to issues seems to offer answers but contains and blocks potentially controversial argument. The article on rape offers sound advice on self-defence and the necessary and demeaning practicalities to adopt having been raped. But masquerading as a 'solution', the

6.7 *Woman's Own*, 14 May 1983

advice proffers only individual survival strategies: 'In the end, confidence is really a woman's most important weapon. If she looks as if she can handle herself she stops looking like a victim.' Why rape should be a hazard all women live in fear of, and a hazard they, not men, are urged to circumvent by keeping off the streets at night, what relation rape bears to more common forms of masculine aggression, contemplating the social conditions under which rape might be eradicated, are simply not raised.

The magazine's cautiousness around feminism – not wanting to upset too many apple carts too quickly for readers – leads at worst to a misrepresentation of the women's movement, at best to an enthusiasm about what women can achieve. In the editorial below Iris Burton does both.

It is a misunderstanding of the women's movement to separate its 'moderate' bit from a supposedly 'extremist' wing, for the former would not exist without the latter. It has often been just those Iris Burton refers to as the 'scatty extremist elements' who, amidst initial hostility, have insisted on issues like lesbianism, porn and rape being placed on the political agenda. On the other hand Iris Burton does persuade readers that they have much to thank feminism for, and much to gain from the women's movement, though her eulogy on women's newfound respect and confidence, inspiring as it may be, errs on the side of wishful thinking. There can be few women who are not occasionally patronised, mocked, silenced by men, or whose confidence is not at times torn with nagging doubts.

In 'Women – then . . . and now. You've come a long way, baby', Claire Rayner suggests, 'We have taken from the men's world what we wanted (well, some of us have – no one will pretend that *every* woman has achieved equality yet) but we still

OUR WORLD

I'm not a feminist. I simply hate labels of any kind – they give people too much scope for knocking the scatty extremist elements while blithely ignoring all the gutsy, common sense, honest aims. For we really do have a lot to thank the feminist movement for. For the first time in hundreds of years, women can not only have their say but be listened to with respect. Whether it's in the context of home, family, at work or in public life, what a woman thinks and says is no longer light-heartedly dismissed or treated patronisingly. Even more important, I believe, is the increasing confidence women have in themselves and their ability to influence events. The 30,000 women of every age, background and political colour who've made Greenham Common one of the best known places in Britain are an example. You may not personally agree with their cause but you have got to approve their incredible determination to bring about change. Passionate feelings and high opinions are all very well, but it's action, in the end, that counts.

I don't know if you tuned in to the fascinating series Inside Women's Magazines on BBC2 a few weeks ago. I watched with both professional interest and not a little personal trepidation as Woman's Own featured in it quite largely. The last programme in the series, looking in particular at Spare Rib and Woman's Own, was titled Feminism and Femininity. It's true that many women will still label themselves as either feminist *or* feminine, but I like to think that the two sides are closer now in spirit than they've been for a decade or more . . .

6.8   *Woman's Own*, 5 February 1983

have the chance to hold on to the best part of our women's world' (16 October 1982). 'We' patently have not, unless Claire Rayner has superwoman in mind and she is not an enviable model of womanhood to aspire to. Some of us, admittedly, are more privileged than others but the point of the women's movement is that equality is not something women can achieve individually. Equality depends on the fabric of society – its laws and work patterns, its family arrangements and sexual mores, as well as its ideas about 'a woman's place', be they in women's magazines, on TV or voiced on the street, all being transformed. The liberal (and implicitly aspirational) version of feminism (cf. chapters 7 and 9), which *Woman's Own* espouses vindicates an individual equality while not allowing the possibility for that in fact to be achieved.

A liberal intent also informs the magazine's moves towards addressing and including Britain's black women. It gestures towards including them, but on white women's terms. On the whole its unashamed address is to white women. Many issues have no black woman anywhere and a black model has yet to grace the cover.

One editorial rationale (having something of the chicken and egg dilemma to it) is that *Woman's Own* only has 4 per cent black readers. The second is a more liberal argument. As Iris Burton put it (interview, 1982), 'I like to think of our readers not as black or white women, but as women who get the same kinds of things from all the features, and not thinking that "Oh I've got a white skin" as I read this, "I've got a black skin" as I read that.' If that were true it would not be a 'problem' for the magazine to use black as well as white models, anytime. It is not.

A third rationale, while denying it, is more clearly racist. Discussing *Woman's Own*'s cover Iris Burton commented,

> I'm fair to our readers, because I don't believe that the bulk of them are anti-black . . . . But they would be unnerved by a black face and you do it two weeks running and they will start to think, 'Oh what's happening, my way of life' . . . . It's the one thing that shakes any race to the roots. 'Is everything I've known and become familiar with going to be shaken up and changed over night?'

Leaping to protect white women as if black women are a threat to them conveniently ignores what has been a much longer-term unnerving – the daily and relentless imposition of white cultural values on black people in Britain. To be fair to Iris Burton (and who am I anyway, as another white woman also deeply implicated in racist practices, to criticise another?), since she made this comment in August 1982 *Woman's Own* has made visible gestures, if not towards confronting racism, at least towards acknowledging that cultures other than a white one do exist in Britain. And by spring 1985 Iris Burton *was* prepared to accept the need for more positive action around including and addressing black readers. A black woman on the cover was, she thought, likely to be a possibility very soon.

So far there has been the occasional cookery feature like 'A taste of the Caribbean' in which 'Cookery editor Alex Barker visited Rustie Lee to learn all about this deliciously different cuisine at her Caribbean restaurant in not-so-tropical Birmingham'. Nevertheless, addressed to white readers it defines West Indian culture in terms of its palatable trappings, leaving unknown the real problems for black people living in Britain. Sometimes, as in 'Job sharing' in Figure 6.9, the magazine has judiciously slipped in the odd black face amongst a majority of white ones. This liberal touch is decidedly forked; it includes and addresses black women; it also renders blackness an irrelevant factor in the issues being discussed. Yet being black carries with it greater difficulties both in finding work – on account of racism – and, since many young black women are single parents, in managing childcare alongside paid work. *Woman's Own* makes no mention of these social factors.

Blackness *is* highlighted as different in the beauty feature 'Yes you can look better'. As 'This week's special' it is notable for giving Sandra Fontain prime place and attention, marking a shift

At Your Service edited by Judith Gubbay

Job sharing

Is half a job better than one, or better than none? For those who want time at home, but need to go out to work, splitting a job with a partner sounds ideal. We've asked job sharers about the pros and cons and found out how to join in. Report by Anne Montague

other people in the office do have to be more co-operative, but it's now established as a permanent share and will stay that way as long as the people involved want it to.

Monica Pereira and Dolores Marsh have been sharing a job in London as audio-typist at Lambeth Social Services Department since 1979. "The whole idea of sharing was a mystery to me before I started," says Monica. "I had two small sons and was looking for part-time work but nobody had the hours to suit me. Dolores was in the same position. Now I work 20 hours a week, and Dolores does 16.

"The great advantage is flexibility. We get on very well together."

Most employers are still cautious about job sharing. Lucy Gaskell of New Ways To Work (see Who Can Help) feels that this can often result from misunderstandings about the nature of job sharing. "Employers are often afraid that it will cost them more—but it hardly ever does."

In fact, the employer pays no more in National Insurance contributions unless the job is worth more than £220 a week (£11,440 a year) and, it could be argued, he will get more for his money. The greatest advantage must be flexibility. The employer no longer has to provide temporary holiday help or sick cover. If one sharer leaves, the continuity of the job is not broken and the remaining sharer can train the new recruit.

Barclays Bank have used a "twinning" system—one week on and one week off—for secretarial and clerical staff since the 1940s. They now have 2,000 out of their

Dolores (left) and Monica were both looking for part-time work but couldn't get hours to suit

involved. Don and I work very well together, but for this type of job, compatibility is so important— matching strengths and weaknesses—and I would stress the importance of communication between the two people sharing."

'You work doubly hard

Don and Jean agree; two brains are better than one

apply jointly for any medical post. Other shared jobs include a production assistant for BBC Schools TV, a research officer at St. Mary's Hospital and a librarian for Lambeth Library, all in London.

Job sharing's most recent boost came on July 28 this year when the

split up to 100,000 jobs from next January. They hope to encourage employers to create part-time jobs by grants of £750 towards any extra costs.

They stipulate that the splitting of a job must take somebody off the unemployment register or save a

have had a guarded response to the government's plans. As Lucy Gaskell pointed out: "We feel that the scheme the government is putting forward is a negative measure which will take people off the unemployment register, rather than a positive approach to introduce more choices in the way people work.

"It also does nothing for a lot of people who we come into contact with—married women—the hidden unemployed who may need jobs just as much as the people on the register. This scheme could discriminate against them even more."

New hope for unemployed youngsters

In the Midlands, two organisations are already using job sharing as a

---

6.9 *Woman's Own*, 20 November 1982

in the magazine's assumptions about its readers. Some assumptions remain unchallenged. In common with the white women, Sandra Fontain appeared on that page because she had 'a problem'. Unlike them, however, her problem is the colour of her skin: 'She shares a problem, along with many dark-skinned girls, of how to choose and use make-up for girls with dark skins.' This may seem (to white women) a trivial point; the issue at stake is not. Sandra Fontain only has 'a problem' about make-up because the dominant white culture in which she lives does not value black skin. It does not produce, nor advertise, nor sell, nor educate women (in women's magazines) on the use of make-up for black skins. Thus 'a problem' which white culture has created becomes her problem. So too in wider fields: the 'problem' of black youth rioting in Toxteth or Brixton, the 'problem' of black children's reading difficulties at school, are rarely seen as the products of a dominant white culture but as 'their' failure.

An article on 'Kailash Puri – agony aunt' at least gives a glimpse into Asian life, albeit that Kailash Puri occupies a very middle-class place amongst the 200,000 Punjabis to whom she is agony aunt. Yet the revelations white readers might pick up about cultural codes manifestly not white, like arranged marriages, are

KAILASH PURI sinks into the green silk settee of her plushly-furnished drawing room. She wears a beautiful orchid-pink sari wrapped gently around her pleasingly-plump proportions. As she munches her way through a packet of chocolate biscuits, a peaceful smile plays around her lips and eyes. She is totally at ease. She has every good reason to be.

Kailash Puri—Indian Agony Aunt, writer, sexologist, nutritionist, Woman of the Year, wife, mother and eternal shoulder to cry on—knows she has arrived.

This week she and her husband Dr. Gopal Puri celebrate their ruby wedding anniversary. Kailash intends to raise a glass to the 40 most important years of her life—years spent with a man she still loves who taught her wisdom, compassion and understanding and made her precisely what she is today.

"I owe it all to my husband," she announces. "When he married me in India I was an ignorant, naïve schoolgirl of 15 and he was already well on the way to being a brilliant scientist. My marriage has been the source of all my learning."

Whatever the source, the wisdom flows and flows in a never-ending stream.

Kailash is Agony Aunt to more than 200,000 Punjabi-speaking people in Britain and Europe. They avidly read her columns in two Punjabi newspapers—the Punjab Times and Des Pardes. Each week hundreds of letters from troubled readers drop on to the door mat of her home in Blundellsands, Liverpool. She answers all of them personally. Her ability to understand and sometimes solve culture-gap problems is widely respected.

As a self-styled sexologist Kailash has written five books on sex, marriage and love. This year she received the Punjabi Literary Academy Woman of the Year award for being able "to reach the depths of women's minds."

'They know I will be sympathetic'

Inevitably, many of the problems she receives centre on marriage and its complications. She begins by understanding and referring to her own marriage and accepting that it has not always been plain sailing, for either of them.

Gopal was the man her parents chose for her. After the marriage they travelled the world together and en route had three children—first a son, Shammy, now 35, then two daughters, Kiran, 33, and Risham, 26.

Her advice is derived from her experiences as a wife and mother who has seen the world, her firm Sikh faith and yoga philosophy and her knowledge of the West, having lived away from India since 1962.

"My readers feel secure in the knowledge that I have shared their experiences or witnessed them," she explains. "They know I will be sympathetic and that I will realise what a large step it is to advise someone, say, to move away from living with their mother-in-law."

Kailash knows how it feels to be homesick and culture-shocked. And though the Puris are doing very nicely now, she also knows how it feels to worry about where the next meal is coming from.

In the early days of her marriage money was a major problem. She smiles indulgently as she remembers how her husband dressed for their wedding 40 years ago.

"He was a post-graduate student, caring for his widowed mother and paying for his younger brothers' education. He simply couldn't afford decent clothes," she says. "For our wedding he wore faded corduroy trousers, though I was beautifully dressed in traditional bridal clothing!

"When we married we lived in his family home. I remember he gave his only decent pair of shoes to his brother to wear to school—he wore slippers.

"All our money seemed to go on books. One day I got so cross I said he'd have to stop buying them. He was really upset but convinced me that even if he did only have two suits in the world, that was plenty."

Throughout the lean years, Gopal encouraged her to carry on with her own learning, too.

"He felt sad that he'd interrupted my education when I got married, so he encouraged me to get my BA in General Arts. Kailash sees the problems of the early days as lessons in the subject of life. "When the children were older and we were living in Ghana, a problem occurred in our marriage," she says. "It was maybe a result of my having to grow up as a person, within my marriage to an older man who was used to looking after his own family.

"One day at a dance my husband came up and said it was time to go. My daughter knew I was having a good time and didn't want to go. It was she who pointed out to her father that he seemed to be making all the decisions. She was right.

"In a way I was being suppressed. My own father wouldn't have consulted the female members of the family. I'd let the same thing happen in my own marriage to some extent, and it was my own daughter who saw it—not me.

"Yet it wasn't my husband's fault—when we discussed it he was delighted to allow me more freedom. It was not he who was suppressing me, but really it was myself."

'All this sleeping around is exaggerated'

"I don't suppose I'm the easiest person to live with. I'm a very demanding woman and, of course, I've had frustrations and problems. But if I'd never had them I don't believe I could ever have been a writer."

Trophies of her own and Gopal's success are displayed in the plant-filled drawing room. There are pictures of Kailash with Indira Gandhi, another with Margaret Thatcher and a third of Gopal with Pope Paul VI.

But amongst this impressive gallery are the family photos of Kailash and Gopal together, snaps of their children and grandson, Shivan. Despite the wealth and the professional accolades, Kailash says simply: "My husband, my children and then my plants. They're the things I would hate to do without."

It's the simplicity she uses to deal with readers' problems.

"Many problems arise out of ignorance," says Kailash. "In Asia there is a very sensational idea of how European women live. Sometimes the freedom they expect within a marriage is taken for bad morals.

"When I was lecturing in India I had to spend so much time telling people that all this sleeping around is exaggerated. The sad thing is that when a village man comes over to marry someone who has been living here a long time, he suspects that she has been sleeping around."

There are more unusual problems like the case of the young girl who was sent over to England in the care of an "aunt" who arranged—for profit—one unsuitable marriage after another and threatened her charge that she would be sent home with her reputation in shreds if she did not co-operate.

But a great proportion of the problems Kailash is asked to answer are about sex.

"There are so many partners worried about frigidity," she says. "Some husbands are going out drinking and then coming home and making too many demands on their wives, whether she is well or not. These husbands want sex every night and behave like animals towards their wives.

"I get many phone calls from poor women who don't know how to stop the vicious circle of drinking and sex. My answer has to be—communicate. Don't be so passive. Control your anger and talk (*Please turn to page 45*)

'How can I stay married to this filthy, short, rude man?'

'My wife shows no interest in me'

'My husband makes too many demands on me'

This week Kailash Puri celebrates 40 years of marriage. She has also won the coveted Woman of the Year award given by a Punjabi literary agency. What for? Kailash is Agony Auntie to over 200,000 Punjabi-speaking people in Britain and Europe. And, as the extracts from the letters above show, the problems of love and sex know no boundaries

"I've had frustrations and problems too," says Kailash

Agony Aunt Kailash advises . . .

Respected Kailash sister, my daughters of 16 and 17 have adopted English ways. They don't want to listen to me. If I stop them from going out they threaten to leave home and live on their own. I lie awake worrying till they return. Please can you tell me how to convince my daughters that they are not English and to live our own way?

Kailash answers: I have all sympathy for your frustration, but as parents we have to understand our children's position. They are educated and brought up in a multi-cultural and multi-racial society and copy their friends.

You have to give them some liberty. Win them over with patience and love. Understand the outside social pressures on them. Let them talk to you. You will find they are normal kids who need love and understanding. If you have an open mind they will discuss all their problems with you.

Dear much respected Kailash, I am married but with no children. You say a woman must be co-operative with her husband in bed, but I am married to a filthy, short, rude man whom I hate. I agreed to this arranged marriage hoping things would improve.

Kailash answers: I would suggest you persevere, but from what you tell me there is no hope. I do not believe in wasting two lives. If his habits aren't going to change then divorce is the only way out.

My friend, I came to this country two years ago to marry an Indian girl who had been living here since she was a young child. When I come back from work, she never even looks up from the television. She is not interested in cooking or keeping the house clean, although she is expecting our baby. I cannot bring myself to have sex with her unless I am really desperate.

Kailash answers: You are new to this country, your wife has lived here for many years. She sounds depressed. Give her understanding, especially because of the baby. Buy her a new dress. Take her out. Women like to be spoiled . . .

6.10 *Woman's Own*, 27 August 1983

undercut by an editorial insistence on the similarities: the emphasis on Kailash Puri's ruby wedding anniversary (surely a white tradition even if some Punjabis in Britain have adopted it?); the extracts from letters making a case that 'love and sex know no boundaries'.

It may be racist to unthinkingly condemn an unfamiliar cultural practice like arranged marriage: to pretend that difference is not there, or of no significance, is liberal folly. It neatly avoids the political issue that black people are oppressed in Britain.

An evasion of politics is also apparent in *Woman's Own*'s treatment of *the* social bogey of the 1980s, unemployment. Ever hopeful in its liberal and pragmatic approach the magazine declares 'Unemployment – at last a positive approach' (31 July 1982), 'Unemployed but don't be down and out' (24 September

1983). Its 'New Venture' slot (replacing 'A day in the world of . . .' on the readers' letters page) has women recounting their successful entrepreneurial attempts to beat unemployment. As survival guides its articles are immensely supportive. But what is saddening is that even as these articles ebulliently open up possibilities for action, 'the problem' of being unemployed and of achieving any success in finding a job is thrown on to 'you' the individual: 'For most young people, being out of a job means being out of life. Yet it need not be the case. There's plenty to do if you try to remain positive . . . . As in any battle . . . the better armed you are, the more likely you are to win.'

Perhaps a few will win, 'haul themselves up' like the successful co-operative venture, the article recounts, Bootstrap. And the articles do invite that hope. Elephants fly too. Individuals experience unemployment as a personal 'battle'; it is hardly one of their making; it is certainly not one many will 'win'. *Woman's Own* never asks why there is unemployment, but simply accepts it: 'Everyone knows that unemployment is a huge problem . . . .' By focusing on individuals, unemployment, and *Woman's Own*, are kept out of politics.

Yet the refusal to engage in political questions is, I'd argue, to abdicate from the social responsibility the magazine would have us believe it has towards its readers, and to misuse the social influence it commands. Raising possible political reasons for unemployment is not useful in finding a job like the pragmatism of '*Woman's Own*'s self-help guide'. What it alleviates, however, is the heavy onus thrown on to individuals to solve 'their' problem, the utter feeling of failure experienced by those who lose in this industrial jungle's version of the survival of the fittest. *Woman's Own* is ominously silent about those who become depressed or are driven to commit suicide. (There is some evidence to suggest a much higher incidence of attempted suicide amongst the unemployed and a definite link between unemployment and physical and mental ill-health (Harris 1984). The liberal option *Woman's Own* extends to readers in these articles does not, I'd suggest, offer the choice that is intended. As the magazine for the allegedly 'liberated woman', *Cosmopolitan* has its head less in the sand. Yet the ideology it is caught in has the same liberal hallmark of seeming to stand for individual 'freedom' while unknowingly blocking its realisation.

Chapter 7

Cosmopolitan: 'who could ask for more?'

Our Cosmo world

'Is *Cosmopolitan* worth it?' was the question asked when the price went up to 60p . . . yes. Tessa Marshall of London gives her reasons: 'Sixty pence buys a slice of Brie, a trip on the tube, or one silk stocking. In the case of *Cosmo*, it also buys dreams, glamour, gossip, laughter, recipes, common sense, sex appeal, stories, love, life and style.' Who could ask for more? D McS. (*Cosmopolitan*, November 1981)

A portrait: 'tough, tender and in touch'

7.1a *Cosmopolitan*, March 1982
7.1b *Cosmopolitan* cover, November 1983

With editions of *Cosmopolitan* in at least seventeen different countries, including Greece, Australia and nine Latin American regions, *Cosmo*-girl has an international reputation. Yet it is less the dungareed (if still attractive) worker image people bring to mind than the sexual hype of the cover: the glamorous and

feminine woman out to lure her men with all the Cosmo-style seduction she can muster. For the magazine – the British edition at least – the discrepancy between its 'tough' and 'tender' faces has always been one to revel in. And if there is a key to *Cosmo*'s commercial success it is in embracing that contradiction to offer a pluralism of opinions, voicing what are potentially mutually exclusive views on the subject of women. It can be pro the women's movement and sometimes against it; in sympathy with men's problems – 'men bleed too, you know' – or very critical; exhort 'Be big, beautiful and fit' in one issue (January 1983) and be back to 'Waist away – exercise with Esme' a few issues later (September 1983). Marriage may be endorsed or it may be condemned, likewise romance, fidelity, having babies over the age of 30, and sexual relationships in some of their manifold guises. Moreover these disparate opinions are presented in a style that can be earnest or funny, or both. They can reflect an awareness of problems for women while always coming up with combative countermeasures. As Bel Mooney on *Cosmo*'s eleventh birthday comments,

> I know that *Cosmo*'s spectacular success is due to a clever editorial
> balancing – one that realises that seriousness and frivolity can co-exist
> quite happily . . . . *Cosmo*'s skill is in offering lots of possibilities on
> a rather pretty plate – ideas about jobs, friends, love, life; always
> the reassurance that although problems abound, so too does joy.
> (March 1983)

Cosmo's selling line could well be that of the Martini ad, 'Fairy tales can come true', with *Cosmo* acting as fairy godmother. It offers readers '*Cosmo* courses: change your life today', 'Win the ultimate ski trip *plus* kit', 'Life as a party', 'Escape from depression', 'Dare to be happy'. And if 'There's a little magic in every glass of Martini Dry', every *Cosmo* has surprise as part of its package. According to Deirdre McSharry (who resigned as editor in 1985, interview 1983),

> It's enormously important to get the balance right . . . like one sex
> article and six emotional articles, and one a negative and one a
> positive article. It's like cooking if you like, it's a kind of recipe . . .
> the readers know a certain amount about what they're going to get.
> That's the sort of reassurance element . . . . But the clever thing is to
> always offer a very strong element which will surprise them, and
> that's really what keeps them going.

More generally, *Cosmo*'s design has a different look from most magazines. Offering a lot to read and think about, its visuals tend to highlight the making of images, therefore also inviting thought and comment rather than simply providing an unreflective pleasure, like 'Style. It's visionary', with its 'visionary' pun and strangely shaded images achieved with a colour xerox machine.

Ads too are often strategically placed in relation to editorial material, encouraging readers to notice them, like the Martini 'Fairy tales can come true' and the Lilia ad, picking up on the sunglasses motif, the wavy deckchair pattern in pink, echoing the ruffled pinky edges to the 'visionary' faces opposite.

Indeed despite *Cosmo*'s glamorous reputation it is less its fashion pages and more its profuse advertising which offers enticing consumer spreads with all the associations of female desire, and pleasure, and fantasy. Unlike most magazines *Cosmo* also uses glossy photos (of posed models) to illustrate its all-important articles about relationships. And these too evoke similar ideals of desire. Unusually, its graphics accompany much more than just fiction – cookery and general articles for example – while a mix of graphics and photography is often used in consumer slots.

This departure from magazine conventions, though it may not be something *Cosmo* has consciously articulated, indicates *Cosmo*'s self-consciousness: firstly, that being a woman involves constantly adjusting one's own image to fit time and place in an ever-changing game of images; and secondly, that 'real life' is constantly thought through '(dream) images'. The corollary of these views is that *Cosmo* recognises (to a small degree) that changing images is an integral part of changing being women and men.

If *Cosmo*'s more basic editorial recipe is sketched by the contents list, there are some pungent flavourings not evident there. 'News report', the opening regular slot since Autumn 1982, is an argued but polemical 'think piece' about contemporary issues: the hypocrisy around contraceptive advertising; men's dominance at the managerial level of nursing; on dieting makes you fat. Similar to *Woman*'s briefer 'We think' editorials, it is notably not an editorial opinion. Likewise 'Articles' more generally are offered as authoritative but individual arguments and opinions. Thus November's 'News report' was 'Women and drink' (of the alcoholic kind): '. . . Richard Smith, Assistant Editor of the *British Medical Journal*, assesses the evidence and gives his personal views.'

'Articles' in *Cosmo* as a whole tend to have a common structure. First they set up a personal problem, potentially if not already 'yours', sometimes a general one – like the difference between women and men (investigated by Tom Crabtree in 'Strong women are good for men') – sometimes the author's own problem. Then they explore it through a combination of knowledge from 'the experts' – psychologists (who are also frequent contributors to *Cosmo*), writers, lawyers, economists – and personal testimonies including, often, the author's own. Finally they come up with numbered or labelled strategies of action (much in the style of Claire Rayner and Angela Willans)

101

Cosmopolitan: 'who could ask for more?'

Unfortunately, Cosmopolitan cannot consider unsolicited articles, poems and short stories for publication.
© **THE NATIONAL MAGAZINE CO LTD, NOVEMBER 1983**

7.2 Double-page spread from *Cosmopolitan*, November 1983

Fairy tales can come true.

There's a little magic in every glass of Martini Dry. In its clean, fresh taste. In its unique blend of the choicest wines and herbs. But, most magical of all, it doesn't have to disappear at midnight.

7.3   *Cosmopolitan*, July 1983

about what-is-to-be-done. 'Articles' are therefore reflective, analytic and opinionated but within a pragmatic framework.

Although 60 per cent of *Cosmo*'s readers are married, the feel of the magazine is single. Deirdre McSharry explains this as 'more an attitude .... It's a way of seeing yourself rather openly ... in a fairly fresh, free light ... but it's got nothing to do with whether you're married' (interview 1983). One of the marks of this is *Cosmo*'s minimal attention to, but applauding of, a bohemian domesticity. It displays rooms that have a strong personal style rather than the homogeneity of Habitat or the British High Street fashion for 'reproduction furniture', in articles such as 'License to paint', and it offers cookery that cheats, as in Bel Mooney's 'The fastest cook in the west' complete with dashing recipes and punning graphic.

Less quirkily individual and more 'establishment', but nonetheless organised around the (often exceptional) individual, is the 'centre' of *Cosmo*: 'Working woman'. In September 1984 and in the face, I suspect, of competition from the new magazine *Working Woman*, *Cosmo* scrapped a special work section but not the emphasis, maintaining, 'No one knows more about women's work and does more to help working women than we do!'

LIVING IN COLOUR

Colour it blue, and keep it sweetly simple—just an iron cot against painted wood walls—but then pile on cushions in subtle shades of pink, crimson, mauve and purple, stick a print on the wall, and you'll be surprised how a quiet corner will suddenly come to life.

Some painters, like Duncan Grant and Vanessa Bell, paint everything within reach—fireplaces, tables, cupboards and the result is a cosy clutter of colour as in this shot of the studio in their Sussex home, Charleston, which has been opened to the public as a museum.

Licence to Paint

brown, beige. "Neutral colours are so easy to live with," you hear people say. So are "nice" people, bland food, sweet music. They take nothing out of you, but by the same token, they put nothing back. I'll qualify that. People living in beautiful natural surroundings may feel no need to compete with the incomparably varied

FOOD

You don't need a freezer full of delicatessen specialities in order to rustle up an unexpected meal. Just a well-stocked larder, and a dash of ingenuity! Bel Mooney shows how.

THE FASTEST COOK IN THE WEST

7.4a   *Cosmopolitan*, November 1982
7.4b   *Cosmopolitan*, March 1983

For the rest it is the editorial backbone, the staples, without which *Cosmo* would be shapeless: fashion, beauty, offers and competitions, fiction, health, problem page and readers' letters. What is interesting editorially about *Cosmo* is that there isn't a strong editorial voice: Deidre McSharry does not voice a line in the quite forceful way Iris Burton does, nor in the rest of the magazine are opinions expressed which are clearly *Cosmo*'s. Rather part of *Cosmo*'s fairy godmother act is to provide the arena for a range of individuals to 'speak out'. And it is the (common) individuality of each voice which creates the unity of *Cosmo*'s apparently contradictory pluralism.

Cosmo manifestly subscribes to an ideology of competitiveness and individual success, and to what I call an aspirational feminism. Ardently committed to women 'winning' and with the focus mainly on 'self-assertion', *Cosmo*'s feminism is limited in what it can achieve generally for women. Insofar as our society is built on competitive individualism it is, however, a 'politics' which has popular appeal.

Back in 1972 it was through a sexual self-assertiveness that *Cosmo* 'took on the world'. By 1984 *Cosmo* has extended its reach considerably but it is its sexual profile which still has a pivotal place in the ideological shaping of the magazine.

A sexual reputation – and why not?

Cosmopolitan was spawned of American parentage, the brain child (or should one say sex child?) of Helen Gurley Brown whose first claim to fame in 1963 was the bestseller *Sex and the Single Girl*. Less sexually bold than might be imagined, the book was more significant, at a time when any unmarried woman over 25 already felt herself stigmatised 'the spinster', for its celebration of being single. Taking on the editorship in 1964 of the Hearst Corporation's long-established but moribund *Cosmopolitan*, she brought that celebration of singleness to *Cosmo*'s rejuvenated pages. The magazine was an immediate and huge commercial success in the USA.

Eight years later in Britain, *Cosmo* girl and her magazine burst on to the scene with all the bezazz of the Hollywood starlet known more for her steamy sexual liaisons than for any sizzling acting talent on the screen. The decision to defy protocol with a nude centrefold – the 'girl's' answer to *Playboy* – enhanced a sexual reputation the USA edition was already brandishing. It gained even greater notoriety from the one-time status of the nude in question as Mr Germaine Greer (Paul du Feu). And with such a redoubtable advertising ploy *Cosmo*'s print-run of 300,000, double that of any of its possible competitors, *Nova*, *Honey*, *19*, *Vanity Fair* and *Flair*, was sold out in one day.

In other ways the nude was anticlimatic, his genitals hidden behind a discreetly arched knee, even his navel airbrushed out

7.5 *Cosmopolitan*, May 1974

(perhaps fancifully signifying the embodiment of Man: immaculately born of no woman!). Two years later the fate of *Cosmo*'s unsatisfying nudes was placed in readers' hands. As one reader nicely put it, 'Well, to be honest, if he *was* in my hands I'd probably send him off to play cricket with the lads or perhaps to have his ears reshaped' (August 1974). The 'Great *Cosmo* pin-ups' were no more.

Yet *Cosmo* itself continued to thrive on the sexual reputation that first gesture established. The publishers of *Cosmo*, Brian Braithwaite and Joan Barrell, retrospectively prided themselves that 'the product was unique and absolutely right for its time' (1979, p. 53). But what exactly was 'its time' and how (assuming the wisdom) was *Cosmo* 'right'? Was it just 'sex' that was right?

Cosmo's readership, mainly 16-25-year-olds (accounting for about 50 per cent of the readership from 1972 to 1983), were the babies of the post-war bulge. Fed on orange juice and cod liver oil as youngsters, they were the generation who had grown up with the Beatles and *Honey*. More of them than ever before had gone away to college, and often on to the pill, and with high expectations of a world at their feet they were set, if nothing else, on ensuring they didn't have to forsake womanly delights, as their spinsterly and not to be envied schoolteachers had, in order to take a public place in the world.

For many of these young, middle-class women in the early 1970s the women's liberation movement seemed, if not plain wrong, unnecessarily extreme. 'Women's lib' had accrued to it thanks, or rather otherwise, to the media, an image of strident women who burned bras, despised men (to wit Valerie Solanas's *SCUM – the Society for Cutting Up Men – Manifesto*) and who, obviously, were-not-a-lot-of-fun. Would you believe they threw

USE YOUR STARS TO HAVE A GOOD AFFAIR

by Diana Hunt

The nicest (and most dangerous) thing about starting a new affair is that you go into it hoping for perfection. Conveniently forgetting all past disasters, you convince yourself that *this time it's going to be different.* Great. It would be sad if experience deprived us of that over-the-moon feeling. On the other hand, the higher our expectations, the sooner disappointment is bound to set in. The ideal lover exists only in fiction, in films and temporarily in your imagination. What do exist are lovely exciting and intellectual relationships, which give physical, emotional and intellectual satisfaction, delight at times and misery at others.

You can have a good love affair, if you take your partner's Sun sign into account and base some of your behaviour on it. Not all of it, though, as this would hamper your spontaneity. After all, everybody's chemistry works in different ways, and the rules of love are made for bending. But the more you know about his personality to his.

If you have time and money to spare you can get an astrologer to compare your man's birth chart with yours and that will tell you how well, how indifferently or how impossibly you are matched. It would be good news to hear that on your birth day the Moon was in his Sun sign or that on his birth day the Sun was in a harmonious position to the Moon in your horoscope. Not that such a comparison of birth charts would or should put you off if you're in love. You don't really want a textbook, just a few pointers so that you can write the story happily yourself.

The great thing about romance with an Aries man (March 21–April 20) is that he insists on taking the initiative. If he likes you he tells you so straight away; if he wants to go to bed with you, he'll make it plain immediately. If you can't stand undiluted frankness leave him alone, but it is a positive quality that this man is no liar except in a dire emergency. Even then he is a poor liar and you'll see through him.

His is the pioneering spirit; he's always looking for activity which leads him away from routine. He'll admire you in the most crazy, outrageous fashion, but a superbly-cut leather coat or jacket would be a good investment in his eyes. You needn't be a super cook—he often doesn't know what he eats or drinks, but don't cook like his mother used to or you'll bore him stiff. Best of all, let him take you to a restaurant which is his own disc...

You'll win his heart if you pro... him to fly to Morocco for a wee... sleighing—anything new that woul... If you can bring a fresh nuance in... gadgets, however, he is proud of... stimulants. But perhaps he has... sponged his back in the bath or... of a roaring fire . . . gently is th... be his.

The man who was born under... 21–May 20): a paradoxical c... day and the next criticise y... rather than finding the cash f... ...ed or give you an antique...

He has an unusually strong sense of personal property, and he isn't a bit ashamed of it (you'd better read the financial pages of your paper to know what's going on). When he loves you, you become one of his beautiful possessions, even more desirable for being alive. He will protect you and be frankly jealous and possessive, though he won't allow you the same weaknesses.

He is warm hearted and passionate in a frank, natural way. He adores smooth sensual textures—your velvet dress, your silky hair, your clear skin. He is turned on by anything that feels and smells good. You'll spend a fortune on soap and scents and, if you're attuned to him, the most luxurious armchair money can buy.

Mr Taurus loves his creature comforts.

You will behave like a lady for him, for although he loves show ing you off to his friends, he has conservative tastes. No swe words in his company, though he can get away with it himse "There's a great difference between what men and women can do he says, and he truly believes it. You may not agree, but be tact hurting his vanity is your big taboo.

Your love life will be gayer, more varied yet far less secure if man was born under Gemini (May 21–June 20). It may star foolish, amusing flirtation meant for a few hours and last a str long time. It's enjoyable to be with a man who appreciate abilities, your wit and your brains. He is a passionate talker even forget about lovemaking over an interesting argument, and cuddling he can do with many girls, he reckons, but brains, wit and patience to be the long-term compan volatile Geminian.

You may think he doesn't notice what you wear unt he admires your babyish nightgown or your innocent-l through shirt. He'll love it if you wear six bracelets an every finger for he is still very much a child and wants you as well as to love you. He is lightheartedly sensuou with the big drama, and thinks there are many things ju ant as love. What about travelling? Or throwing a par an Alfa Romeo? Don't breathe a word about mu like money. He likes dreaming of such things and y in and discuss his ever-changing projects.

Of course he'll flirt with your girl friends but, be mind your flirting with his chums. Jealousy?

"Darling, we're modern people."

...the nervous, highly sensitive ...Geminian pl...

7.6 *Cosmopolitan*, November 1972

Belle Epoque elegance is easily achieved with just a couple of judiciously placed hairpins. Remember, it doesn't have to *last!*

GO-T
HAIRS

COSM
Yours t

Slip into something immediately you li Cosmo silk shirt. T ultimate status sy feels, we're offerin for a shirt that wo ladylike vamp an trousers or with that such a fragr its keep. The shi

HE

Brenda Arnau, six year old appeared in *Oh!* nothing more than recommends this e was compulsory to the show. We've bo to be ashamed of makes for a lot o Appearing nude taug If it hadn't I'd c fool of myself."

"Until *Oh! Cal* appeared nude on the l She shook her head got to it was working but there I had an elab "How did you com *cutal?*"

"A friend of mine tions with the show to auditioning for it."

I ask Brenda wha first audition. She told had to do was sing. Wh to know if she would be part, she hesitated. She You see, I come from a to a Catholic all-girls scho "What thoughts bothere "At that stage, silly thin out ways to place them so with a chuckle, "I also tri ty boobs look larger. It w own I was very insecure ab Before the second auditio on as many other clothes as way through, the produ very easily. She was as d in front of just the p sionalism came to the re were ten in the cast hours every day they re wearing leotards. T going to happen—wh nbarrassed with guys h playing one of the to accept each oth embarrassed in front looked around and ht all hell had bro ment I had joine custom ourselves to us were insecure more embarrassed

you?"
d. "The first. We fi t but interesting ction of myself. k at other wome understand what w es with other i

Men and Super Men

In an extract from her new book*, JILLY COOPER gives you some vital and witty advice on her favourite subject

The male is a domestic animal which, if treated with firmness and kindness, can be trained to do most things. It is important to have one in your life to turn on your bath water, do up your zips, carry your suitcases, work out tips, tell silly jokes to, use as a threat when you are having trouble with tradesmen or unwelcome suitors and ultimately to arrange your funeral. Men, according to legend, want only one thing, are deceivers ever, are not interested in gossip, like a cosy armful, need two eggs, and seldom wash behind ears. They come in all shapes and sizes except for their organs which, according to all the sex books, are exactly the same size when erect and similarly capable of giving pleasure.

Although I love a few individual supermen very deeply, as a sex men drive me up the wall. I resent the fact I can't live without them, that they hurt me emotionally, that I hate yet secretly enjoy being bullied by them, that they can do tasks domestic far better than I can, that they enjoy the company of other men so much, and on the whole prefer a bat to a bit on the side. This article from my book* is about men—at work and play, in bed and out of bed, in sickness and in stealth. At one extreme there is perman—he is a cross between Charles Atlas and Einstein, eps his figure by lifting dumb blondes above his head before eakfast, and is sent to stud like Nijinsky at the age of twenty-ne. And at the other extreme there is an individual called Sexual orm.

Sexual Norm is married to wife called Honor whom he has 2.8 imes a week. Honor is sometimes satisfied. Norm thinks continually about other girls, but never does anything about them unless it is handed to him on a plate. He always has a bath in the morning —just in case—and, although he has never dared enter a strip.club, if a girl makes him promise not to look he usually does. He is inclined to get out of hand at office parties. His lifelong ambition is to meet a nymphomaniac.

Apart from Sexual Norm and Superman, most men a girl meets will probably fit into one or several of the following categories.

YOUTHS. In my youth, youths used to breathe heavily, say thank you three times if you gave them a cigarette, open the matchbox upside down so that the matches cascaded on to the floor and, finally, knock over the ashtray.

Today youths are extremely cool, have lean and hungry pelvises. They often marry at seventeen and refer to their father in law as "baby." They don't talk if they don't feel like it, but this is probably because in the places they frequent the music is so loud as to make conversation impossible. They wear clothes which disconcert their elders, including tight jeans to emphasise a bulging crotch. They spend most of their time strumming on guitars or trendy-looking girls. Secretly these girls will worry about tight jeans making a ...nsant. ...d unfair to me that no one bats

man can have a ball with any dolly he chooses.

As a result the world is now full of seventy year old ravers, locks clustering over the collars of their shirts, sideboards laddering their artificially tanned cheeks, and fifty year old ton-up boys, forcing themselves into tight jeans, brushing their thinning hair forward, and touching up the grey roots of their jet-black Viva Zapata moustaches. In the evening they wear sawn-off kaftans to hide their pot bellies.

In an attempt to keep up, they exhaust themselves going on vegetarian diets, giving up drink, and dancing all night in disco theques, then they go round with grey faces saying they feel twenty years younger. In trying to be Peter Pan, they look more like petered-out pansies. They also embrace all the phoney mystic-ism that surrounds smoking pot, and at parties they can be seen going furtively into back rooms and tearing cigarettes apart. Later they gaze into young girls' eyes and say: "My dear, you've made an old man very hippy."

Dolly birds like them—because it gives them kudos in the typing pool to be going out with an older man. Older men can also take them to trendy restaurants younger men can't afford, and are said to be "experienced" sexually. (I shudder to think what rubbish is dished up in the name of experience.) They also take them occasionally for dirty weekends at a Truss House in Hernia Bay.

FIANCES. Fiancés are out of date and not getting it. If pressed they will say, "My fiancée and I have slept together all night in the

"But of course there's nothing wrong with you, Adrian darling—I just can't stand red hair. . . ."

same bed, but we haven't actually slept together." Fiancées never give their fiancés their all—only about seven-eighths.

Fiancés have soft curly hair, pink faces from permanently blushing at their predicament, starry eyes, and a mosaic of scarlet lipstick on their downy cheeks from having been embraced by so many aunts-in-law. They also manage to appear vacant and many aunts-in-law. They also manage to appear vacant and engaged at the same time by having a far away abstracted expres-engaged at the same time by having a far away abstracted expres-... People naturally assume they are dreaming of ...hed will be one flesh;

BED
LES

ENSUAL SILK SHIRT OFFER
s than a fiver

possibility detailed with two mother-of-pearl buttons, the
sleeves snip. Even its sleeves are elegant at its abit of the slit, it is cut
those lines extraordinarily deep, and it feels comfortable to gather
there lines are so sopally deep, and it feels comfortable to gather
generously to laid to you get in onto a stick so unique is just that
to. Based on a fraction of inch col-around. X2. As an Cosmo's are
am-clement. A glowing silken. Candy pink. Marvellous. Friends
really childbad cream and is any broder. It you can once so long
you, in after you can't take it – – – better turn to page 155
and get your complete on that modern Francs?

LOVE LESSONS
FROM AN
OLDER WOMAN

A worldly lady shares her man pleasing secrets.
You could try them all.
by Jessica Andrews

[body text fragment, illegible]

Brenda Arnau talks to Jack Gratus about
HOW NUDITY CAN
OU DISCOVER YOURSELF

herself whilst singing, something which had
never been done before on the legitimate
stage. This, she told me, really
stretched her inhibitions to the
limit. "I found out a lot about being a
woman. The only vision outside of herself
that a woman has is what she finds in the
media. She has to compare herself all the
time with those beautiful models. No
wonder she's so unsure of herself, as I
was. But during that song I had to stand
there alone, with no protection. It taught
me to be proud of myself as a woman."

I asked her if she was nervous at first.
She told me that they all were, but this
was compensated for by the fact that they
felt they were doing something important,
breaking new ground. A real stripper
wants to turn her audience on. Did
Brenda? "No. I wanted to prove to myself
and to other people that one could accept
nudity. It can be an intelligent thing, you
know. I didn't want them to be shocked
or embarrassed by it. Particularly the
women, because if you alienate them,
they'll take their men away. People get

and cried. "I was in a daze.
d, more important, I went
rcome that in one go." I
in the nude?" I asked.
ot big feet. I tried to figure
and out." Then she added
ways of turning to make
of the wrong kind. Deep

silly about nudity. They become childish. A reversion to their upbringing, I
suppose. But, surprisingly enough, they seemed to get used to it very quickly. I
only once heard an embarrassed snicker from a woman when I came out to
sing my song. I also got quite a few letters. Do you want to see them?"

She disappeared for a moment, returning with a large envelope filled
with letters, most of them very complimentary. Some, like one from a
university professor, were on formally headed notepaper. Only one was of
causing "innocent girls and women to be sexually assaulted". We read
through the others together, and we agreed that even in those from very
angry women you could feel the underlying envy, not so much for Brenda
as a woman, but for the freedom and unselfconsciousness she had achieved.

As all psychologists know, some people get a thrill from taking off their
clothes in public. I asked Brenda if she had. "It'd be dishonest to say that
it wasn't exciting. Once I'd loosened up I remember being very excited.
But I think it was more the feeling of being free. It was really lovely. I felt
reborn."

"What do you think feelings in general were towards you when you were
doing the show?" I asked. "People tend to look down on conventional
strippers. How do you feel about them?"

"I admire them, but I think it's easier to turn people on than to do what
we were trying to do. I felt I had a responsibility to my audience, but I think
that some of them saw me on a lower level than a stripper. They couldn't
quite place me. To a certain extent we were being rejected by society. I felt
the show."

It was obvious that *Oh! Calcutta!* was a profound experience for Brenda
Arnau, and she confirmed this. She said she had at first been worried it
might affect her career. I asked her if it had. "For the good," she replied
promptly. "Without clothes to hide behind, I learnt how to hold myself,
how to use my body properly. This has been good for my whole stage presentation. I learnt where real sexuality lies, and I'll tell you this, it's not
in a low-cut dress. Clothes are unimportant to express real sexuality. That's
something which comes from deep within. As a singer I can now come
out of myself, but more than anything it has made me pleased to be a
woman. I tell you, it's beautiful to be a woman, and not to be afraid of it."

Looking at her sitting there, calm, confident and, indeed, very beautiful,
I had to agree with her.

uld have to strip. Brenda
hat, by the time she was
ld stop her. In fact, it all
e small scene which was
grapher – and then her
had to do and I did it."
men, five women – and
to get into shape. But
r all of them was when
strip?" "I wondered if
happened so suddenly
rapher devised to en
the risk of any of us
mped into each other
around with nothing
clutched at myself.
ade to stare at each
bodies. I found out
old with clothes on
naturally shy when

ach other's bodies.
g another woman
said, if you're a
ut we had to look
lves and to each

ppear naked in

from close observations of my friends, and their husbands. In addition, all
of my three children are sons, and from them I've learned what seemed at
times almost too much about the male animal. Finally, for the last several
years, I've been a partner in a thriving theatrical agency, handling the
careers of many young actors.

None of this, of course, makes me any more of an authority on men than
any other woman of forty-nine who's had a fairly full life. However, I have
one additional reason to claim better than exceptionally successful with
wishing to sound immodest, I've always been average expense. Without
men – not with every man, of course, but with most. My successes have
included lovers and sons, professors, scientists and poets, homosexuals
and Don Juans. By now I take my happy relationship with men for granted,
put as I have learned to accept the fact that I will never be able to
remember the simplest melody.

Now, assuming that you are interested first in getting, then in keeping
one or several men, and taking into account that there aren't enough good
men to go around, a woman who wants one must use all the feminine wit,
available to a forty-nine-year-old brain and place them in the twenty-two-
year-old body. So, to work.

1 When I was nineteen I had a blind date with an absolutely stunning
man. He was the silent sort, but I was determined to make a devastating
first impression on him. Drawing on all my freshly budding wit, intelligence
and anecdotal ability, I tried to intrigue and entrance him. After I had
scintillated over the veal piccata at the fashionable trattoria, we took a long
walk. Suddenly he seemed to be limping a little. I didn't want to be tactless
told war wound?) but, as his limp grew worse, I reluctantly interrupted
myself long enough to ask if he would like to sit down. He stopped short,
swung around, and delivered his longest and last speech of the evening.
"I don't have a thing wrong with my leg," he hissed. "I started pretending
three quarters of an hour ago to see if I could get you to stop
talking! What does a person h___ ___ at___tion – fall into
the gutter." L___ ___

healthy ___ man___, there's a
your ___ ___ ego at first

with a man
not what
was not
od in a
True I
was
hich
her

NOVEL

A SINGLE
GIRL

by Mary Danby

If she had known how things were going to turn out,
she would have danced naked in the streets rather than
deny him the slightest intimacy.

Some people can live with unopened letters. Share their homes with
them. Pass them calmly in the hall. Even sensible telephone messages
on them I can't.

That glorious July Monday there was a postcard of Vesuvius from
Dorothy, a statement from the newsagent and that form from the Embassy.
I put the newsagent's bill behind the kitchen clock. Eight thirty-five
and no time for standing around. I looked at the last envelope. "Official
Business," it said. It was as I had expected, a long questionnaire, and I
can my eye over it without taking in what I was reading, seeing in its crisp
type only a precious milestone between the old life and the new.

Cramming the remains of my breakfast toast into my mouth, I put the
dirty plate in the sink and propped the Embassy form against the bread
bin. Had I got change for the Tube? Lipstick and comb? Kleenex? Door
key? A last minute check in front of the long mirror in my bedroom, just

109

children's smoke bombs into the auditorium at Mecca's Miss World contest? It wasn't playing cricket; it wasn't feminine either, and many women as well as men didn't like it.

At the same time large numbers of young women *were* concerned about a sexual and economic equality with men. What *Cosmo* appealingly extolled was not anger and discontent but an optimistic *joie de vivre* about what women in 1972 could enjoy and achieve. The magazine enthused that women could successfully combine 'independence' and more traditional aspects of femininity; brains and beauty could be a winning combination. And any problems with that combination simply didn't surface. An early competition, *Cosmo*'s 'Supergirl contest', aimed to find 'the prettiest, best dressed, most *alive* girls around .... Much more than a model contest, this is the search to find the girl with something extra – a mind of her own' (April 1973). Casual readers, however, could be forgiven for believing that 'mind' and 'work' took a back seat to an overwhelming preoccupation with all things sexual, as a selection from just one issue indicates.

In the 1980s the magazine is still thought by some to be concerned with little more than 'How to get a man into bed' and 'Bed time beauty, fashion and psychology' to say nothing of 'sexual acrobatics' (aerobics even?) to keep him there once you have. The caricature catches something but also misses the point of what *Cosmo*'s pursuit of sexuality was and is about.

If *Cosmo* turned the tables on *Playboy* by playing it, in a minor way, at its own game of pin-ups, it also shared with *Playboy* a similar permissive or sexual liberation ideology. Hugh Hefner's '*Playboy* philosophy' (1962) linked individual fulfillment not just to work and achievement – the puritan heritage – but to sex (uncompromisingly heterosexual), play and pleasure. And the expression and enjoyment of the latter was regarded as a critical commentary on the shackles puritanism imposed on individuals. Sex wasn't just unbridled fun though, it was necessary to emotional and psychological health. 'Liberating' your sexuality – as if it were an essential life force trapped inside you – would bring you in touch with your 'true self'. Such views had pretensions to liberalism: '*The Playboy Philosophy* is predicated on our belief in the importance of the individual and his rights as a member of a free society'. 'Natural' sexual expression was just one of those rights (*Playboy*, January 1979).

Notwithstanding the coining of the term 'sexual revolution' in the mid-1960s, with its inferences about *women's* new found (pill) sexuality, it was not until the early 1970s and the burgeoning of ideas about a wider equality for women that a feminine version of 'sexual liberation' could be popularly addressed to women.

Cosmo contributed to that. Its early basking in sexuality was partly a symbolic rejection of puritan and masculine styles of work; it made a provocative statement by upturning feminine

7.7 *Cosmopolitan*, April 1973

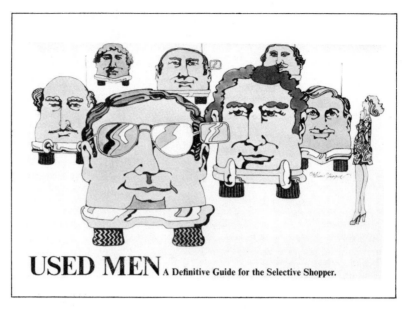

USED MEN A Definitive Guide for the Selective Shopper.

codes, relishing a humour about sex and relationships and making men, for a change, the butt of laughter. As in 'Used men: a definitive guide for the selective shopper' (though admittedly 'revenge' is limited here: the piece is written by a man) (April 1973). *Cosmo* dismissed as anachronistic the old double standard: rather, nice girls do, and they (should) enjoy it:

> The cliché of the Wicked Lady slinking by and, with bat of an eyelash, luring the Nice Young Man to destruction while the Nice Girl Who-Always-Loved-Him wrings her hands in helpless frustration, is history. That Nice Girl has learned some tricks the Wicked Lady never knew – for one thing, she honestly and openly enjoys sex. ('Nice guys make lousy lovers', July 1972)

Sex was a woman's right too: 'The ability and right of women as well as men to enjoy sexual expression and satisfaction is as important and relevant a subject today as any other physical ability or civil right' (The ostentatious orgasm', July 1972). And *Cosmo* was concerned that women should know and talk about sex: 'Mention the word orgasm in some circles and eyebrows still go up, women giggle or look guilty, men look vaguely hostile or protective. By the defensive silence that ensues, you feel the subject is not discussed even between married partners. It's about time these defences came down' ('The ostentatious orgasm'). Pulling down these defences, through the endless half-serious, half-fun quizzes *Cosmo* has always delighted in – 'Are you really permissive?' (July 1972), 'Are you sexually adventurous?' (August 1974) – and through articles helped to dispel old myths and banish women's feelings of shame/guilt/abnormality about their sexuality: it accepted as commonplace that women do masturbate,

111

have sexual fantasies, sometimes desire sex more than their male partners, enjoy times of non-monogamy, sex without deep commitment, and so on. Such articles provided for the first time in magazines a legitimate space for women to contemplate their own desires, not simply their responses to men's.

Yet this emphasis on sex also made it increasingly like another area of personal work and in this respect, ironically, *Cosmo* was following in the hallowed footsteps of magazine tradition: 'domestic work', 'beauty work' and now 'sex work'. In the early days the work was as much of a *sportif* variety as about relationships: 'There is no doubt that a well-trained and practised internal musculature is an important factor in sexual pleasure for both' ('The ostentatious orgasm'). In the 1980s sex is no longer a terrain for exercised gymnasts; in pursuit of the body beautiful *Cosmo* women have branched out into other sporting activities – 'Train with zest', 'Exercise with Esme', 'Shape up for life' with *Cosmo*'s book and tape 'for total health' – but they have hardly been allowed to relax on the sexual front.

Cosmo explores a variety of possibilities around relationships: 'Pillow friends' (September 1978), 'Is marriage dead?' (June 1981), 'Sex and the single parent' (August 1981), 'Sexual commitment: can it satisfy?' (September 1983), 'Licensing your live-in lover' (November 1983). It always has a new 'angle' on sex: 'What next for sex?' (on if women were as tall as men! March 1982), 'Skin to skin – clothing the erogenous zone' (October 1983), 'A little more than breakfast in bed' (July 1982), 'Your most personal sexual experience' (November 1983) which, while enlightening – well maybe – and compulsive reading, also elevate sex to the prime place in social life. Sex is a means of discovering yourself; sex is the centre of a relationship; sex is a step to other things; sex is always something that can be bettered or varied; sex is potentially always a problem; sex is something you-never-can-forget.

Lurking within *Cosmo*'s verbosity about sex is the sexual liberation notion that 'true' individuality is found and fulfilled in the (hetero)sexual quest: 'How I fought my way to sexual freedom' by Arabella Melville, 'from academic psychologist to editor of a sex magazine' (March 1976). More recently, Irma Kurtz introducing *The Making of Love* comments that the book is full of cases where people needed to review themselves and their rules of sexuality 'before they could discover who they really were and thereby discover where the well spring of their own particular sexuality lay' (June 1983). Prudence Tunnadine, the author and a doctor and therapist, maintains, 'Ideally, we like to make the individual so free that he or she can take freedom to his [sic] partner'.

What I question about this 'talking sex therapy' – the most common approach *Cosmo* takes to thinking about relationships –

is the emphasis it places on finding yourself through sex; its tendency to cut sexuality off from the rest of social activity; and its belief that so long as a heterosexual couple communicate frankly their different sexualities can be mutually satisfied.

It is illusory to think that hidden away behind our inhibitions is our 'true' sexuality and 'freedom'. Sexuality is as culturally constructed and learnt as is the language we speak. Nor is it just about what goes on in the bedroom. Yet in '"It's lovely but . . ." Telling the truth in bed' (October 1982) the authors never once move from that bed to consider that the conditions for 'sexual criticism' may hinge on the state of a couple's more mundane criticisms about who, for instance, supplied the new loo-roll (cf. page 117). As the writer Angela Carter has put it, 'We do not go to bed in simple pairs; even if we choose not to refer to them, we still drag there with us the cultural impedimenta of our social class, our parents' lives, or our bank balances, our whole biographies' (1979, p. 9). And what women and men centrally drag into bed are the uneven and protean power relations insidiously working to support masculine sexuality.

Sexual difference, even sexual conflict, is acknowledged, but the 'solution' to such clashing is to understand the differences and then compromise. Thus, describing one couple in 'Sharing the same sexual wave' Ann Hooper writes of their sexual relationship, 'Caroline and John didn't find it easy to marry their different needs . . . . They agreed to take turns in supplying the other with the nearest each could get to their ideal. Even though this didn't work out very often . . .' (July 1983). There is no hint either of any power relations between them or that those 'needs' and 'ideals' could be transformed. Similarly, Ann Dickson in 'Be true to yourself and your sexuality' suggests that most women at some time have participated in sex out of fear: 'Fear of being accused of being frigid or a tease. Fear of invoking a hostile response, of being attacked verbally or physically. Fear of . . .' (December 1982). Rather than confront the issue that 'fear' points to – that it is men who have the power to pull the sexual (and other) strings – she advises women to be self-assertive and negotiate as sexual equals, carefully warning of the danger of assertiveness becoming agression. Thus, in accord with a sexual liberation ideology, not only is equality deemed to lie in women's hands, so too does the responsibility for not becoming, God forbid, the sexually dominant partner, with its dreaded consequence, male impotence. That 'problem', like an allergic reaction to feminist assertiveness, erupts recurringly in *Cosmo*'s pages: 'Tender loving care: an (almost) infallible cure for impotence' (December 1973); 'Passive men and how to arouse them' (August 1976); 'Helping him through the night' (March 1983).

His problem is thrown on to her shoulders; above all as the 'sexually liberated' *Cosmo* woman she must be careful about *him*:

'Be liberated but discreet . . . . Do be wary . . .' (December 1973); 'Nothing is more fragile than the male's ego, so don't tread on it' (March 1983). It is advice which undercuts the injunction that she assert *her* ego: 'Be a feminist but mind you don't upset him' is simply impossible. One woman's assertiveness *is* another man's impotence – in a manner of speaking. Because whatever her actual behaviour he is likely to experience it as threatening and aggressive; and if he does not 'fight back' with a 'problem' of impotence, he will do so in other subtle and less subtle ways. Men do not easily relinquish power (and why should they?).

In 'Helping him through the night' Phillip Hodson appeared to understand the relation between men's sexuality and their power: 'A large majority of men confuse their sexuality with power. If they can't have sex, they think they lack *puissance*. The very word they have chosen – impotence – indicates what they think.' Unknowingly nevertheless, he perpetuates the linking of sex with power – and naughtiness. His ten-point plan of action addressed to the bereft *Cosmo* woman may alleviate *his* symptoms; it hardly tackes the root of the difficulty which *she* bears the brunt of. He advises, 'Abandon the direct approach altogether . . . . Any man will find it easier to perform when sex is no longer compulsory and perhaps impossible to resist an erection if it's forbidden.' Exactly so! If sex (still a performance note) is no longer compulsory then he, not she, is back at the helm; if he can get an erection when sex is forbidden then he is flaunting his power (naughtily in her face?) in breaking the taboo. The 'problem', and the extensive column inches devoted to 'solving' it, only displaces and hides the real problem: the 'normal' construction of men's sexuality as powerful and performing – and fuelled by 'naughtiness'.

To put it in its strongest and most controversial terms, the 'problem' of impotence – not impotence *per se* – is part of the same problem as rape. If the 'problem' of impotence is naughty power having 'failed', rape is a brutal insistence of it. And neither impotence nor rape can begin to be eradicated without an understanding by men as well as women of the need to transform masculinity. And if that is to be anything more than gestural on men's part it is likely to involve immense personal upheaval. As far as women are concerned a negotiation as equals in a heterosexual relationship can only begin to occur when the conditions of that social inequality are carefully taken into account.

Although *Cosmo* has become more feminist and cognisant of those inequalities over the years, its acknowledgment of the tensions between femininity and masculinity in social life continue to be displaced on to a repetitive attention to sexual relationships. It is as though personally solving sexual problems provided the panacea to women's equality: a 'sexual liberation' ideology still has its echoes. It is an element of individual effort also which, whether on the sexual or work fronts, centrally characterises *Cosmo*'s feminism.

Aspirational feminism: one woman's gain, other women's loss?

Having no allegiances to the women's movement when it was launched, *Cosmo* has, according to Deirdre McSharry, gradually heeded 'the rumbles' and responded to them, and by 1983, in contrast to its American counterpart, British *Cosmo* is 'more out of the closet' (interview 1983). Many feminists, however, would probably dismiss and disown *Cosmo*'s inclinations towards feminism as variously reformist, recuperative or compromising. *Cosmo* in rejoinder would probably agree, but argue that it's no good living in cloud cuckoo land and that compromise is the stuff of everyday life — for feminists as much as anyone else. My own view is that it is cutting off our nose to spite our face to outlaw wholesale what *Cosmo* stands for, to say nothing of manifesting the worst aspects of a political 'holier than thou' moralism. Nevertheless, though I respect *Cosmo*'s efforts on behalf of women and its ability to carry along with it a readership of over a million, I also think there are problems to its feminism. And if there are points of coincidence, some aspects — like *Cosmo*'s unreflecting white, heterosexual and aspirational focus — completely cut across the grain of *Spare Rib*'s radicalism, as will become clearer in the next chapter.

Cosmo's strongest appeal, and perhaps its feminist strength as well as weakness, is that it constantly tries to have its cake and eat it: 'We've reported the battle of the sexes and helped to discuss how to make the peace' (tenth birthday issue, March 1982). Wanting both, *Cosmo* therefore tackles some of the contradictions about being a woman that feminism and independence throw up, and in characteristic *Cosmo* style it lauds their pleasures as well as despairing of their problems.

As *Cosmo* girls have grown up, so having babies and combining work with childcare have more frequently been discussed in the magazine. Unlike *Woman's Own*'s, *Cosmo*'s articles like 'A woman's place is in confusion' (December 1982) and 'Kids and careers — the great balancing act' (November 1983), don't short-shrift the difficulties. In the latter, Angela Phillips soberly recounts how the lack of flexible work patterns, unhelpful employers, sometimes hostile colleagues, problems of childcare, all contribute to 'guilt mixed with exhaustion and stress' for the mother with a young baby. At the same time the article is not all gloom and doom: 'Having a child to come home to after work is like getting a present every day in the post', even if some days it doesn't live up to expectations. And the pleasures women describe are often mixed ones: 'Since I stopped working full-time, it has been marvellous. All the pressure is off. Mel and I now have a far more equal relationship and more time and energy but I do feel frustrated about the loss of my career.' The value of the article is less in offering overall solutions than in simply speaking about those conflicts, sharing with readers those necessarily *ad hoc* survival strategies adopted by individual women.

Cosmo also admits to enjoying (sometimes) the supposedly feminist '*verbotens*': 'Cosmo goes soppy over the wicked weekend (ahh . . .). It's naughty . . . but it's nice' (February 1982); or 'high heels, shimmery dress, elaborate make-up'. In 'Fashion is a feminist issue' Eileen Fairweather maintains, 'There's a time and a place for everything – including being sexy' (July 1982). Its articles acknowledge too the contrary demands we make in heterosexual relationships: '"Don't treat me like a child, but take care of me," she says. "Be independent, but need me," is his refrain. "Don't be a chauvinist, but act like a man not a wimp," she says' ('Driving each other crazy on the way to liberation', September 1983).

In the interests of the battle and enjoying a truce, *Cosmo* gives unusual prominence to men's views – about feminism, their contributions are barbed. Claiming 'post-liberation' status they whinge defensively and then stab the women's movement in the back. They rarely see themselves as 'the problem', rather, 'the problem with the feminist movement is that it liberates women but not men.' And why the hell don't you women show us what to do: 'The day the feminist movement comes of age will be the day when it stops despising men for their chauvinism and starts a positive way of educating men and women to accept equality of the sexes' (November 1981).

On a more regular basis Tom Crabtree laments the state of manhood: 'In years to come, a man will be judged more by who he is than by what he is and he'll need more skills to cope. So come on chaps, start living!' (January 1983).

Occasionally a male writer seems to have seen the feminist light, and grasping the problems of masculinity, unlike Tom Crabtree, includes himself in the thick of it. In 'Rape: this man says it's unforgiveable' Peter Martin may not link the problem of male impotence to rape (a link immensely difficult for men to stomach), but does argue, 'There are many ways of putting and keeping women down . . . rape is a form of terrorism which supports – and perhaps even holds together – a status quo. Unlocking this equation will not be easy. We men will need to discover and dismantle the full ruthlessness of our attitudes towards women in ways we have barely begun to comprehend' (May 1983). In another delightfully entitled article he blows 'The myth of the loo-roll fairy' or on how the fairies *don't* do the housework.

These masculine voices and *Cosmo*'s visual attempts to break the conventional codes of 'real manhood' are a journalistic attempt – and there are few such forums addressed to a mixed audience – to transform masculinity. Whatever their limitations –

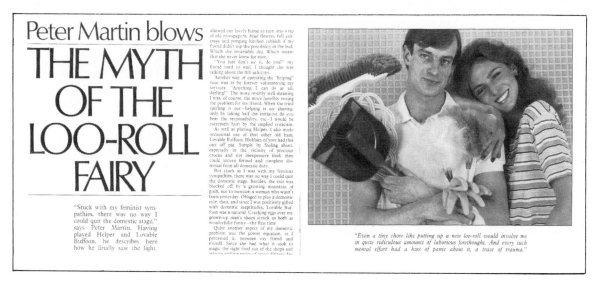

Peter Martin blows
THE MYTH OF THE LOO-ROLL FAIRY

"Stuck with my feminist sympathies, there was no way I could quit the domestic stage," says Peter Martin. Having played Helper and Lovable Buffoon, he describes here how he finally saw the light.

allowed our lovely home to turn into a tip of old newspapers, dead flowers, toll ashtrays and ponging kitchen rubbish if my friend didn't nip the possibility in the bud. Which she invariably did. Which meant that she never knew for sure.

"You just don't *see* it, do you?" my friend used to wail. I thought she was talking about the roll ashtrays.

Another way of operating the "helping" ruse was to be forever volunteering my services: "Anything I can do at all, darling?" The more overtly well-meaning I was, of course, the more horribly vexing the problem for my friend. When she tried spelling it out—helping is *not* sharing; only by taking half the initiative do you bear the responsibility, etc—I would be extremely hurt by the implied criticism.

As well as playing Helper, I also made occasional use of that other old ham, Lovable Buffoon. Hobbies of yore had this one off pat. Simply by fooling about, especially in the vicinity of precious crocks and not inexpensive food, they could secure formal and complete dismissal from all domestic duty.

But stuck as I was with my feminist sympathies, there was no way I could quit the domestic stage. Besides, the exit was blocked off by a growing mountain of guilt, not to mention a woman who wasn't born yesterday. Obliged to play a domestic role, then, and since I was positively gifted with domestic ineptitudes, Lovable Buffoon was a natural. Cracking eggs over my grown-up man's shoes struck us both as wonderfully funny—the first time.

Quite another aspect of my domestic problem was the power equation, as I perceived it, between my friend and myself. Since she had what it took to magic the right food out of the shops and into an endless series of never-dinners, by

"Even a tiny chore like putting up a new loo-roll would involve me in quite ridiculous amounts of laborious forethought. And every such mental effort had a hint of panic about it, a trace of trauma."

highlighted in the 'Men bleed too (but differently)' scenario – these efforts at masculine reconstruction ought not, I think, to be wholly scorned.

But the other, less constructive, side of *Cosmo*'s obsessive attention to heterosexuality is its relatively minimal attention to other relationships: friendship between women (or with men for that matter), familial relations, work friendships, and, noticeable by its conspicuous absence as an acceptable practice and identity, lesbianism. When the rare article about lesbianism appears it is addressed, somewhat voyeuristically, to heterosexual women and expresses and urges a liberal tolerance rather than a feminist understanding. Candace Lyle, for example, in 'Women who love women' argues, 'Like heterosexuals, lesbians struggle through their relationships, savouring the happy times, enduring the disappointments .... Only one of the problems lesbians face is truly unique – and that is they must confront the hostility of homophobes, people with an irrational fear of homosexuality' (April 1983). That is, they must confront people who are 'prejudiced'. But as two ads illustrate, with their symbolic and actual play around heterosexuality and their incidental placing either side of an earlier article by Anna Raeburn 'On lesbianism', the 'problem' is both more than that and one that implicates all of us: the social construction of a 'normal' female and feminine sexuality as heterosexual.

The liberal view of lesbianism is that women should be able to adopt a lesbian identity if they 'choose'; it assumes, but without considering it, that heterosexuality is also a choice. And yet for all *Cosmo*'s explorations of 'choice' within heterosexuality the identity itself is never questioned. That *Cosmo* cannot ask 'what makes a woman heterosexual' (in the way it can ask what makes a woman lesbian), and that advertisers cannot possibly portray a lesbian

117

7.9a *Cosmopolitan*, April 1979

7.9b *Cosmopolitan*, April 1979

7.9c *Cosmopolitan*, April 1979

sexuality, mark the degree to which not just individuals but our culture as a whole is deeply homophobic. As the American feminist and writer Adrienne Rich has persuasively argued, the 'problem' of lesbianism arises because heterosexuality is 'compulsory' and culturally pervasive, and until that 'compulsion' is recognised and challenged lesbianism will continue to be regarded as socially 'aberrant'.

If, on the sexual front, *Cosmo* opens up 'choices' for women only to tie them to heterosexuality, on the work front it opens up job possibilities for women only to catch them in a competitive individualism. And this despite Deidre McSharry's sardonic comment, 'It isn't just work away like a man and sacrifice everything and you will finish up with a heart attack and managing the company age 49. I don't think women want to work like that' (interview 1983). Certainly from its early days of featuring only the glamour jobs – 'Girls in the gilt-edged jobs' (September 1973), 'Working in the world of art' (May 1974), and 'Work where the men are' (at the Stock Exchange, just opened to women, April 1973) – *Cosmo* has moved on to embrace anything from farming and engineering to 'the new glamour jobs – microchips', and to devote space to 'work training, retraining, changing jobs, job sharing, flexitime. I think we've been rather good at discussing these new ways of working' (Deirdre McSharry interview 1983).

Yet the language in which work is considered is one of individual self-assertiveness, competition and success. Women are encouraged to aspire and are congratulated on winning; the caption to a reader's letter was aptly 'Who asserts herself wins' (June 1983), and *Cosmo* praised readers who took part in the questionnaire: 'You're aiming high! … *Cosmo* readers are ambitious, well-educated and career-minded' (April 1982).

Cosmo's *Guide to Getting Ahead* by Brenda Jones (one of its 'Save your life' books 'to help you run your life more efficiently'); its Saturday development courses (started in 1980 and ranging from courses on radio, TV, and video to 'getting to grips with the mighty word processor') and its awards, like the 'Perform Award'

7.10a *Cosmopolitan*, May 1983
7.10b *Cosmopolitan*, May 1983

119

for 'outstanding performance', have all opened up opportunities for some women while tending to reward the jobs in which it is possible to achieve individual success. *Cosmo*'s 'winners' are either 'creative artists' dancers, writers – or entrepreneurs. Moreover there is an easy fit between the styles of individualism these jobs flaunt and the values extolled by the companies who fund these awards.

Beecham Hair Care, providers of the 'Perform Award' (Perform is also a hair conditioner), and other capitalistic benefactors have no qualms about their philanthropic support of 'the arts' or their encouragement to 'free enterprise'. It would be another matter if *Cosmo* saw fit to sponsor collective achievements on the shopfloor to improve women's working conditions and training possibilities. The latter would undoubtedly serve considerably larger numbers of women. It is however on the 'wrong side' of the capitalist equation, smelling therefore of class politics, trade union militancy and disruption; *Cosmo* rewards individual, not political success.

By sustaining the dream that individuals *can* win, and by constantly affirming individual success, *Cosmo* obscures the fact that, in the class society we live in, for every woman who 'wins' there are many 'losers'. Its address to middle-class women, and its (indeed helpful) pragmatic approach obviates any questioning of work structure as a whole. It wouldn't look behind, say, the 'Perform Award' to wonder about the working conditions for those on Beecham's shopfloor producing and packaging 'Perform'. It does not see the hierarchical social divisions in which one group has power and success, or the possibility of them, on the backs of those who, largely, do not. *Cosmo* rather persuades that power is individual, to be grasped by one and all: 'failure' therefore, implies only that you have failed to master *Cosmo*'s 'highly recommended self-assertiveness scheme'; it does not imply failure of the structure. Whatever its gains for individual women, an aspirational feminism works within, not against the competitive organisation of work. It is about 'I' rather than 'we'.

More generally, though, there are contradictory elements at play in *Cosmo*. The magazine is a veritable tribute to the capitalist marketplace, in which, above all, each looks first to herself. A vehicle for ads, offering a wealth of consumer goods for readers to choose, and buy, and enjoy, editorially, *Cosmo* also 'sells' its monthly surprises. But like any reputable retailer it also listens to its consumers' angry complaints as well as to their praise. On the last page is 'Dear Cosmopolitan' where readers write about *Cosmo*'s 'mismatched wares', 'faulty goods' and, less often, its 'quality merchandise'.

PORNOGRAPHIC PICTURES?

Cosmopolitan publishes articles which aim to raise female conscious-ness, decrying male chauvinism, yet the pictures seem to contradict these views. I was prompted to write by the picture taken at the Porchester Baths (*Style* May). Although I'm a keen Turkish bather, the image projected was not very appetising. Who was the picture aimed at? Surely not women. The picture of four tousled girls lounging around looking provocative in white corsets and damp muslin, their thighs spread, could not have been more pornographic.

If it had not been for the News Report about Maggie's Family Policy, I could have had the impression that I was reading some magazine designed to feed male fantasies.

Suky Best, London
(July 1983)

STICKING UP FOR STOPES

I was shocked and annoyed that you should allow space for an attack on Dr Marie Stopes – and by a man too! (*Sex and the literary earthmovers* by Phillip Hodson, November). For your readers under forty, may I elucidate?

Dr Marie Stopes was not a novelist, she was the inventor of Birth Control (as it was then called) and gave instruction on how to use it in a book called *Married Love*. This was so revolutionary that many members of the Establishment – and particularly of the Church – would have liked her banned – and burned too! For she suggested:

That having more than six children was harmful to a woman's health (this was an *average* family). That contraception should be available to all women. That men, instead of raping their wives every night should actually try making *love* to them (and how to do this). That women, freed from the fear of pregnancy, might actually get to *enjoy* sex!

OK, so her descriptions of what sex could be like were a trifle lyrical, but probably in an attempt to encourage people to try it. And maybe she actually experienced it herself that way.

So don't knock Marie Stopes – she did more for women in practical terms than all today's 'liberators' put together.

Dora Poole, Bath
(January 1983)

... AND NOW FOR SOME PRAISE

I would like to tell you how much I enjoy your magazine. It is a source of useful information and intelligent comment. Unlike the other women's magazines, *Cosmopolitan* urges women to expect and actually achieve more in their lives than 'keeping a better home'. I also have a suspicion that the men who read *Cosmopolitan* now realise that women have much the same needs and feelings as they do. More important – I believe that you have helped a lot of women to realise that. Keep inspiring us!

Sally Langston, Gloucester
(August 1983)

As the 'end word' it seems that readers are the final and powerful arbiters. Yet in the context of *Cosmo*'s overall package these small voices are, like that of any individual consumer confronting 'big business', soon forgotten. On the other hand *Cosmo*'s cover image, in many ways belying its contents, is still the wholly appropriate image by which to remember *Cosmo*. Often the named and recognised individual, by spoof of make-up and hair style, photography and printing, the image is manufactured in *Cosmo*'s sexual mould. 'She' has become a desirable commodity: 'Buy me, buy *Cosmo*, and buy my recipe to individual success.' Who could ask for more?

In *Spare Rib*'s view, all of us.

Chapter 8

Spare Rib: 'a women's liberation magazine'

'. . . I sometimes feel that *Spare Rib* is the voice of sanity in a world which won't listen or try to understand. You certainly cheer me up and make me feel strong and hopeful, and able to carry on – you are as much a sister to me as the women I know and love. *Thanks.*'
(Letter from Sue Regan, *Spare Rib*, August 1983, no. 133)

Cultural shock; political radicalism: 'I used to be a Tupperware groupie until I discovered *Spare Rib*'

To compare *Spare Rib* with commercial magazines is like evaluating the appeal of a spartan wholefood diet by reference to the rich diet of junk food. It is found, inevitably, to be lacking: no layers of sugary icing between the editorial cake and no thick milk chocolate as palliative to the 'hard nuts'. Instead a heavy textured pudding, dingy in colour, and somewhat hard work on the jaws. Or as Brian Braithwaite and Joan Barrell dismissively describe *Spare Rib*, 'It appears drab and colourless, a bit like a political tract . . . not the kind of magazine one could recommend for a jolly good read' (1979, p. 60). But then that depends . . . .

'Jolly' *Spare Rib* is not; a 'good read' of a different sort *Spare Rib* assuredly is, and the publication of the Penguin *Spare Rib Reader* to celebrate one hundred issues of *Spare Rib* is just one witness to that. Undoubtedly too, *Spare Rib* is something of a cultural shock. Unlike commercial magazines it expresses less a fragile contentment with women's lot than a critical discontent; it is less a women's magazine than a women's liberation magazine.

Editorial production, design and administration of the magazine, what appears and how it is represented, and *Spare Rib*'s relation to its readers are all informed by a sense of responsibility to women in the women's movement. Nevertheless another strand of its editorial policy has always been not to assume but to explain the women's movement to women unfamiliar with it and to 'kidnap readers from other magazines' (Sue O'Sullivan, interview 1983). Thus one of its recurring editorial issues is 'how to be popular, accessible and reach more women without toning down what we want to say' (April 1977, no. 57).

At one level this mixed editorial address has worked: *Spare Rib* has after all been around for fourteen years (1986), much longer than many commercial magazines, and been read by and influenced many more women than its print-run of 20,000 copies a month might indicate. But at another level, *Spare Rib* is trying to meet incompatible demands from 'inside' and 'outside' the women's movement that are not easily accommodated in the editorial mix of one magazine. As Sue O'Sullivan commented, the main attack on *Spare Rib* is that it falls between two stools: 'You don't satisfy feminists and you don't satisfy the reader who hasn't come across feminism.'

In this chapter I want first to try and understand what it is that makes *Spare Rib* so different from the commercial magazines, and in many ways much more stimulating. Secondly, I want to disentangle some of the dilemmas *Spare Rib* faces.

One of the difficulties of talking about the women's movement is that it is not a centralised and clearly defined political party and has therefore come to mean different things for different people. One way of thinking about it is in terms of its component groups (Women Against Violence Against Women, Rape Crisis, or Women Oppose the Nuclear Threat, for example); another is in terms of its political tendencies, from radical feminism, with its stress on men as women's universal oppressors, to socialist feminism, with its concern for class differences and with how women's oppression is also rooted in the organisation of production. Some of that heterogeneity I will go on to explore through *Spare Rib*'s pages, but in particular I want to draw out some underlying principles which cut across the women's movement and, more relevantly here, contribute to the shape *Spare Rib* takes.

The radicalism of the women's movement lies less in the simple assertion that women are oppressed than in questioning and opening up all the taken-for-granted patriarchal assumptions about femininity and women's lives: motherhood and family life, heterosexuality and the feminine sexual image, divisions of labour in the workplace and women's emotional dependence within marriage. *Spare Rib* is constantly thought-provoking, often about the social unmentionables, from facing death to hairiness, always informative, about health or the law. Rather than the world brought home (like *Woman's Own*'s 'Caribbean cookery'), *Spare Rib*'s horizons look to the world: 'Comiso Peace Camp – Sicily's Greenham' (January 1984, no. 138). *Woman's Own*'s complacency, the overwhelming heartiness radiating from *Cosmo*, are simply not there. *Spare Rib* resonates with strong feelings, sometimes of exuberant energy, warmth and humour, often of pain, sadness and anger.

As the feature titles (Figures 8.1a, 8.1b and 8.2) show, the political touchstone of the women's movement is always at some level women's individual experience: thought and action around women's position starts on just that ground of personal life over which commercial magazines so endlessly, if restrictedly, tramp. The women's movement begins with 'I' but stoutly refuses the codes of femininity and the ideological hold of individualism to which the latter are so closely bound. In a key and condensed

8.1a   *Spare Rib* cover, September 1982
8.1b   *Spare Rib* cover, May 1983

phrase of the women's movement, 'The personal is political', rendered so through the process of consciousness-raising. Originally associated with special small groups, it has become an ongoing (if submerged) practice for feminists. By sharing and making public what seem individual and private experiences, women begin to understand the social roots to those experiences; they muster from a common oppression a supportive strength to help each other transform their lives. As an early slogan declared, 'Sisterhood is powerful.' Such a politics, beginning and constantly referring back to individual women's experience – as Lucy Goodison wrote in her article 'Falling in love', 'We are as we are and we have to start from there' (November 1983, no. 136) – potentially strikes chords of recognition for most women and has an immediate relevancy to their lives which other politics do not. Potentially, it leads to a wider politics of engagement and transformation of the central ideologies and institutions of society.

It is however in tension with a second strand of the women's movement's politics which, by seeming to dismiss many women's experience, undercuts that relevancy. Many women are less attracted to feminism than intimidated by what it seems to stand for: a wholesale rejection of all the personal and institutional baggage associated with femininity, whether it be consumer

125

FEATURES

6 **An approach to Death** — Sue Cartledge describes, in her diary, the last years of her life.

18 **Racism: Black to Black.**

19 **Marriage Money and Women's fight for independence.**

26 **Coming Out: An Asian woman's experience.**

27 **A to Z of Feminism.** AmaZing Pull Out, part 1—.

32 **'Excessive' Body Hair** — How do women feel about it?

52 **Falling in Love** — An Excerpt from a new book called 'Sex and Love'.

POETRY AND FICTION

49 *Back* by Cheryl Lee and *Woman Mother Lesbian* by Alison Longford.

50 *Ursula* by Al Garthwaite.

REVIEWS

Films: *Come back to the 5* and *Dime Store Jimmy Dean*, by Robert Altman. *Querelle*, Fassbinder's last film, and a selection of the films at the National Film Theatre Festival in November.

Theatre: *Dear Girl* by the Women's Theatre Group, the Devil's Gateway by Sara Daniels, and *Slipstreaming* by Diane Biondo.

Exhibition: Unusual Exhibition: Bemba, People of Central African Plateau· Afro-Portuguese Ivories; Black Arts & Crafts Fair.

Books: *Paris France* by Gertrude Stein; *Intruders on the Rights of Man* and *A Very*

Music: *Opening nite in Heaven, September in the Pink*, and *Poppie Nongena*; a Black South African Production.

REGULARS

Letters: *This mag is alive, Black Neglect, Blind and Proud*, and more . . .

News: Women ride for peace, Divorce — Women blamed, Sri Lankan News and more . . .

23 **Shortlist:** Events, Centres, Campaigns, Projects.

35 **Classifieds:** Homes, Jobs, Groups.

56 **Subscriptions:** Tug your hair and get a subscription.

Please don't send any more poetry or fiction until the first of January.

Spare Rib is produced collectively by full timers Maxine Angus, Arati, Susan Ardill, Farzaneh, Petal Felix, Rachel Lever, Loretta Loach, Manny, Sona Osman and Sue O'Sullivan and part-timers Sue Hancock, Carole Spedding and Ruth Wallsgrove. Special thanks this month to Jill Dawson, Stephanie Wallis, Cordelia Donohoe, Susan Bennett, Gina Ploszajski, Tinuke, Maggie Fagan, Cathy Sellers, Susan Hemmings, Alice, Irene, Dianne; Ravinder, Alison, Joelle, Sara Dunn, Barbara Norden and Joy Whiddett.

8.2 *Spare Rib*, November 1983

culture which sells and nurtures 'false' images of womanhood, or marriage. This oppositional politics appears to abandon 'the centre' (where most women like to think they are placed) to create alternative lifestyles on the fringes of society. It advocates therefore that 'I' leap into becoming someone quite other than who I am at the moment.

But if feminism wholly rejects patriarchal institutions, it is less a dismissal of women's current experiences or needs than a refusal to relax into what could be detrimental compromise. Importantly, too, radical changes of lifestyle (by some) affirm and herald a feminist utopian vision (for all) in the future. All this is part of the women's movement's strength; it is also a potential weakness.

The women's movement's idealism slips into a purist and puritan and morally overlaid politics: the fringe becomes the only politically OK place for feminists to occupy: alternative ways of living and working become the only 'pure' political action, and a moral disapprobation of the hazy 'centre', with all its contradictory pains and pleasures for women, ensues.

For example, *Spare Rib*'s March 1984 cover carried the following sell-lines: 'CHILDREN: some women really do want them'; 'MEN: some women do have them'. A tone doubtless intentionally tongue-in-cheek, but still the sell-lines make abundantly clear the supposed 'norms' and 'shoulds' for feminists: not to want children; nor to have relationships with men. Inside Ann Cunningham wrote about having children. She was, she declared, scared about 'speaking out'; scared about defending her own and other women's decision to have and bring up children as a choice politically as well as personally right and positive: 'Whatever we do [as mothers] we are told constantly we are WRONG. *WE ARE NOT*. All of us, whatever choices we make within the limitation of our own situations, are strong women who love our children and are doing the best we can for them – and ourselves.'

Her article indicates well that tension between what 'I' hold to politically, though it takes the form here of 'I' within a group – 'we mothers', and what 'the movement' is allegedly committed to (*not* the institutions traditionally constituting society's 'centre'). In the last section I return to what I have described there as 'sisterhood' v. 'me'.

Here I want to take up another aspect of *Spare Rib*'s oppositional and alternative politics and examine the contradictory effects of *Spare Rib* as an alternative magazine and a cultural commodity set apart from commercial magazines. It is politically anti-capitalism and its consumer culture, and materially produced on the edges of capitalist organisation.

Until 1985 *Spare Rib* looked strikingly different from commercial magazines (see Figures 8.1a and 8.1b). Neither cover nor inside pages visually exuded consumerist hedonism, and there are no glossy ads in *Spare Rib*. The ads it does carry are, with the exception of books, the occasional film and record album, and, oddly though understandably, the Orion 'Harmony Personal Vibrator', either public information ads, or for jewellery (political as well as decorative), shoes and clothes (practical rather than fashionable), all produced under non-capitalist conditions: co-operatively and/or by craft production. In design the ads are largely small, black and white, and information packed (see Figure 8.3).

As I have explained earlier (chapter 5), the 'look' of commercial

8.3 *Spare Rib*, March 1984

Spare Rib 24

magazines is inseparable from the 'look' of advertising and the latter's colour and codes are bound to ideas of romance, desire and successful femininity all to be pleasurably satisfied by consumption. Without explicit statement (though many articles do indicate *Spare Rib*'s anti-capitalist and anti-Tory politics), its visuals and advertising show it refusing capitalist consumption in general (though worthy exceptions can be made), and women's identification with it in particular. *Spare Rib* also rejects the style of visual imagery associated with that.

The gains, in addition to a reprieve for readers from an aggressive bombardment by sexual and domestic imagery, are that *Spare Rib* is not fettered, as commercial magazines are, by the need to harness the magazine editorially to a section of the advertising market. It has an editorial license the latter do not have, and the space to develop innovative ways of working non-hierarchically. Members of the all-women collective each take responsibility for administrative and routine office duties as well as for editorial work. Everyone receives the same pay (which in recent years, thanks to support from the Greater London Council, has been set at a respectable level), though many volunteers give help for free. Articles are, as much as possible, written by readers in conjunction with the collective and the writers are paid a nominal fee.

What's important for *Spare Rib* is not only the final product but trying to implement – and learn – feminist ways of working at all stages of production. Sue O'Sullivan explained, '*Spare Rib* strives to meet high standards but it isn't going to feel it's failed if it doesn't manage it.' After all, the magazine has enabled hundreds of women, not just a handful of already trained journalists, to gain experience at writing; many of the collective have tried their hand at design, and without a house style for either articles or design *Spare Rib* has lent itself to experimentation.

The problems with this alternative production are financial and political. Spurning glossy advertising, *Spare Rib* relies for revenue on subscriptions, sales, some small and classified ads. It endures therefore an almost continual financial crisis and for this reason the magazine is a relatively austere production. Not only no glossy colour ads but no full colour editorial pages either. Its front and back sixteen pages are usually in two colours, the rest, forty pages or so, of cheaper quality paper, are black and white. Even if *Spare Rib* wanted to, it could not afford to pay for the team of designers – at any one time *Spare Rib* has just one trained designer – or for the equipment and printing processes necessary to produce the kind of slick, colourful commodity that most commercial magazines are.

Spare Rib's appropriate, 'spareness' accords with its sentiments about women's lives. As Sue O'Sullivan explained (interview 1983), 'The magazine isn't entertaining in the sense that other magazines are entertaining. We keep being struck, day after day after day . . . how serious women's position still is. The material that comes into us just keeps reiterating that women still have so far to go and all this stuff about it being over is completely bullshit.'

Quite.

But at the same time, whatever the interest of *Spare Rib*'s articles, its visual look is, I would argue, one which assumes an already feminist readership who understand the politics behind that choice. It is not one guaranteed, on any large scale, to win readers from commercial magazines, whose chief attraction (maybe) is their colourful and glossy look. In itself that would not matter – without doubt the women's movement needs a magazine primarily addressed to its concerns – except for the following political ramifications.

As an alternative magazine *Spare Rib* not only doesn't compete with commercial magazines economically – it's not out to win either their advertising or, substantially, their readers and circulation revenue – but also doesn't, at one level, challenge them ideologically. That is, *Spare Rib* less engages with those associations between capitalistic consumption, femininity and certain forms of visual pleasure, that I discussed in chapter 4 than evacuates from that whole area. It offers something quite else. Meanwhile commercial magazines continue visually in much the same oppressive-but-often-pleasurable ways. If the mark of feminism is to be found in their pages it is not, on the whole, in their visual imagery.

For those reading *Spare Rib* the lie is that feminists, no less than other women, are still caught, one way or another, in those associations: we may not be quite consumer junkies but necessarily still have to consume the goodies capitalism offers; or, hooked on the visual fix and pleasure commercial magazines provide, continue with some sense of hypocrisy to devour the politically, dubious pleasures of those glossies. And *Spare Rib* hardly allows the opportunity to work through those contradictions.

I'm not really suggesting here that *Spare Rib* should carry ads for Miss Selfridge and run articles and pics in the style of *Options*'s 'Field Days'. Rather what I want to highlight is, firstly, that *Spare Rib*'s distinctively different 'look' from commercial magazines is the outcome of a feminist politics, not simply anti-sexism – for commercial magazines are sometimes that – but also anti-consumer culture and capitalism – which commercial magazines definitely are not. Secondly, that *Spare Rib* opposes consumer culture, and the representations it has spawned, by rejecting them for alternatives: it offers a fringe consumption and uses visual styles and codes other than those of commercial magazines. And thirdly, that as a consequence of this politics *Spare Rib*'s practices on the one hand give it a space to be editorially flexible and make it 'the readers'' magazine in ways commercial magazines cannot be, and on the other restrict it financially and tend to shape it as primarily a magazine to be read by 'insiders' but, arguably, less for enjoyment than as 'a duty'.

When *Spare Rib* was launched in July 1972 its politics and practices were somewhat different: measured against *Spare Rib* in the 1980s, the early issues had much more in common with commercial magazines.

A feminist approach; 'the feminist line'

Spare Rib – the name began as a joke and stuck – was both a product of and a feminist reaction to the alternative press of the 1960s. In the introduction to the *Spare Rib Reader* Marsha Rowe explains how she and the small group who set up *Spare Rib* intended it as 'a new magazine' that would be 'calmer, clearer and easier to read' than the alternative press and would not only appeal to women – *It*, *Oz* and *Frendz* hardly addressed women and were often blatantly sexist – but would 'also use and test our own capabilities', hitherto little further stretched than envelope-licking and coffee-making (Rowe 1982, p. 16). Organising themselves on conventional lines with a separation of editorial, design and publicity jobs, *Spare Rib* raised a meagre £2,000 with which to launch a first issue.

Its cover mix and selling tone of address held much the contradictory cover combination of commercial magazines in the 1980s – the political slant of 'Does the government care about pensioners?' alongside the almost titillating and flippant 'George Best on sex' and 'Growing up in the Bosom Boom' (the articles themselves adopted a quite critical tone). Inside *Spare Rib* was careful to address women on the terrain they were already accustomed to, offering alternative variations on 'beauty', 'home' (do-it-yourself floor-laying in a 'Spare parts' slot), 'fashion' and 'family', with some added ingredients: political issues, news (soon a substantial central insertion on coloured paper) and history, but relatively little about paid work.

Some of the early design, like superimposition of print on visuals and coloured print, had much in common with the alternative press. But *Spare Rib* also borrowed and reworked the visual forms and codes of commercial magazines: the smiling (if not glamorous) woman on the first cover, full-page tinted cookery pic, illustrated short story, model photo accompanying a dress pattern.

Men were included and tolerated – John Cleese even appeared on the cover – in ways which echo *Cosmo*'s practice in the 1980s: 'we wanted men to write exploring their feelings' (Rowe 1982, p. 20), though it often seemed to mean an assertive 'exploration' of all-things-sexual. To wit, Jonathon Green on pornography: 'I'm sexist. An unashamed exploiter of femininity and all its assets' (November 1972, no. 5). And the presumptuous letter from Phillip Hodson (then editor of the sex problems magazine *Curious*), the self-same who contributed 'Helping him through the night' in *Cosmo*: 'Dear Spare Rib, With reference to your second issue men will also visit prostitutes so long as they continue to want to explore their environment, and little more, like Kafka and James Joyce and me' (October 1972, no. 4).

Spare Rib's 'Man's World' slot was intended as a satirical reversal of Fleet Street's women's page. But as the contributions from men also indicated, it was a fine editorial line between an

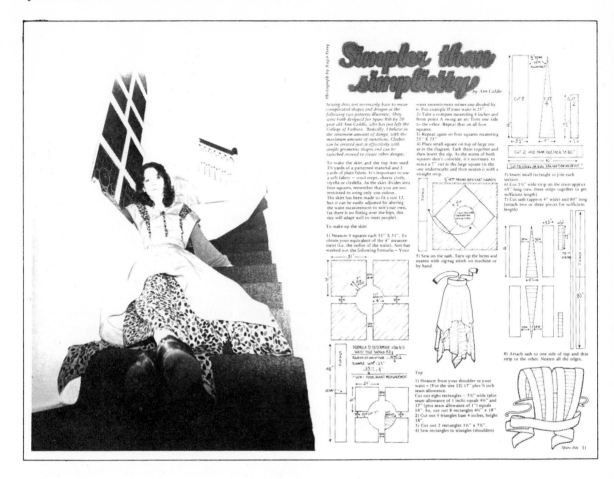

8.4   *Spare Rib*, March 1973

exposé of masculinity, and the all-too-familiar exposure of women to a male gaze and definition. In fact the first issues of *Spare Rib* were regarded with suspicion by the then burgeoning women's movement and at one National Conference a send-up – *Spare Tit* – was circulated. Certainly *Spare Rib* did not have its later sharpness around manifestations of sexism: the occasional blatant record sleeve was commented on while *Spare Rib* itself used not wholly dissimilar images (see Figure 8.4), and ads like those for Evette blusher and Sabre's men's toiletries graced its pages. Certainly, too, shades of the counterculture's politics of sexual liberation – 'frank' discussion and 'free' expression of (hetero)-sexuality – not unlike early *Cosmo* – were also in evidence: 'The liberated orgasm: what is it?' (January 1973, no. 7). And a quick gloss of 'What's up front?' (on the manufacture and sale of bras) might well have revealed *Spare Rib* as, indeed, *Spare Tit*.

But how could *Spare Rib* have been other than what to its

8.5   *Spare Rib*, January 1973

8.6   *Spare Rib*, January 1973

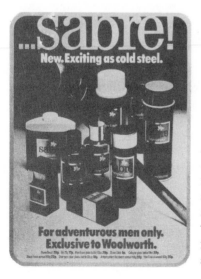

present-day readers seems contradictory? The women's movement and feminism in Britain simply did not exist in the
elaborated intellectual, political and social forms of the 1980s.
Instead of the hundreds of books now available on women and
gender there were a mere handful. Otherwise there were local
news-sheets and reams of stencilled papers circulating at
conferences. *Spare Rib* could hardly straightforwardly adopt a
'feminist approach' when it wasn't wholly certain what that
involved politically, or journalistically.

If there was an underlying politics in early *Spare Rib*s it was one
of moving off from the counterculture's 'personal liberation' to
engage in an ideological and cultural politics around femininity.
Age-old problems for women ('Why are most women so worried
about the size and shape of their breasts?'), desires ('Carry on
romancing: the novels of Georgette Heyer and Barbara Cartland'),
and myths ('What Emily did: Antonia Raeburn looks at the
suffragette movement and disproves the myth that those involved
were merely a bunch of hysterical women') were subjected to this
new but as yet unfocused eye; this was the excitement and
adventure of the early issues. It was a process of discovery,

intellectual, personal, and political. As Caroline Charlton commented in 'The First Cow on Chiswick High Road', 'Those of us who have become part of Women's Aid have found it's changed our lives for the better, given us new friends (real friends) and woken us up to what ordinary women can do to help each other' (June 1972, no. 1).

As the women's movement developed, so its politics and analysis became more assured.

By *Spare Rib*'s fourth birthday it too was a more overtly political and uncompromising magazine: it had long lost the most obvious elements it shared with commercial magazines, had been working collectively for over two years, and now came out as 'a women's liberation magazine'. Over the years it has worked through many changes, its politics moving from a cultural and personal emphasis through to a more socialist feminist feel (with articles on work, campaigns against the state, international questions), to a more radical feminist stress (with articles on sexuality, men's power, subtle and otherwise, and 'women's culture'), through to a more anti-racist stance (with articles on racism and a more conscious address to black women).

Spare Rib's design, if not in neatly corresponding steps, has also undergone alterations: from the use of subdued colours and news photos, often showing 'strong women', in a socialist realist period, to a more punky and less documentary look, with brighter (if not sickly) cover colours, angled sell-lines and 'shock' images, humorous as well as politicising. Design has moved from a brief period of overly intellectual and self-conscious design challenging the primacy of words to again, a more selling look, instigated by the turn both to new printers, allowing use of bolder colours, larger format and typeface, and to the commercial distributors Comag (they also handle *Cosmo*), well-trained towards the winning image. It has changed from an assertive 'leftie' style, starkly black and white, using cut-out photos, hyperrealist illustrations, blocks of print and chunky type – what Ruth Wallsgrove referred to, in a talk she gave on *Spare Rib* at the Extramural Department, University of Birmingham in 1984, as 'the fat black lines school of thought' – to a softening of that and a carryover of an anti-racist politics into the design itself.

Notwithstanding political and editorial shifts, there are some areas *Spare Rib* has consistently covered, like health, paid work and education. *Spare Rib* always carries fiction and poetry. But its sense of continuity is mostly attributable to its 'regulars'; perhaps also to the 'conceptual tools' deployed in articles.

Through readers' letters, news section, short list, classifieds, ads and reviews, *Spare Rib* takes part in the creation and affirmation of a collective feminist culture beyond its pages. Its short list and classifieds, for example, publicise what would otherwise be isolated events in far-flung places. Unlike com-

8.7 *Spare Rib*, August 1977

8.8a *Spare Rib* cover, December 1977
8.8b *Spare Rib* cover, July 1978

mercial magazines it does not leave you on your own once you have closed its pages but offers a range of possible ways in which to get in touch with other women to share problems, experiences and leisure time. For women committed to feminism in an often hostile world *Spare Rib* provides the support to feel neither mad nor bad, nor alone in those beliefs. As Sue Regan put it, 'I

8.9a *Spare Rib*, February 1981
8.9b *Spare Rib*, January 1983

8.10a *Spare Rib*, November 1983
8.10b *Spare Rib*, November 1983
8.10c *Spare Rib*, December 1983

sometimes feel that *Spare Rib* is the voice of sanity in a world which won't listen or try to understand' (August 1983, no. 133).

For a time *Spare Rib* had a column similar to *Woman's Own*'s 'A day in the life of ...', but the content and tone, in the interrogation of the gamut of contradictory feelings experienced, were very different. Janice, for example, spoke about watching her young children playing in the park: 'I thought how wonderful and comical they were, and wondered what justification there could be for me feeling resentful, frustrated, bored, which I often do ...' (December 1977, no. 65).

Such accounts, and *Spare Rib*'s letters, are not, as they might be in *Cosmo*, simply voicing opinion. Rather women participate in an ongoing dialogue and share experiences, and in this way begin to take hold of their lives. An article based on readers' letters, 'Excess hair – you're not the only one!', illustrates well *Spare Rib*'s different approach to women's problems. It acts neither as 'Auntie' nor offers practical solutions; but rather it sparks off discussion: 'These "small" individual, debilitating worries and realities about our bodies ... still cloud our lives and sap our energies. Taking these areas of our lives on board isn't luxury ... the way we feel about ourselves, the way other people respond to us doesn't just drop out of the sky; it comes from the kind of society we live in' (November 1983, no. 136).

The letters tell of the means, successful and catastrophic, resorted to in order to combat 'unacceptable' hair. Uncovering this 'bad' experience, understanding it socially, women try to redefine it in more positive ways; collectively, they begin to reconstruct the boundaries of 'normal' womanhood. The upshot for writers and readers may not be that 'the problem' is solved, or even that the feelings of unacceptability disappear; but at least the pain is, in part, endured together. More generally guilt, failure, the paralysing loneliness of womanhood is dissipated through these exchanges. As Madhi Patel wrote, 'I hope that other *Spare Rib* readers will learn something from my experiences. I would like to thank *Spare Rib* for putting me in touch with other Asian lesbians – so now I know that I am not the only one in the world!' (November 1983, no. 136).

Much of the fiction in *Spare Rib* also reads like a slice of personal life, and some of the 'real' accounts read like stories (for example Anya Bostock's saga 'In the shit no more – or the tale of a lone woman's attempt to mend her long-broken lavatory seat', reprinted in *Spare Rib*'s book of fiction *Hard Feelings* (February 1976, no. 43). Telling 'real' experiences in fictional form and therefore externalising them is, again, a means of control and reinterpretation. To place them in a narrative structure is to give them, perhaps, a poignant pleasure, and an order and meaning previously missing when the writer felt victim of events that 'just happened'. In much this way Minnie Cowley related the tale of her first love for Tommy, a delivery boy who kissed her – 'I had a lovely feeling all over and wanted to fly' – only shortly afterwards to renounce her for a bike (he couldn't afford both!). He 'rode away without a wave, leaving me broken-hearted . . . I was in my seventeenth year, and although Mum had told me two years before that I had become a woman, I reckon that it was then that my childhood really came to an end' (August 1982, no. 121).

In the feminist political armoury history too is a conceptual weapon. It is not simply the fascinating spectacle or validation of a so-much-better present as in commercial magazines. Historical accounts in *Spare Rib*, whether personal like Minnie Cowley's or more analytical, are attempts to grasp a collective social heritage in order to wrestle with contemporary womanhood. An early article, 'The word for embroidery was work', clearly throws into relief this historical blind spot of commercial magazines. Though noted for their encouragement of crafts, and with knitting patterns still a staple of many, the association of women with these activities is a 'fact' taken for granted. Yet the history of embroidery at least is a fascinating and salutory one. Rozsika Parker recounts that in the Middle Ages 'English embroidery was considered to be equal if not superior to painting' and embroiderers, women and men, 'played an important part not only in the cultural but also in the economic life of the country'. By Victorian times, partly to do with the rise and status of figurative painting, partly to do with the amateurisation of embroidery amongst middle-class women, a mutually destructive

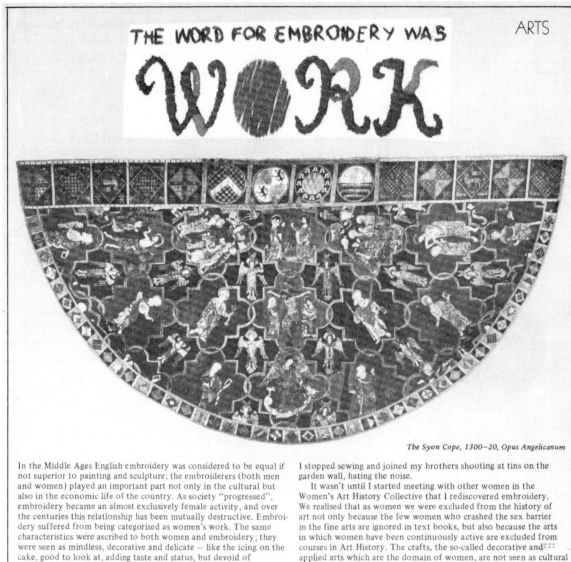

THE WORD FOR EMBROIDERY WAS

WORK

ARTS

The Syon Cope, 1300–20, Opus Anglicanum

In the Middle Ages English embroidery was considered to be equal if not superior to painting and sculpture; the embroiderers (both men and women) played an important part not only in the cultural but also in the economic life of the country. As society "progressed", embroidery became an almost exclusively female activity, and over the centuries this relationship has been mutually destructive. Embroidery suffered from being categorised as women's work. The same characteristics were ascribed to both women and embroidery; they were seen as mindless, decorative and delicate – like the icing on the cake, good to look at, adding taste and status, but devoid of significant content.

Women in their turn have suffered from their connection with embroidery. While it may have been sanity-saving art therapy for women imprisoned at home, at the same time it absorbed their restlessness and rebelliousness. It cost many others their eyesight and it set the precedent for women's exploitation in industrial workshops

I stopped sewing and joined my brothers shooting at tins on the garden wall, hating the noise.

It wasn't until I started meeting with other women in the Women's Art History Collective that I rediscovered embroidery. We realised that as women we were excluded from the history of art not only because the few women who crashed the sex barrier in the fine arts are ignored in text books, but also because the arts in which women have been continuously active are excluded from courses in Art History. The crafts, the so-called decorative and applied arts which are the domain of women, are not seen as cultural transmitters like sculpture and oil painting.

When painting and embroidery were different but equal

In the 13th and 14th centuries, English embroidery, known as *Opus Anglicanum*, was greatly admired and was exported all over Europe. It was exceptionally fine embroidery but its value did not lie in its

relationship had developed; both women and embroidery 'were seen as mindless, decorative and delicate – like the icing on the cake, good to look at, adding taste and status, but devoid of significant content' (July 1975, no. 35). It is a hangover we, and embroidery, have still not entirely lost.

Some of the best articles in *Spare Rib* bring a combination of historical knowledge, personal experience and social analysis to bear on politically knotty issues. On the other hand some of *Spare Rib*'s reviews trade in a particularly heavy-handed criticism of others and are also prone to 'forget' some women's experience.

The criterion of 'good' or 'bad', the praiseworthy or unworthy, is the manifestation of feminist sentiments. Does the book or play, TV programme or musical event, confirm feminism or not? It is lauded if it represents women's lives allegedly 'as they really are' with none of the ideological haze that more usually befogs images of womanhood, like Tessa Hankinson's review of Caryl Churchill's play *Fen*: 'Fen is a moving, sad, funny but above all a realistic portrayal of East Anglian women .... Les Waters directs a very strong cast in an extraordinary and moving play which evokes the harsh reality, not only for the brave fen women, but for women everywhere' (April 1983, no. 128).

So too if it is 'honest' and 'truthful', celebrating women's lives and skills – and the practices of feminism. Diana Scott writes of an exhibition in Leeds entitled *Mother, daughter – two related artists*, 'Woven hangings ...; bright dancing figures of women .... The underlying theme of the exhibition surely is support ...' (March 1984, no. 140). Or if the performance, or text, shows women exhibiting qualities feminists value; there is the active and exuberant woman who gets the better of men, like Julie Walters in *Educating Rita*: 'She just knocked spots off the tutor ... Julie Walters does give a brilliant performance but I also think that the way the script was written made this film a celebration of a strong woman character. I haven't seen a commercial film on general release with so much to offer women in a long time' (Eileen McNutty, September 1983, no. 134). Without doubt, but whatever the contribution of Michael Caine's performance as the tutor-with-his-spots-knocked-off it's simply ignored.

If what is being reviewed cannot be read for signs of incipient feminism – its representations are 'unrealistic' and therefore the fantasy creations of the masculine mind – then it is summarily dismissed and readers curtly advised not to see or read it. Susan Hemmings on *Kramer v. Kramer* says, 'I can't believe this film is going to change lives up and down the Odeons of the land. Go if you want, but you'd get just as much feminist input by staying home watching *Dallas*' (May 1980, no. 94). Bertha Freistadt on *Juliet Bravo*: 'I watched ... for signs of real understanding of women. Sadly everything was as usual .... She is a man's creation .... Stephanie Turner plays her with a compelling singleness of mind. But finally not even the excellence of her performance makes it worth watching' (November 1981, no. 112).

But can we really expect that commitment to feminism in such programmes? Is it really the case that 'sadly everything was as usual'? Surely not. And the interesting feminist questions are around how and what has shifted on the gender front as well as the limits to that. These reviews, however, bolster the reviewer's position and raise feminism and feminists to the lofty pedestal of 'having seen the light', with the consequent dismissal not only of a whole range of cultural events but also of many women's pleasurable and interested experiences of them. Whether intentionally or not, feminists are setting themselves distinctly apart: 'us' who know and reject most popular cultural forms (including women's magazines); 'them' who remain in ignorance and continue to buy *Woman's Own* or watch *Dallas*. The irony, however, is that many of 'us' feel like 'them': closet readers and viewers of this fare.

There are two misconceptions behind these reviews. Firstly, there is the belief that if only directors, authors and editors desired it, feminist principles could, immediately and directly, be translated into popular cultural forms. They cannot, and it may well be an even longer haul to win round audiences to the enjoyment of non-sexist entertainment, whatever that might be. Secondly, there is the belief that the 'correct' political analysis guarantees the 'correct' experiences, that is, to propound feminist arguments is, in itself, to have already transformed our ideological feminine selves who enjoyed the 'bad old things'. Unfortunately ideologies cannot be changed only by the assertion that they should be. Feminists we may be, but as individuals our emotional responses and our sense of ourselves have been learnt within older codes of femininity. In spite of 'knowing better' we also find ourselves behaving and feeling according to other ideological patterns. And it is important that we recognise that contradiction not as a sign of weakness, to be pushed behind our public feminist veneer, but exactly that which feminism has to deal with.

If I seem to have made much of these reviews it is because they seem to me to be emblematic of a wider tendency in the women's movement: the espousal of a feminism which partly denies not only the experiences of other women but also our own experiences. We find ourselves uncomfortably oscillating between what we think 'we should' as feminists and what, for social and ideological reasons, we actually want or are still compelled to do.

It is this tension, and *Spare Rib*'s management of it elsewhere, that I want to turn to next.

A question of sisterhood; but what about me?

In December 1983 *Spare Rib* declared the following in its editorial:

> *Spare Rib* is no longer a white women's magazine. All issues have a connection, white with Black, wealth/poverty with Imperialism, and we must pursue that recognition. *But*, issues on which Black/Third World women want exclusive space will be acceptable to *Spare Rib*. We are not denying the difficulty of all this for many of our white

8.12 'Sisterhood . . . is plain sailing', cartoon in *Spare Rib*, July 1983

readers. But who ever said that taking on an overdue challenge is easy? We are all committed to feminism, to women's liberation, but not at the expense of fighting racism, including white feminists' racism. We ask you, our readers who are white, to learn about and engage *with* us in the process of change. (December 1983, no. 137)

The statement came after months of painful discussion for *Spare Rib*'s collective and its transformation from an all-white one to half Women of Colour. (The latter phrase has a currency in the USA it does not have in Britain and *Spare Rib* later dropped it. Not wholly satisfactorily, but for reasons of brevity, I've used the term black women to refer to all non-white women except when referring to the particular grouping within *Spare Rib*'s collective.)

Concomitantly the editorial shape and content of *Spare Rib* also changed fundamentally. *Spare Rib* had always covered international issues but for the first time it also confronted racism in Britain, within the women's movement and in its own practices. This broadening of its address to include black women and to take on an anti-racist politics is part of a longer, often tortuous endeavour in which *Spare Rib* has shifted from its early preoccupations with the interests of white, middle-class, heterosexual and relatively young women to a wider politics, embracing, for example, the concerns of working-class women, lesbian women, girls and young women of school age, older women and women who are not able-bodied. It has tried to foreground

141

groups both oppressed and placed on the margins. What I want to consider here is that wider endeavour, whose problems were thrown up in a particularly acute form for *Spare Rib* by the issue of racism.

As the editorial statement earlier highlights, if the challenge to *Spare Rib* from black women was not easily made, its take-up was by no means smoothly accepted, either by *Spare Rib*'s white collective members or its white readers. And the debates still continue.

The inability to accept differences is, I want to argue, engendered by the form of our politics, comprised of two not easily reconciled strands – to put it crudely, one that demands 'what about me?', the other 'what about her?'. The women's movement *is* a politics insisting on women's individual experience as the political touchstone. 'The personal is political' allows 'me' the space to take my experiences seriously, to respect my thoughts and needs, and to begin, with sisterly support, to transform my weaknesses as a woman into strengths. It is an unsteady process: insecurity, self-hatred and low self-esteem are the ingrained marks of the oppressed severely hindering any assertion of 'I'. And when other women whose experience is different disagree with me I feel, above all, threatened; I either crumble or attack with anger.

Such occasions are further complicated by a second strand of the women's movement's politics. This recognises the social divisions of power, a hierarchy of oppression, and therefore the 'inequalities' of those experiences, but also conceptualises politics, and those differences, precisely through a language of 'doing battle'.

The two strands derive from rather different political traditions: the 'personal is political' from a 1960s libertarian politics with its stress on individual liberation from society's repressive structures; the recognition of inequalities (and also the need for collective action) from a more socialist politics focusing on class hierarchy and working-class oppression. Not, however, a socialism of the Labour Party but, as Elizabeth Wilson describes, the 'sometimes romantic but always highly militant and usually vanguardist notions of revolution as embodied in Trotskyism' (1980, p. 206). This latter input is often less visible to the women's movement than to its critics. A young reader wrote to *Spare Rib* to say how much she had enjoyed her first issue despite the fact that 'My father says it is a communist magazine' (April 1984, no. 141). Polly Toynbee in the *Guardian* sniped, 'The magazine is written heavily in Left-speak, that curious jargon of Marxism that sounds only half translated from the German. Everyone is "fighting" or "struggling" in this "arena" or that "forum", "confronting" the "contradiction" and the "violence" of the "system"' (1982, p. 8).

A caricature; but the politics of the women's movement and

Spare Rib is a 'revolutionary' one (even when it is not strictly socialist) and its rhetoric is often militant and anti-reformist. Women's liberation cannot be achieved without upturning society and that involves, necessarily, power 'battles', around ideas and responsibilities – yes, in this 'arena' or that 'forum', or in this bedroom and that workplace. The strength of this 'revolutionary' vision is to settle for nothing less than women's liberation; its weakness is that it isn't on the whole the stuff recruitment is made of.

Created from the female margins of those libertarian and left groups of the 1960s (themselves 'recreated from the margins' of society by 'the new dissidents: the young, the alienated, the mad' (Wilson 1980, p. 193)), the women's movement has continued to regenerate itself in this manner: by a radicalisation from its own 'dissident' margins, its middle-class politics challenged by working-class women, its heterosexism by lesbian women, and so on. Yet these new growth points can also be endangered as 'the personal' for some groups is rendered more 'political' than for others. The upshot, when the experiences of different groups clash, is that a tangled chain of accusation – 'you oppress us'; 'you have power, we do not' – and of uncomfortable guilt is set in play. The guilt of the vulnerable turns to anger, a defensive 'counterattack' ensues and dialogue becomes a virtual impossibility.

Feminist practice is similarly 'judged' (though it is never clear who exactly is making the judgment: one's own conscience?). To be at the forefront of feminism is, if not to *be* working-class/lesbian/black, then to give priority to those struggles. To be a proper/right-on/good feminist is to be politically involved with certain prescribed issues.

Spare Rib is caught in these tensions; its editorial task is perhaps more fraught since the demise of the women's movement's annual conferences in 1978. Those unwieldy events (3,000 women attended the last two) provided the occasion for, among other things, a public airing of political differences and the discussion of controversial issues. Despite their limitations, of size and time in particular, something like a political agenda and priorities that had some semblance of having been collectively worked out usually emerged, to be carried back to local groups for debate and action during the year.

The 1978 conference in Birmingham was notable for its sharp chord of political disagreement – what turned out to be the sounding knell of those yearly events. Subsequently differences within the women's movement have largely been contained within separate political groups who rarely come together. To some extent, too, the women's movement has lost the space to publicly define itself, and there are both ill-defined and conflicting notions in circulation as to what is meant by 'the women's movement' and who is 'in' it.

It is in this dispersed context that *Spare Rib* has become a key national institution where the terms of the women's movement are set out and argued over in a fairly public way and new issues at the forefront of the women's movement are dealt with, like an anti-racist politics. The form of the crisis *Spare Rib* weathered over this issue was manifest earlier around a pro-lesbian politics (this was one of the issues at stake at the 1978 conference). The storminess of both was partly for the reasons I've outlined above; it was also compounded by *Spare Rib*'s editorial role. *Spare Rib* has managed controversies, and subdued conflicts, by a gate-keeping operation, selectively presenting arguments, and maintaining silence on some important differences. At both these times, nevertheless, pressures have so built up in the women's movement that dissonant voices have erupted into *Spare Rib*'s pages – all the more angrily for having been partly suppressed – while *Spare Rib*'s own collective voice has also cracked under the strain. In July 1980 the collective raised what it saw as its editorial intractables and convened a readers' meeting to discuss them.

> Controversial articles have always been a problem area ... articles which raise issues basic to feminism in lively new ways, and articles which expose and explore differences within the women's liberation movement.
>
> We want to be accessible and interesting to new readers while stretching and surprising older readers; we want to be honest about the movement without 'betraying' it to the world outside.
>
> The *Spare Rib* collective itself contains a variety of feminist opinion. Do we tend to suppress our differences to keep the peace, and so arrive at a safe but boring 'common denominator'? How much should *Spare Rib* be an open forum, and how much should we develop our own 'line'? We have certainly had bitter disagreements over some articles – do they stimulate debate within and about the movement? Is it necessary to publish such material in order to open issues out and move us all forward? Or are the views expressed so offensive to some collective members that we shouldn't print them? Could they be harmful to certain groups of women – lesbians, separatists or black women, for instance? Where does responsibility become censorship? (July 1980, no. 96)

What lay behind this editorial was a disagreement over the publication of 'Feminism for her own good' by Ann Pettit, dealing with what she considered a dominant idea in the women's movement that women should have nothing to do with men. *Spare Rib* had decided to publish the article 'because it touched on real tensions in the women's movement'. Then three of the collective felt it was anti-lesbian. 'Publication was blocked. Personal rifts and political disagreements opened up .... Since then it has been difficult to produce work and get along in a sisterly spirit' (September 1980, no. 98).

None of this did *Spare Rib* readers learn about until after the readers' meeting in London where a necessarily select group was able to read the disputed article. Some went on to write about it in *Spare Rib* while most, since it never was published (except in the women's movement's internal newsletter *Wires*), were not so privileged. This graded 'censorship' and the uneven relationship it set up did not enamour *Spare Rib* to many readers. Justifiably Ann Pettit complained that it was 'unspeakably crass' that she had been named and her article discussed without her being able to defend it (November 1980, no. 100).

Nor, though readers were appealed to for their thoughts about these editorial problems, did *Spare Rib* go on to share with them how they had or hadn't resolved their differences, or what the collective thought they had leant from the crisis. Its engagement with readers around editorial dilemmas was an exceptional moment brought about by crisis. (Its subsequent articles, nevertheless, seemed to open up the contradictions around heterosexuality and men's power, and show a more pro-lesbian stand. For example, an article about cancer, featuring a couple who were lesbian, was a significant public acknowledgment that lesbianism wasn't just about sex (November 1980, no. 100)). All these difficulties resurfaced around the argument which began as an issue about an appropriate politics on Zionism and the Israeli-Palestinian conflicts, and broadened out into a question of an anti-racist politics. Readers had some inkling that something was amiss but didn't quite know what that was. *Spare Rib* didn't, for example, wholly explain why some articles appeared; it hinted at political differences but didn't wholly spell them out. And despite the collective's political disagreements, for a long time they maintained a veneer of editorial consensus. As the pressures on and off the collective built up, so *Spare Rib* began painfully to divulge some of the hitherto hidden political backcloth and the repressed tensions on the collective itself. By July 1983 the enormity of the editorial crisis was such that in the middle of going to press the collective decided to publish their differences publicly and explore the difficulties of working as a mixed collective (in 'Sisterhood . . . is plain sailing'*). That speaking out

---

* 'Sisterhood . . . is plain sailing' appeared almost a year after the article precipitating the arguments had been published. 'Women speak out against Zionism' (August 1982, no. 121) was written after the Israeli army's so-called 'Peace for Galilee' operation, in which 14,000 people, mainly civilians, were killed in South Lebanon. By a Palestinian, an Israeli and a Lebanese woman, it was introduced with the following: 'If a woman calls herself a feminist she should consciously call herself anti-Zionist.' *Spare Rib* received a 'flood of letters' which readers later learnt were particularly critical of that statement. (*Spare Rib* also suffered heavy harassment and racist threats, some from pro-Zionist groups.) The letters became the (symbolic?) nub of political disagreement, largely between Women of Colour and white women on the collective. The

then allowed readers to respond and share in a dialogue around an anti-racist politics which until then *Spare Rib* had tended to monopolise. It seemed too that the collective was also enabled to move beyond the impasses.

Clearly *Spare Rib* did not wilfully conspire to keep its readers in ignorance, nor intentionally make its editorial problems worse by maintaining relative silence about political differences. Retrospectively it's easy to see that *Spare Rib* might have weathered this storm less biliously, and not lost support from white readers – Jan Parker lamented that 'Unfortunately what *Spare Rib* has been experiencing recently is an increasing withdrawal of support from the women's movement' (July 1983, no. 132) – if it had shared with readers more of what was going on. So why did it lock the floodgates, so to speak, against the incoming tide?

One good reason for *Spare Rib* subduing conflicts is out of fear of 'betraying [the women's movement] to the world outside' (July 1980, no. 96): revelation of 'internal squabbles' can so easily be turned against the women's movement and *Spare Rib*. Another is the responsibility *Spare Rib* bears towards women who are not familiar with feminism. Its editorial role in relation to them has to be a more pedagogic, authoritative one, introducing feminist ideas and politics, steering readers through possible conflicting positions. Selectivity and simplification are essential to make *Spare Rib* readable; such readers do not want to be, nor are in a position to take on *Spare Rib*'s editorial dilemmas; judicious silence is preferable to a plethora of confusions.

Spare Rib's responsibility and relation towards the women's movement is more complex. Though it might be expected that *Spare Rib*'s preferred editorial role here would be to provide, as much as possible, an open forum for women's movement debate, there are pressures working against that. As a key national institution *Spare Rib* undoubtedly occupies a special place, with its collective likely to have a much more comprehensive sense of the women's movement than most other groups of feminists. The collective also strives to be representative of the women's movement's groupings and interests. Thus when differences arise *in* the women's movement they tend also to be ones between collective members. Perhaps for these reasons the collective is inclined, as Jane Bryce pointed out, to slip into 'carrying the can

former maintained that they were all Zionist, racist and shouldn't be published; white women, on the whole, thought some of them, from Jewish feminists, should have been published. None were. Instead *Spare Rib* commissioned the London Lesbian Jewish Feminist Group to write 'About anti-semitism' in which they explained that in their experience anti-Zionist sentiments could easily become anti-semitic and racist ones. This was followed up by several other articles and editorial statements, though few readers' letters. It was during this period that the composition of the collective changed to half Women of Colour.

for the movement' (September 1983, no. 134), pre-empting discussion in the movement and critical judgment of issues by readers themselves. To slightly reword her comments, *Spare Rib* seems to feel the responsibility of representing [how] the women's movement [should be] to itself. *Spare Rib* edges into being the women's movement's conscience, editorially presenting and prescribing its 'shoulds'. Whatever their disagreements white women on the collective were committed to supporting the Women of Colour within their collective, and to have publicly disputed their decisions [over the letters, say] was, I suspect regarded by them as well as by Women of Colour to be a racist betrayal. Something of the latter was also felt by white readers. Fran Wheat wrote saying she thought many white women were 'nervous of writing about their true feelings . . . I felt that you would dismiss my views as reactionary and irrelevant'. (September 1983, no. 134)

The risk for the women's movement and *Spare Rib* is that if 'my' feelings and experiences as a feminist, whether they be as white or black, married or unmarried, or whatever, are rendered not-OK politically by my sisters and therefore returned to 'the personal and the private' or to a more local sisterhood, then the women's movement vulnerably leaves itself open for those issues to be dealt with outside *Spare Rib* and the women's movement – not least in the pages of commercial magazines – and to be less transformed by feminist principle than co-opted, again, to individualist ideologies. If that is not to be the case then, as Bea Campbell once contentiously said of heterosexuality, a politics that begins with 'I' 'has to feature in our politics as more than a guilty secret' (1980, p. 1).

By 1985 *Spare Rib* no longer had to carry the feminist flag alone. With the launch of *Everywoman* and *Women's Review* new possibilities opened up. And it is to these, and other, more recent events that I finally want to turn.

Chapter 9

Shifting categories: magazines in the 1980s.

Social trends; market factors

'I think it's a pity there isn't a halfway house between *Woman's Own* and the women's liberation publications – it would do a lot of good for a lot of women.'

(Fran Wheat, *Spare Rib* no. 134, September 1983)

If the contours of the women's magazine market post-Second World War were defined in the 1950s, and if retrospectively those years appear as a magazine heyday, then the mid-1980s may well turn out to be the time when the 1950s heritage was finally jettisoned and the profile of the market fashioned anew.

Yet the movements afoot seem to be contradictory. Whilst most commentators are suggesting that the women's magazine market is contracting, a welter of new titles has been launched. That giant of magazine publishers, IPC, is engaged in the biggest axe-wielding exercise of its twenty-four-year history – magazines are being sold off and jobs are being cut. And yet several other, sometimes shoestring, operations have not only burst on to the magazine scene but against seeming odds been unusually successful, such as *The Face* and *Just Seventeen*.

The profitable market has increasingly been tilting in favour of relatively expensive and specialist middle-class publications at the cost of cheaper and mass working-class titles. ('The middle-class become wealthier as the working-class are further impoverished.' Campbell 1984) And yet *Chat* has appeared, the first mass women's weekly to be launched since *Woman's Realm* in 1958. Sales of magazines in the young women's sector have been falling off; demographic trends indicate that the numbers of young women under 25 is declining. And yet *Just Seventeen* achieved sales of over 200,000 in under a year.

The media has begun to talk about post-feminism; the women's movement in Britain has become a highly dispersed one. And yet in addition to *Spare Rib*, relaunched with glossy cover and a new inside look, two nationally distributed feminist magazines now grace the major newsstands: *Everywoman* and *Women's Review*.

So how to begin to plot and understand these changes? One problem for me commenting now (April 1986) is that whatever I say about current trends may well be partly outdated by the time you read this. Indeed much of the detail, if not the arguments, I have made about *Woman's Own*, *Cosmopolitan* and *Spare Rib* has already changed. Such are the difficulties of discussing a contemporary cultural form, subject to the fluctuations of the marketplace in a period of social change, and with a short shelf life. (How many of us, after all, bother to keep, let alone read, old magazines?) All I can hope is that what I offer gives particular purchase on events occurring now, whilst also providing some general guidelines for thinking about the future.

It would be easy, but wrong, to suggest that a new era in women's magazine publishing is being precipitated by the tight market and high unemployment. Nevertheless those economic factors are pervasive even as their effects are neither simple nor obvious. What's interesting is how those economic factors have been cross cut by ideological and social developments so that the category of 'women's magazine' is, at least partly, being redefined.

The development I specifically want to point to is the 'success' of feminism. The long-term contraction of the women's magazine market is partly the result of television's (and other media's) more dominant role as provider of the 'survival skills and daydreams' long offered only by women's magazines. But the contraction can also be accounted for by a reduction in the number of women who 'need' women's magazines. If, as I discussed in the opening chapter, women's magazines address the 'lonely' woman who in a patriarchal society is, necessarily, on the margins, then as women have increasingly engaged with that society and chipped away at patriarchal culture (though I wouldn't want to be too optimistic about how far that process has gone); the *raison d'être* for traditionally styled women's magazines is gradually being under-mined and a space opened up for new sorts of magazine.

The term post-feminism, if it means anything useful, suggests something of this change. With the 'success' of feminism some feminist ideas no longer have an oppositional charge but have become part of many people's, not just a minority's, common sense. At the same time post-feminism does not mean that feminism has been and gone, that we no longer need feminism because its demands have all been met (though that *is* one interpretation). Rather it suggests that feminism no longer has a simple coherence around a set of easily defined principles (throwing into question whether it *ever* had such a coherence) but instead is a much richer, more diverse and contradictory mix than it ever was in the 1970s. It isn't really possible any more to label the dominant strands of feminism, nor does feminism exclude all men, whatever their politics and personal style, in the quite hostile manner characteristic of the 1970s. The upshot is that the boundaries between feminists and non-feminists have become fuzzy and with that the demarcation between feminist magazines and the more commercial glossies has also become less rigid.

However there are minuses as well as pluses to these

149

developments. In the absence of 'the women's movement' and clear-cut arguments on any given topic, the space is opened up for feminism becoming whatever you, the individual, make of it. This is all very well, perhaps, so long as those feminisms are not reduced to so many forms of the individualism I've discussed earlier. As Susan Ardhill and Sue O'Sullivan argue, that variety of (post-)feminism tends to mean 'an appropriation of the cultural space feminism opened up minus most of the politics' (*New Statesman*, 8 November 1985). Personally, I'm inclined to think that feminism will only proceed by those cultural (and it should be said, market) spaces being pushed to their limits, hence revealing their impasses and inadequacy. The expansion of magazines catering to 'superwoman' perhaps illustrates such a case (see p. 155).

But the flip side to the category of 'women's magazines' shifting ground is that a new category of 'men's magazine' is slowly opening up. The influence of feminist ideas, the rise of the gay movement in transforming masculinity, together with unemployment and capitalism's relentless penetration of new consumer markets, all account for this development.

It is IPC's vigorous clear-out and refurbishment of remaining magazines which perhaps best marks the turning point. For it was IPC, after all, which was born from, and consolidated, the rich pickings of the 1950s. By the mid-1980s the company's long-standing problems turned from bad to worse and strict financial straitening was called for. The company had an over-centralised and inflexible organisation (in a costly and over-large building, King's Reach Tower), and since the 1970s this factor had contributed to its missing out on nearly every growth sector. In the 1970s its monthlies lost out to the National Magazine Company's *Cosmopolitan* and *Company*; in the 1980s the *enfant terrible* of publishing, EMAP, had clawed at IPC's young readers with *Smash Hits* and *Just Seventeen*. The company was also relying too heavily on the mass women's weeklies. By February 1986, with their circulations decreasing and 'all but one of its five recent launches trading at a loss' (*Campaign*, 22 November 1985), IPC was in deep trouble.

Having the strength of Reed International behind it IPC is unlikely to go under. But further changes seem likely, with the mass weeklies one sector due for a grand overhaul, or IPC will have to look elsewhere to make up their 75 per cent contribution to its profits. For some time the weeklies have been facing stiff competition from newspapers. The daily tabloids now woo women readers in ways they hardly deigned to ten years ago; their Sunday equivalents have flooded the market with something like 8 million 'free' colour supplements tussling over the same female readership, the same advertising, and with their cut-rate practices they often have the edge in winning the latter.

Against that competitive background the idea for *Chat* (launched in Autumn 1985 by the owners of *TV Times*) was an inspired one, even if copied from a German publication *Bild der Frau*. A sort of hybrid magazine, it has taken over some of the features of a weekly magazine but offers them in a cheap newspaper-style package which, with its colour pages, fore-shadowed the use of new printing technology by the daily newspaper *Today*. Indeed IPC's claim is that *Chat* poses less challenge to its weeklies than it does to Tuesday's tabloids (Tuesday is *Chat*'s sell day) If *Chat* is a newspaper and its design as well as editorial content are judged alongside that of other newspapers, then there is much to be said in its favour. The newsy feel, without the unrelenting sexism of the tabloids, a mix of columns on welfare rights, women's issues and politics, together with the more conventional (for women's magazines) stuff of fashion and food, marriage and sex, is a refreshing one to address to women who are, in magazine terms, 'older' (25-45) and downmarket.

But as one commentator scathingly described, the magazine is 'like a cross between *Weekend* magazine and a D. C. Thomson comic' (*Campaign*, 2 August 1985). Compared to the weeklies like *Woman* and *Woman's Own*, *Chat*'s visual and colour quality are poor. Using non-glossy paper, *Chat*'s colours are harsh and its mix of them garish. Its photos can't achieve subtle effects with light and shade but have a flat, sometimes smudged and rough feel. The overall design effect is busy but also jarring so that readers cannot flick through *Chat* for the visual fix most other magazines provide.

Chat is not a feminist magazine even though feminist sentiments may be expressed, and there's none of the 'gender-bending' so visible in magazines for younger women. Yet it is a sign that women's expectations and demands for their reading matter are changing that *Chat* can introduce a less intimate format and editorial approach. Editors and contributors aren't anonymous but they do not present themselves in a way which encourages familiarity as do Richard Barber, *Woman*'s editor, and Polly Graham, *Woman's Own*'s columnist, for example.

More generally, Joan Barrell, once *Company*'s publisher, has predicted that *Woman* and *Woman's Own* will move more in line with the monthlies: circulations will drop to around 500,000; and each magazine will become more segmented in its readership – 'The name of the game is to get particular groups with distinctive lifestyles to identify themselves with specific magazines . . . [they] will need to attract specific age groups, rather than covering everything from changing a baby's nappy to claiming your old age pension' (*Advertising Age's Focus*, May 1984).

Certainly *Woman* and *Woman's Own* have switched to higher quality glossier paper for their covers in a bid to differentiate themselves from the cheaper weeklies, whilst switching to web offset printing to give more flexibility and colour on their inside pages. Under Richard Barber's editorship *Woman* has, arguably, begun to offer a stronger editorial mix than *Woman's Own* of the almost-political and the traditional, of the shocking and the comforting. But IPC's revamps are hardly innovative in the way *Chat* was.

New-Style day dreams?

For all *Chat*'s breaks with the old order, and its success, it has had a low profile. Precisely because it *is* for downmarket, older women and carries low-budget advertising, and above all because it *looks* tacky, the professionals are not particularly interested in it. In contrast, the most touted and influential magazine of the 1980s is not a women's magazine at all: *The Face* is an image, style, fashion, music magazine which offers 'street credibility' – for the young – and does so in a design package which is much lauded in publishing circles. Yet there is something worrying about a hierarchy whereby the young and middle-class are both arbiters and recipients of 'good' visual design and the old, working-class are only given an opportunity to enjoy (or is it endure?) what those arbiters of taste would describe as visual disasters. It's not that I want to recommend a *Face* make-over for *Chat* but I do think it ought to be possible to create an aesthetic design which does justice to *Chat*'s editorial approach and is appropriate for its readership.

The significance of *The Face*, however, reaches beyond (although partly through) its design. Its launch indicated the ability of small companies to spot the market gaps and take the risks which the likes of IPC, ossified by time and size, dared not. And the editorial it offered spoke to, whilst also partly creating, the changed consciousness of young people in the 1980s.

Dick Hebdige, in a difficult but thought-provoking essay (1985), suggests that *The Face* foregrounds image-making so that even the written word, the typography becomes an image. Along with that shift in design emphasis goes a shift in how the world is represented: 'There is nothing underneath or behind the Image and hence there is no hidden Truth to be revealed' (page 41). Moreover there is no way of judging one image (and one 'truth') against another: 'Thus the impression you gain as you glance through the magazine is that this is less an "organ of opinion" than a wardrobe full of clothes (garments, ideas, values, arbitrary preferences . . .)' This impression is reinforced by the magazine's characteristic style of making statements: 'never straightforward. Irony and ambiguity predominate' (page 46).

Dick Hebdige measures *The Face*'s difference against the academic magazine in which he is writing, *Ten:8*, which offers debates around photography. If, however, *The Face* were to be set against women's magazines which, you might remember from chapter 1, have long been thought to be 'schizophrenic', delivering images in which, allegedly, 'experience and make-believe merge in a manner conducive to the readers' utter bewilderment', then its difference would not seem so great. The coherence of women's magazines, like that of *The Face* (and this isn't something Dick Hebdige takes up) lies not *in* the magazines but in, or through, the reader – or rather in the relation between the representation in the magazine and the social life in fact experienced by readers. If women's magazines are a counterpoint for women to the 'man's world' and its 'truth', from which they are marginalised or excluded, then it could be argued that *The Face* and other 'style' magazines (*ID*, *Blitz*) are a counterpoint for the young to the values and 'Truth' of a Britain which supports a low inflation rate and defence but not jobs and people, and which denies them a valid social place and real hope for the future. As the new oppressed group, young people construct themselves through consumption; shops and their merchandise provide a vocabulary through which to fantasise (cf. chapter 4). As Dick Hebdige puts it, describing a Levi jeans cinema ad in which *The Face* is also a key commodity, 'The articulation of commodity consumption, personal identity and desire which characterises life under hypercapitalism has here been universalised. There is nowhere else to go but to the shops' (1985, page 45).

In the 1960s young *women's* access to commodities, particularly clothes, provided a means, however contradictory, by which they could explore and construct an individuality and assert their difference from older generations of women. Oddly, as it appears retrospectively, the mini-skirt in the 1960s symbolised young women's newfound liberation; unlike their mothers they were stepping out into the world alongside men (cf. chapter 4).

By the 1980s the capitalist commodity market had begun to realise the potential of a young men's fashion and 'beauty' market. And under changed social conditions of what it means to be a man, these commodities enable a tentative exploration of new expressions of masculinity (which isn't to say that the commodities can't be mobilised to express old modes of masculinity too. Under many a new man fashion look lurks a diehard wolf.)

In the 1960s the expanding consumer market addressed to young women's wants also gave rise to magazines like *Honey* and *19*. In the 1980s publishers are attempting to launch men's (life)style magazines, partly to push men's products. So far the efforts have not been an unqualified success. Both *Cosmo* and *Options* have published quarterly supplements for men, *Cosmo Man* and *OM*, which borrow as much from *Playboy* and *Gentleman's Quarterly*, with their emphasis on power, money, business, sporting and sexual success for white, middle-class men, as they do on any New Man ideology. On the other hand *The Hit* (a magazine from IPC which was withdrawn from publication after just six weeks) and *Hero*, a one-off pilot publication from D.C. Thomson and associated with the young women's magazine *Patches*, were still magazines for 'the lads' but tried to offer something of the style of *The Face* blended with a mix borrowed from women's magazines (fashion, make-up and skin care, and emotional problems).

The problem of succeeding with this kind of young men's magazine is that although there is no problem garnering sufficient advertising, young men, unlike young women, do not like the idea of a magazine which suggests that other men have the same desires and angsts. Young men's preoccupations with self and self-image still have to be catered for by safely removing them from the volatile terrain of emotions to 'things', whether that be BMX bikes or the sophisticated package offered by *The Face*.

Yet amidst the parody and irony of *The Face* (in themselves techniques of self-distancing?), emotions surface. Dick Hebdige regards this as evidence, if I read him correctly, of an emergent and potential *political* consciousness, the basis on which justice and truth can, in fact, be judged. But I'd like to think, too, that the '80s sensibility', the 'emergent structure of feeling' to which *The Face* contributes, is also about changing feelings of *masculinity*. Currently, however, it is in some of the young women's magazines, *Just Seventeen* and *Mizz* in particular, that those feelings are safely explored (for example the short stories often have young men trailing the tortuous paths of romance).

I have discussed these magazines in detail elsewhere (see 'A girl needs to get streetwise', Winship 1985). Suffice it to say here that these young women's magazines share something of the 1980s sensibility of *The Face*. Their editorial is built on the premise that young women in Thatcher's Britain largely *don't* have the money to buy consumer (and other) choices that the market economy so relentlessly continues to sell them, but that they do still desire. Thus Brenda Polan reported that 'Sally from Grantham, an unemployed 16-year-old', was '*Just Seventeen*'s (wo)man on the Clapham omnibus'. If Sally wouldn't like an article 'then out goes the feature' (*Guardian*, 4 April 1985).

The magazines don't, quite, engage in political discussions of 1980s problems. Yet there is sometimes a humour in the magazines which *is* that of the disaffected and of post-feminism. Some of the fashion images, as in 'Prime cuts – bare all in a flash of flesh', featuring young woman in 'turquoise cotton bustier', a sort of 1950s strapless boned bra, are anathema to a 1970s-style feminism. Yet such a self-parodying approach marks less a reneging on feminism than the degree to which the observations feminists have made (in this instance, the notion of women as meat) can now be taken for granted.

At the same time these magazines hold to new versions of the well-worn ideology of individualism. Hopes for the future, the fulfillment of desires, lie, in the end, in the hands of the individual. And in the text certain individuals, variously referred to as 'upstarts' or 'art throbs', lend the promise of those good things to come, beyond the pages of print. They are young women and men making their name in the artistic fields of fashion and music, art and design. They have, above all, style and are in the business of creating the style(s) young women want to buy: clothes, records, design goods .... More than that, having themselves often once been unemployed, 'art throbs' do not lose their individuality in any nine-to-five routine; not for them work as drudgery. They retain both control over their work and a perception of the world which, at the cultural level at least, is challenging and positive. That relatively few readers are in fact going to enter these artistic spheres doesn't really matter. After all, when you don't have a job, when your chances of *any* job are not high, you might as well contemplate work that is appealing. Why else dream?

Superwoman: 'I'm all right sisters!'

The problems of individualism apart, this is a rather different dream from the conservatism offered by the superwoman model of *Options* and *Working Woman*. In the USA, where superwoman is thicker on the ground than in Britain, she and her problems have featured in a group of magazines for the 'independent woman' appearing from the mid-1970s onwards. Elizabeth Cagan, in an article called 'The selling of the women's movement', takes issue with these magazines which include the American version of *Working Woman* (Cagan 1978). She suggests that they concentrate on

> advice and information for women who seek to move independently and successfully in their personal, professional and social lives. The tone is decidedly optimistic and congratulatory rather than critical, angry or concerned. Theirs is a feminism of rising expectations, not analysis and critique; feminist ideals are expressed almost entirely in personal terms and are totally depoliticised.

They offer, she continues, 'fantasies of liberation' dependent upon

> no more than personal qualities of self-confidence, assertiveness and determination, combined with a measure of practical know-how. The image of the 'new woman' ends up being remarkably similar to the image of the successful male in a competitive, materialistic society.

The prevailing conditions of unemployment and recession in Britain in the 1980s have brought a less brazen sell of superwoman and the women's movement. But superwoman is certainly alive and kicking in *Options*, the magazine for the grown-up *Cosmo* girl with domestic responsibilities, even if many of its readers are probably made of 'weaker' stuff. The basis for the magazine lies in the greater spending potential of middle-class women aged 25-plus. Not only is this group growing numerically but the steady post-war rise of married women's employment and the effects of sixteen years of the women's movement have meant that these women tend to have personal spending money beyond the purely domestic sphere. If the High Streets in Britain have witnessed a crop of Next, Principles and Country Casuals shops springing up to provide for these 'mature' women's fashion needs, so too the magazine world has begun to look to her custom. *Options* occupies a niche now in part shared by *Working Woman* (launched Autumn 1984), *Elle* (which launched in Autumn 1985, also looks towards *Cosmo*'s younger readers) and, to some extent, *She*, the median age of whose readers is 35.

She has lost some of its quirkiness but is still, in the words of editor, Eric Bailey, 'idiosyncratic' (*Guardian*, 19 February 1985). Domestic topics are covered but these are not what you'd buy *She* for. It's more notable for the somewhat unpredictable range of articles it carries, though they usually have a tendency to be stories of the elite or the eccentric rather than of everywoman. *She* tends towards a news look rather than towards the self-indulgence of colour photography and is thus both less glamorous and less aspirational than its competitors. *Elle*, on the other hand, creates in its pages, and espouses for its readers, the careful chic the French have long been renowned for, while *Working Woman* has a thrusting style reminiscent of its American namesake.

From the outset *Elle* had the advantage that it was a magazine 'concept' already known by many in Britain. Readers were familiar with French *Elle*'s fashion and cookery spreads, while amongst designers and the magazine trade the magazine has consistently been held up for its quality. As well as building on that estimable reputation (rather than trying the more precarious venture of starting afresh from the drawing board), Rupert Murdoch also made sure of an initial readership by including a preview of the British *Elle* in the *Sunday Times* magazine. In that way the magazine secured a high visibility amongst its target readership. (Such a ploy had been successfully used earlier by EMAP who brought out the first issue of *Just Seventeen* with *Smash Hits* and later included a preview of *Looks* with *Just Seventeen*.)

Working Woman, whose USA equivalent was unknown in Britain, has had a choppier ride. Whatever you think of the package, to 'come out' as primarily concerned with paid work is a more notable event, given the largely domestic history of women's magazines, than the launch of *Elle*, with its emphasis on style. For that reason, perhaps, it has been a trickier exercise getting the pitch right. The resignation of both publisher and ad director after '18 months of frustration' (*Campaign*, 15 November 1985), followed by the sale of the magazine and resignation of Audrey Slaughter as editor, would seem to be an indication of that.

The problem has been that, although the magazine declared that 'there are 10.2 million working women in Britain', it has geared itself to 'top and middle management' (plus aspirants) of whom there are very few indeed. Originally to be called *Verve*, rather significantly the title of a magazine in Shirley (*Superwoman*) Conran's novel *Lace*, the magazine has pushed self-motivation and drive.

Audrey Slaughter called *Working Woman* the magazine for 'realists'. To be deadly serious about career achievement, and money, may not in themselves be any bad thing for women. But an efficient, businesslike ethos shapes all aspects of the magazine, including fashion, food and entertainment, in a style that is unpalatable for most women. It thus offers *Cosmo*'s aspirations (several rungs up The Ladder) stripped bare of the latter's hedonism, hesitancies and tongue-in-cheek approach to life. Do some women really want or aspire to this sort of realism? Or is it not anyway, as Suzanne Lowry quipped, 'a soap opera image of success . . . . Liberation through clawing your way with scarlet nails to the Top' (*Guardian*, 20 September 1984).

What is disturbing about *Working Woman* is that, while it is not *anti*-feminism, it adopts the style of aspirational feminism Elizabeth Cagan describes (and decries). Superwoman is only the elitist and individual success story – 'I'm all right sisters' – which leaves untouched the deep problems for most women of how to satisfactorily combine 'home' and 'work' without being made to suffer for it.

And feminisms

It was partly in response to the inadequacy of the superwoman 'solution' and to the kind of magazine represented by *Working Woman* and *Cosmo* that *Everywoman* was launched (Spring 1985). It called itself 'the REAL WOMEN'S magazine'. But the small collective who produced the magazine was also aware that by the mid-1980s the climate of post-feminism (and hence of feminisms) had made *Spare Rib*'s heavy, sectarian editorial stance less tenable. There was a new generation of young women for whom the 1970s-style hard feminism – popularly referred to as 'that strident, serious "sister" stuff' (*Options* June 1984) – if not feminism *per se*, was inappropriate. Sarah Mower, writing about the new *Elle* magazine, suggested that 'sex, relationships and emotion are out of fashion as core subjects for young women's magazines'. Interpreted in a more feminist context, 'the personal is political' had also become *passé*.

The launch of *Women's Review* as well as *Everywoman* and the relaunch of *Spare Rib* were all responses to these changes. But what is also indicated is that, like most markets, the feminist magazine market is expanding and diversifying: different magazines address distinct groups on particular areas of interest. (As yet nevertheless the diversification is not, as is usually the case, for the sake of improving big company profits; cf. chapter 3).

Everywoman, focusing on news and current affairs and largely steering clear of 'the personal', pitches itself towards women who might not think of themselves as feminists but who are interested in a wider range of issues than the women's glossies deal in. But the magazine would also like to appeal to those who *are* feminists. As a *Guardian* article put it, '*Everywoman* treads a dangerous line in trying to be all things to all women' (11 March 1986, page 10). Whereas it probably succeeds with the former I'm doubtful, as I'll explain in a moment, of its appeal to the latter.

Cheaply produced, it has a plain, black-and-white look relying on a documentary use of photos. Its cover adopts full colour and often carries a woman's face, though not of the glamorous made-up variety; it features 'real women'. It doesn't offer quite the familiar address of the women's weeklies but is less intimidating than the old style *Spare Rib*. So too is it more liberal and politically diverse in the voices that it allows to speak: a Townswomen's Guild member, Conservative as well as Labour MPs. The heart of the magazine lies, I think, towards a campaigning and pressure-group feminism to improve conditions for women (whether maternity care or the work environment) and make women more visible and powerful within various institutions (whether in parliament or on the sports circuit). Its articles therefore tend towards the informational and as such are useful, but they are often without much critical debate for more seasoned feminists to cut their teeth on. Similarly, reviews are sketchy and *Everywoman*'s 'style' section on food, fashion, shopping, etc. (which themes are borrowed from the commercial glossies) seems tokenistic rather than an important element of the magazine's mix.

Even without the competition from *Everywoman* the almost impossible dilemmas *Spare Rib* was facing editorially (see chapter 8) meant that the magazine had to change. The readers' survey which was commissioned revealed that a high proportion of *Spare Rib*'s readers were younger than had been thought. (Undoubtedly at least some long-term readers had got fed up with the strident tone.) *Spare Rib* consequently redesigned its logo, cover and inside pages, notably selecting a designer from *The Face* to do that. And with the introduction of some new slots like 'Feminists' bedrooms' the surface feel of the magazine at least was lightened. The magazine became more 'user-friendly'. Some feminists, however, found no comfort at all in the redesigned *Spare Rib*. Ruth Wallsgrove, writing in the *New Statesman*, commented,

I don't blame *Spare Rib*, for they are only doing what everyone on the left is doing: rediscovering 'style' .... But what are we actually trying to do? Are we working on putting our ideas across clearly? Or are we trying to package a product we suspect isn't very attractive – by lying, or even removing altogether the nasty bits?

Ruth Wallsgrove went on to suggest that style is 'a shadow, fickle thing, no substitute for – well, you know, passion, commitment, and vision. Glossy magazines are made to be thrown away' (15 November 1985, page 24). And leftie feminist magazines should not be?

Though I'm inclined to agree that awkwardly adding 'style ' as a section to an otherwise newsy magazine as *Everywoman* does, or cosmetically giving a face lift to some bits of *Spare Rib*, is not wholly satisfactory, I do not agree that 'style' or design is a sugar coating that can be dispensed with by those with political 'vision'.

On the High Streets of Britain retailers have been discovering the importance of design in selling their products. That is, customers respond not simply to the quality of the product, but to the kind of packaging and to shop display and environment, all of which create the 'brand name' and an associated lifestyle.

Magazines, too, be they commercial glossies or more feminist magazines, are commodities. They have to sell to readers who are increasingly (though not necessarily consciously so) attuned to design and its differences. The difficulty for a feminist (or left) magazine is not the consideration of whether or not design *is* important but of establishing a design that fits comfortably with the 'vision' Ruth Wallsgrove talks about.

In contrast to *Everywoman* and *Spare Rib*, *Women's Review* has achieved a pleasing design fitting for the kind of magazine it is striving to be. Perhaps because *Women's Review* doesn't begin from a political position, and in market terms has a more clearly defined and simpler profile – to provide a female perspective on the arts and culture – it has been easier for it to create a more coherent look. Editorially it tends towards coverage of women's writing and interviews with authors (which since the idea for the magazine emerged from the 1984 International Feminist Book Fair is not surprising). Its articles on popular (as opposed to 'high') culture are fewer and sometimes promise more than they deliver but still *Women's Review* does try to take on board, intellectually and politically, contradictory aspects of femininity: the appeal of Madonna, romantic fiction, the rise of female body-building. These articles are ones *Spare Rib* in its purism always had difficulties in presenting, for to come up with a 'correct feminist line' on such phenomena usually means not to do justice to their complexity.

The market *Women's Review* appeals to is, however, a relatively small one and there seems a risk, which the magazine can hardly afford in the light of its financial difficulties, of it erring towards a too intellectual feminism which will further reduce the number of readers.

Nevertheless, what has become apparent since the launches of *Everywoman* and *Women's Review* is that *Spare Rib* no longer occupies the pre-eminent position it once held within feminist circles: in the late 1970s, it was obligatory to know what was going on in *Spare Rib*'s pages, even if you didn't read the magazine regularly. Yet it is more a gain than a loss that there are several nationally distributed feminist magazines (and many more newspapers, magazines and journals, like *Outwrite*, *Trouble and Strife*, *Wsafiri* and *Gossip* which are available through subscription or alternative bookshops). As Nicci Gerrard, one of the group who 'hold together' *Women's Review*, suggests, 'The more widespread the alternative ... the safer such publications become. Isolation makes us vulnerable' (*Guardian*, 11 March 1986, page 10).

It has also become clear that the social conditions of production for feminist magazines, since the demise of the Greater London Council (both *Women's Review* and *Spare Rib* were partly dependent on GLC grants) and in a context where other subsidies are hard to come by, are very different from when *Spare Rib* was establishing itself in the 1970s. Feminist magazines aiming for a widespread distribution profile have to be more commercially viable on the basis of sales and advertising revenue. This doesn't imply that they have to be the *same* as the commercial glossies but that they do have to measure up on the criteria that market demands, of attention not only to design but also to marketing. Marketing criteria require any magazine to be very clear about *whom* it is addressing. And selling the magazine to advertisers is at least as important as delivering a good editorial idea to readers. With the introduction of new technologies for typesetting and printing, making it easier and cheaper to publish high-quality but relatively small circulation magazines, the proliferation of feminist magazines (indeed, of all types of magazine) will certainly continue.

One (post-) feminist magazine I'd like to see is one which reworks some old themes to new ends. I'd like it to address two areas which have been neglected elsewhere. The first is what Sarah Mower describes as the unfashionable, that is, 'sex, relationships and emotion'. Personally, I feel that the way in which commercial magazines still monopolise those concerns (constantly assuming heterosexuality and the social norm of marriage and monogamy, and posing dilemmas and solutions in terms of the individual (cf. chapter 5)) is a problem that should be confronted. The second would be to engage with the 'mental chocolate' which women's magazines conventionally provide.

Women's Review, especially, is a visually engaging magazine but, for all that, it has a black-and-white, 'arty' look with ads for cultural events but no colourful consumer advertising. The commercial magazines still have the monopoly on colour and its visual pleasures, but what they construct is, on the whole, that oppressive nexus of femininity-desire-consumption (see chapter 4).

The tensions of emotional and personal life do find fictional expression in the novels and poetry some feminists are currently producing and in a range of semi-academic books (for example, Lynne Segal's *What Is To Be Done About The Family?* (1983), Sue Cartledge and Jo Ryan's *Sex and Love* (1983), Stephanie Dowrick and Sybil Grundberg's *Why Children?* (1980), and Ann Oakley's *Taking It Like A Woman* (1984). But there is no popular, non-academic, regular and public forum for a discussion of personal issues informed by a more radical politics than the glossies dare explore except, perhaps, in the *Guardian* women's page (now known on certain days as 'Open Space' or 'First Person'). Why is this so?

In the early days of the women's movement consciousness-raising groups and discussions of personal life were (whatever their shortcomings) part and parcel of most feminists' political involvement; by the 1980s the expansion and development of the women's movement has brought with it a 'professionalisation'. Inevitably and necessarily, 'the personal' has become partly separated from 'the political'. Any area of feminist politics in the 1980s has its own accumulated knowledges and skills. If the political touchstone at some level is still individual experience, for most of us the arena where we discuss and shape our 'politics' is different from the context in which we attempt to sort out our 'personal' lives.

In addition, there isn't a precedent for the choices it is now possible for some of us (mainly white, educated and middle-class) to make, and while that can be exhilarating it is also scary and sometimes paralysing. We can be caught either between the political 'shoulds' of feminism and our apparently 'unreformed' wants and desires; or between the pull of new but uncertain possibilities and that of old and comforting but nevertheless constraining or destructive patterns of living.

But with the separation of 'the political' and 'the personal' so these conflicts of personal life – around sexuality, family and work – have been returned to the semi-private sphere, where they risk becoming our 'weaknesses' and our 'guilty secrets'. As one way that mainly well-off feminists can work through some of these conflicts it is not surprising that feminist psychotherapy has been a growth area. I don't doubt the benefits of analysis but I am concerned that it can't and maybe ought not to be the 'answer' for everyone. For is it not another way in which personal problems are yet again individualised?

For others the conflicts are endlessly ploughed over between (women) friends. It is mainly in that context (of friendship as the new sisterhood) that we try to work out how to carve out our independent pathways, not according to some imposed feminist blueprint but as a way of life in accord with each of our personal histories – and dreams.

What I'd like to consider alongside these approaches is the possibility of thinking again about a more public and collective discussion of personal issues. Otherwise we continue to allow the glossy magazines and the popular press to define the parameters of personal life. We allow the space for an aspirational feminism, with its focus on individual opportunities and choice (super-woman hovering in the wings) and its tendency to believe that while we're all quietly and individually edging our way along a feminist pathway, men are shaping-up-very-nicely-thank-you, to become the public and acceptable voice of feminism (as in Betty Friedan's *The Second Stage*). And in so doing we make it more difficult for ourselves to ask certain troubling questions and to live in ways that do not meet the commonly assumed expectations about personal life.

Finally, I'd like a new magazine to strive to create non-oppressive visual forms of indulgent pleasures and fantasies, a new form of 'mental chocolate'. Unless we try to do that it is difficult to see how that nexus of femininity-desire-consumption which commercial magazines and their adverts trade in can be broken or how a different visual vocabulary around femininity and masculinity can be developed. Such a visual project would have to give high priority to colour, glossy paper and to advertising. It would probably involve re-using, making fun of and commenting on the colour and stylistic conventions customarily used by women's magazines rather than wholly breaking away from that format as *Spare Rib*, *Everywoman* and *Women's Review* have largely done. We might learn much from the 'style' and young women's magazines here as well as from the work of artists like Barbara Kruger, who parodies popular images from a feminist perspective. In order to finance that kind of magazine it would be necessary to be more catholic about the kinds of advertising admitted, whilst also trying to take issue with the ways in which most advertising represents gender. The post-modern reliance on retro styles which raid the past for its images and re-present them in contemporary contexts makes such a design and visual project more feasible. If *The Face* can exclude ads on aesthetic grounds and persuade advertisers to create ads apposite to 'the look' of *The Face* it ought not to be beyond the bounds of possibility (though admittedly more difficult because of the politics involved) to persuade advertisers to create ads which are more suitable for a feminist – post-feminist? – readership. After all, these days the feminist readership is a large one; more importantly, feminists also have a lot of money to spend.

Potential publishers, please take note.

Afterthought

As I wearily reached what I believed, somewhat optimistically as it turned out, was the home straight on this book, on an equally failing typewriter, my horoscope in *Woman* went as follows: 'There is always a danger that after a whole year of restraint, effort, control and forbearance, you will, when in sight of victory, blow the lot!' (No, I wasn't on the verge of throwing it in the dustbin though I was on the brink of something – a toss up between physical collapse or getting very drunk before I'd quite finished.) 'Don't let anyone give you the satisfaction of riling you on a minor point now, just when many of your ships are limping into port! *Contacts*: bragging. *Spirits*: flagging. *Outlet*: shopping' (22 September 1984).

Are horoscopes and feminism compatible? I wish they were, but while others, I hope, ponder the issue and take up the more general challenges I've posed I'm, well – belatedly off shopping, of course.

Tables and appendix

Notes on tables and appendix

1   Tables I, II and IV are largely taken from the Institute of Practitioners in Advertising National Readership Surveys (JICNARS, Joint Industry Committee for National Readership Surveys). These have been carried out from 1956 and are currently done twice yearly. Not all magazines are included however: the long-established *Lady*, for example, was only added in 1984.

2   Most magazines submit their circulations to the Audit Bureau of Circulations (whose figures the NRS relies on). D.C. Thomson's magazines, *Spare Rib* and *Tatler* and a few others do not, hence some gaps in Table II. *Willings Press Guide* (annual) and *BRAD* (*British Rate and Data*, for advertisers and published monthly) also provide circulations and more comprehensive details of currently published magazines.

3   In Table II:
    Ideal Home and *Slimming* are each the 'leaders' in their respective groups (of 'house' and slimming' magazines respectively), the range of which I've excluded from the table – *House and Garden, Homes and Garden; Successful Slimming, Slimmer Silhouette*, etc.

4   In Table III:
    Given that women are not usually 'head of household' there are problems about the use and interpretation of 'class' labels which are not their own but usually husbands' or fathers'. Nevertheless they provide some scale for comparisons. For Social grades according to the NRS see table on opposite page.

5   In general I have simplified all numbers to three figures, aiming less at statistical accuracy than to give numerical shape to some of the patterns and trends discussed earlier.

6   NA means circulation figures are not available.

	social status	*head of household occupation*
A	upper middle class	higher managerial, administrative or professional
B	middle class	intermediate managerial, administrative or professional
C_1	lower middle class	supervisory or clerical and junior
C_2	skilled working class	skilled manual
D	working class	semi- and unskilled manual workers
E	those at lowest level of subsistence	state pensioners or widows, casual, lowest-grade workers.

Social grades according to the NRS.

Table I Readership – magazines and newspapers   January – June 1984

| Unweighted sample | | | Total 13.9 | | Men 6.41 | | Women 7.44 | | Housewives 6.38 | |
Estimated population 15+	(1000s) (1000s)		44,100		21,100		22,900		19,400	
	Circulation ABC (1000s)	Readers per copy	1000s	%	1000s	%	1000s	%	1000s	%
Sun	4,170	3.0	12,300	28.0	6,580	31.2	5,740	25.0	4,730	24.5
Daily Mirror	3,350	2.9	9,820	22.3	5,320	25.2	4,500	19.6	3,720	19.2
Daily Telegraph	1,260	2.5	3,180	7.2	1,720	8.2	1,460	6.4	1,260	6.5
Guardian	473	3.4	1,630	3.7	943	4.5	683	3.0	580	3.0
News of the World	4,250	2.7	11,600	26.3	6,000	28.4	5,590	24.4	4,640	24.0
+ magazine			10,300	23.4	5,290	25.1	5,040	22.0	4,150	21.4
Sunday Express	2,600	2.8	7,320	16.6	3,690	17.5	3,620	15.8	3,090	16.0
+ magazine			7,020	15.9	3,490	16.5	3,530	15.4	2,960	15.3
Sunday Times	1,310	3.0	3,900	8.9	2,160	10.2	1,780	7.8	1,520	7.9
+ magazine			4,100	9.3	2,170	10.3	1,930	8.4	1,620	8.3
Mayfair	192	7.0	1,340	3.0	1,230	5.8	106	0.5	100	0.5
Fiesta	275	4.8	1,320	3.0	1,170	5.5	148	0.6	134	0.7
TV Times	3,110	3.2	10,000	22.7	4,410	20.9	5,610	24.4	4,640	24.0
Radio Times	3,210	3.0	9,530	21.6	4,220	20.0	5,300	23.1	4,460	23.0
Woman's Own	1,210	3.8	5,510	12.5	871	4.1	4,640	20.2	3,790	19.6
Woman's Weekly	1,280	2.5	3,740	8.5	463	2.2	3,280	14.3	2,810	14.5
Woman and Home	592	4.1	2,750	6.3	303	1.4	2,450	10.7	2,230	11.5
Cosmopolitan	387	4.8	2,280	5.2	410	1.9	1,870	8.1	1,260	6.5

Table II Circulations – women's magazines   1950–1985

Frequency	Title		Launch date	Publisher	Price 1986	Circulation (1000s) 1950	1957	1965	1973	1978	1981	1984	Six months 1985
Romance/fiction													
M	True Romances / True Story / Woman's Story	Argus women's three	1934 / 1922 / ?	Argus Press	70p	NA	NA	NA	438	338	298	244	241
W	Red Letter / Secrets / (My Weekly)	Feminine three	1929 / 1932 / 1910	D.C. Thomson	20p	NA	NA	311	250	170	100	88.1	64.5
	Loving		1970	IPC	30p				211	152	105	91.3	82.3
Young women/pop													
W	Jackie	Thomson's teenage three	1963	D.C. Thomson	24p			250	1,000	550	439	384	329
W	Blue Jeans		1977	D.C. Thomson	26p					NA	211	179	176
W	Patches		1979	D.C. Thomson	26p						157	131	127
W	Just Seventeen		1983	Emap	45p							268	270
	Oh Boy!		1976	IPC	32p					NA	146	129	141
	My Guy		1978								202		
Mass weeklies													
W	My Weekly		1910	D.C. Thomson	22p	188	87.3	305	858	872	786	713	696
W	Woman's Realm		1958	IPC	27p		(1958) 1,300	1300	951	781	660	619	637
W	Woman		1937	IPC	33p	2,150	3,480	2,960	1,760	1,540	1,330	1,150	1,120
W	Woman's Own		1932	IPC	33p	1,760	2,560	2,150	1,570	1,600	1,410	1,190	1,147
W	Woman's Weekly		1911	IPC	30p	1,600	1,760	1,480	1,490	1,460	1,380	1,380	1,390
W	People's Friend		1869	D.C. Thomson	22p	NA	NA	425	665	700	670	656	653
Young women/Non-domestic													
M	Look Now		1972	Carlton	70p				203	198	149	140	129
M	Over 21		1972	MS Publishing	75p				106	136	107	100	91.9
M	Honey		1960	IPC	80p			193	189	195	163	122	118
M	19		1968	IPC	75p				178	177	140	132	128
M	Company		1978	Nat. Mag.	80p					(1979) 284	252	212	214
M	Cosmopolitan		1972	Nat. Mag.	80p				349	440	435	387	395
M	Woman's World		1977	Carlton	80p					288	246	213	222
Domestic													
M	She		1955	Nat. Mag.	70p		300	299	302	292	257	221	228
M	Annabel		1966	D.C. Thomson	55p				160	257	243	184	172
M	Living		1967	Standbrook	60p				608	516	485	423	411
M	Family Circle		1964	Standbrook	49p			779	1,060	718	635	543	566
M	Woman and Home		1926	IPC	75p	957	776	722	655	645	603	600	611
M	Options		1982	Carlton	90p						220	221	
M	Good Housekeeping		1922	Nat. Mag.	85p	200	207	159	257	333	349	353	353
M	Woman's Journal		1927	IPC	85p	373	258	222	179	188	247	237	237
M	Vogue		1916	Condé Nast	£1.60	143	130	139	99	98	116	137	164
	Harpers Bazaar		1929				56.5	42.9					
M	Harpers & Queen		1970	Nat. Mag.	£1.70	NA	50.0	NA	60	64	68	88	103
	Queen		1861										
M	Ideal Home		1920	IPC	90p	113	233	191	184	197	208	207	202
F	Slimming		1969	S.M. Publications	80p				330	350	311	277	287
W	The Lady		1885	Lady	43p	76.5	81.4	79.1	76.0	71.0	73.9	71.1	76.1
M	Spare Rib		1972	Spare Rib	80p				Estimate 20–30.0				

Table III Recent launches

Frequency	Title	Launch Date	Publisher	Price 1986
M	*Working Woman*	Autumn 1984	Wintaur Publications	£1.25
M	*Everywoman*	Spring 1985	Everywoman	60p
M	*Women's Review*	Autumn 1985	Women's Review	£1.00
M	*Elle*	Autumn 1985	News International – Hachette	£1.00
F	*Mizz*	Spring 1985	IPC	45p
M	*Looks*	Autumn 1985	EMAP	70p
W	*Chat*	Autumn 1985	ITP	18p
M	*Fitness*	Spring 1984	Stonehart Leisure, bought 1985 by Cover Publications	£1.20

Table IV Readership profiles: women's magazines January–June 1984, women readers only (percentages)

	Age						Social grade					
	15-24	*25-34*	*35-44*	*45-54*	*55-64*	*65+*	*A*	*B*	*C₁*	*C₂*	*D*	*E*
Estimated population aged 15+	19	16	15	13	14	22	3	13	23	27	19	15
Woman's Weekly	15	13	14	15	17	25	2	13	25	28	18	13
Woman's Own	25	19	14	13	12	16	2	13	27	29	18	11
Woman	26	20	14	14	12	14	2	13	26	31	17	10
Woman's Realm	17	14	15	15	16	22	2	13	25	30	18	13
My Weekly	13	12	14	15	18	28	1	9	22	30	22	17
People's Friend	6	9	11	15	21	38	1	7	20	27	22	22
Woman and Home	14	14	16	18	19	18	5	21	27	23	15	8
Family Circle	19	24	22	16	12	7	4	19	28	27	15	7
Annabel	25	16	14	11	16	18	3	13	24	31	18	12
Good Housekeeping	18	21	19	15	14	13	8	27	31	18	11	5
Ideal Home	20	23	20	14	13	11	7	24	25	24	13	6
Options	44	22	17	8	6	3	7	21	33	24	11	4
She	29	20	17	16	9	9	6	20	29	26	13	6
Cosmopolitan	49	22	13	9	5	2	6	19	36	23	11	5
Slimming	29	25	22	15	7	3	3	15	29	32	16	5
Harpers & Queen	26	18	16	15	15	10	11	30	29	19	8	3
Jackie	64	8	15	8	2	3	2	10	19	36	21	12
Argus women's three	37	20	14	12	9	8	less than 0.5	5	17	37	27	14

Tables and appendix

Table V Advertising expenditure – magazines and newspapers, 1982

	£ millions
Daily Mirror	56.5
Sun	53.8
Daily Telegraph	38.8
Guardian	12.3
News of the World	17.2
Sunday Magazine	25.5
Sunday Express	25.7
Sunday Express Magazine	27.9
Sunday Times	21.0
Sunday Times Magazine	26.4
TV Times	30.0
Radio Times	23.4
Woman's Own	16.6
Woman's Weekly	8.4
Woman and Home	0.5
Cosmopolitan	0.7

Source: *Admap*, February 1983

The publications above, up to and including *Woman's Weekly*, are in the Top 30 list. The majority of the next twenty titles, including *Woman and Home* and *Cosmopolitan*, are women's monthly magazines.

The figures are based on card-rates for advertising. In the particular case of the colour supplements card-rates have been estimated to be 40 per cent *above* the actual sums paid by advertisers.

Appendix
The capitalist cake; or who owns whom and what

D.C. Thomson & Co., Dundee

Newspaper and magazine printers and publishers, e.g. women's
magazines and children's comics.
Established 1905; private company.
Nominal capital £6,000,000.
Sales £59,261,000 (31 March 1982).
Employees 3,000.

Standbrook Publications, London

Established 1962; private company.
Nominal capital £10,000.
Subsidiary of International Thomson Publishing ultimately
controlled by International Thomson Organisation, Toronto,
Canada. The latter is an information and publishing business
with strong interests in travel and natural resources. In Britain
they also own Thomson Holidays, Hamish Hamilton, Michael
Joseph and Sphere publishers, Britannia Airways and
Thomson Directory.

National Magazine Company, London

Publishers of good housekeeping books (Ebury Press) as well as
women's magazines.
Established 1910; private company.
Nominal capital £300,000.
Sales £46,000,000 (31 December 1982).
Employees 487.
Subsidiary of Hearst Corporation USA, which also owns Comag
(i.e. Condé Nast and National Magazine's combined
distributor).

IPC Magazines, London

Publish fifty magazines.
Established 1961 (though component company in 1891); private
company.
Nominal capital £3,230,000.
Sales £147,000,000 (1982).
Employees 3,000.

Subsidiary of International Corporation who owns the USA publishers Cahners, who publish specialist trade magazines and who are ultimately controlled by Reed International. The latter used to own the Mirror Group of Newspapers and Sanderson's fabrics. They still own Twyfords loos, Hamlyn books and Crown paints – among other things.

Argus Press plc, London

Newspaper and periodical publishers, book and directory publishers and general printers. Responsible for *I-Spy* books.
Established 1982; public company.
Authorised capital £2,000,000.
Sales £34,706,000.
Employees 1,255.
Subsidiary of Argus Press Holdings plc ultimately controlled by the British Electric Traction Company plc, which is an industrial holding company for subsidiaries engaged in consumer and capital electronics, entertainment and leisure, printing and publishing, etc. They own Thames TV (50 per cent), Advance cleaners and laundries, Wembley Stadium Ltd and Rediffusion.

Condé Nast Publications Ltd, London

Publishers of magazines.
Established 1917; private company.
Nominal capital £250,000.
Sales £12,600,000 (31 December 1982).
Employees 222.
Subsidiary of Condé Nast Inc. New York, ultimately controlled by Patriot-News USA.

News International, London

Parent of group of subsidiaries as printers, publishers, papermakers, transport services and travel agents.
Publish *News of the World, Sun, The Times, The Sunday Times*
Established 1843; private company.
Nominal capital £22,000,000.
Sales £411,809,006 (1983).
Employees 11,140.
Subsidiary of Newscorp Investments Ltd controlled by the News Corporation of Australia.

ITP, London

Independent Television Publications, publish *TV Times* and
    Look In.
Established 1967; private company.
Nominal capital £100,000.
Sales £58,207,325.
Employees 245.

EMAP National Publications, Peterborough

Publish a range of magazines including *Bike, Camera* and *Creative
    Photography, Educational Computing, Steam Railway.*
Part of East Midland Allied Press plc, a holding company for
    printers and publishers.

(Information extracted from: Kompass *Register of British Industry
and Commerce, 1985*, Kompass; *Britain's Top 20,000 Companies*,
Dun & Bradstreet, 1985; *Who Owns Whom 1985*, Dun &
Bradstreet, 1986.)

Bibliography

Many of the readings below cut across chapter areas. I've listed them in this way to guide further study.

Chapter 1 Introduction: survival skills and daydreams

Adams, Carol and Laurikietis, Rae (1980), *The Gender Trap 3: Messages and Images*, Virago, London.
Adamson, Lesley (1977), 'Cooking and sewing – the woman's world', *Guardian*, 3 November.
Berger, John (1972), *Ways of Seeing*, Penguin, Harmondsworth.
Braithwaite, Brian and Barrell, Joan (1979), *The Business of Women's Magazines*, Associated Business Press, London.
Connell, Myra (1981), 'Reading Romance', MA thesis, University of Birmingham.
Coward, Rosalind (1983), *Female Desire*, Paladin, London.
Curran, Charles (1965), 'Journalism for squaws', *Spectator*, 19 November.
Ferguson, Marjorie (1978), 'Imagery and ideology: the cover photographs of traditional women's magazines', in Gay Tuchman, Arlene Kaplan Daniels and James Benet (eds), *Hearth and Home*, Oxford University Press, New York.
Ferguson, Marjorie (1983), 'Learning to be a woman's woman', *New Society*, 21 April.
Greer, Germaine (1972), *The Female Eunuch*, Paladin, London.
Hall, Stuart, Hobson, Dorothy, Lowe, Andy and Willis, Paul (eds) (1980), *Culture, Media, Language*, Hutchinson, London.
Hughes-Hallett, Lucy (1982) 'The cosy secret of a jolly good Reed', *The Standard*, 8 February.
King, Josephine and Stott, Mary (1977), *Is This Your Life?*, Virago, London.
Lefebvre, Henri (1971), *Everday Life in the Modern World*, Allen Lane, London.
McRobbie, Angela (1977), '*Jackie*', stencilled paper, Centre for Contemporary Cultural Studies, University of Birmingham.
McRobbie, Angela and McCabe, (1982) Trisha, *Feminism is Fun: An Adventure Story for Girls*, Routledge & Kegan Paul, London.
Reed, Jane (1982), 'The story so far', *Guardian*, 20 October.
Root, Jane (1983), *Pictures of Women: Sexuality*, Pandora, London.
Sharpe, Sue (1976), *Just Like a Girl*, Penguin, Harmondsworth.
Tolson, Andrew (1977), *The Limits of Masculinity*, Tavistock, London.
Toynbee, Polly (1977), 'At the end of the happy ever after trail', *Guardian*, 21 June.
White, Cynthia (1977), *Royal Commission on the Press, the Women's Periodical Press in Britain 1946-76*, Working Paper 4, HMSO, London.

Chapter 2 Looking back – with thoughts on the present

Adams, Carol (1982), *Ordinary Lives A Hundred Years Ago*, Virago, London.
Cooper, Susan (1964), 'Snoek Piquante', in Michael Sissons and Philip French (eds), *The Age of Austerity*, Penguin, Harmondsworth.
Dancyger, Irene (1978), *A World of Women*, Gill & Macmillan, Dublin.

Davidoff, Leonora, L'Esperance, Jean and Newby, Howard (1976), 'Landscape with figures: home and community in English society', in Juliet Mitchell and Ann Oakley (eds), *The Rights and Wrongs of Women*, Penguin, Harmondsworth.

Drawbell, James (1968), *Time on My Hands*, Macdonald, London.

Hall, Catherine (1982), 'The butcher, the baker, the candlestickmaker: the shop and the family in the Industrial Revolution', in Elizabeth Whitelegg *et al* (eds), *The Changing Experience of Women*, Martin Robertson, London.

Hoggart, Richard (1963), *The Uses of Literacy*, Penguin, Harmondsworth.

Leman, Joy (1980), '"The advice of a real friend": codes of intimacy and oppression in women's magazines 1937-55', *Women's Studies International Quarterly*, vol. 3, no. 1.

Minns, Raynes (1980), *Bombers and Mash: The Domestic Front 1939-45*, Virago, London.

Morris, Rupert (1985), '*The Lady* marks a stylish centenerary', *The Times*, 20 February.

Marwick, Arthur (1982), *British Society Since 1945*, Penguin, Harmondsworth.

Riley, Denise (1981), 'The free mothers', *History Workshop Journal*, no. 11.

Sissons, Michael and French, Philip (eds) (1964), *The Age of Austerity*, Penguin, Harmondsworth.

Spence, Jo (1978), 'What do people do all day?', *Screen Education*, no 29.

White, Cynthia (1970), *Women's Magazines 1693-1968*, Michael Joseph, London.

Winship, Janice (1984), 'Nation before family: *Woman*, the National Home Weekly, 1945-1953', in *Formations of Nation and People*, Routledge & Kegan Paul, London.

Chapter 3   Selling and buying

Abrams, Mark (1959a), 'The home-centred society', *Listener*, 26 November.

Abrams, Mark (1959b), *The Teenage Consumer*, Press Exchange, London.

Dix, Carol (1975), 'Nova news is bad news', *Guardian*, 2 August.

Douglas, J.W.B. (1956), 'The feminists mop up', *The Economist*, vol. 179, no. 5879.

Drawbell, James (1968), *Time on My Hands*, Macdonald, London.

Economist (1953), 'Modes and morals', *The Economist*, 28 November.

Economist (1959), 'Petticoat battleground', *The Economist*, 21 November.

French, Marilyn (1978), *The Women's Room*, Jonathan Cape, London.

Friedan, Betty (1963), *The Feminine Mystique*, Gollancz, London.

Grieve, Mary (1964), *Millions Made My Story*, Gollanz, London.

Ingham, Mary (1981), *Now We Are Thirty: Women of the Breakthrough Generation*, Methuen, London.

McClelland, W.D. (1965), 'Women's press in Britain', *Gazette*, vol. II, no. 2/3.

Mitchell, Juliet (1971), *Woman's Estate*, Penguin, Harmondsworth.

Myrdal, Alva and Klein, Viola (1956), *Women's Two Roles: Home and Work*, Routledge & Kegan Paul, London.

Scott, Rosemary (1976), *The Female Consumer*, Associated Business Programmes, London.

White, Cynthia (1970), *Women's Magazines 1693-1968*, Michael Joseph, London.

Wilson, Elizabeth (1980), *Only Halfway to Paradise: Women in Postwar Britain 1945-68*, Tavistock, London.

Winship, Janice (1981), 'Woman becomes an "individual" – femininity and consumption in women's magazines 1954-1969', stencilled paper, Centre for Contemporary Cultural Studies, University of Birmingham.

Chapter 4 Work and leisure: feminine pleasures

Barthes, Roland (1972), *Mythologies*, Jonathan Cape, London.
Berger, John (1972), *Ways of Seeing*, Penguin, Harmondsworth.
Chappell, Helen (1983), 'Big Sister', *New Society*, 5 May.
Equal Opportunities Commission (1982), *Adam and Eve*, Equal Opportunities Commission, Manchester.
Goffman, Erving (1979), *Gender Advertisements*, Macmillan, London.
Hayne, Beverley (1981), 'Dying for a chocolate ... but what a way to go!', *Company*, September.
Holland, Patricia (1983), 'The page three girl speaks to women, too', *Screen*, vol. 24, no. 3.
Millum, Trevor (1975), *Images of Women*, Chatto & Windus, London.
Myers, Kathy (1982), 'Fashion 'n' Passion', *Screen*, vol. 23, no. 3/4.
Myers, Kathy (1983), 'Understanding advertisers', in Howard Davis and Paul Walton (eds), *Language, Image, Media*, Basil Blackwell, Oxford.
Pollock, Griselda (1977), 'What's wrong with images of women?', *Screen Education*, no. 24.
White, Cynthia (1977), *Royal Commission on the Press, the Women's Periodical Press in Britain 1946-76*, Working Paper 4, HMSO, London.
Williamson, Judith (1978), *Decoding Advertisements*, Marion Boyars, London.
Winship, Janice (1980), 'Advertising in women's magazines, 1956-74', stencilled paper, Centre for Contemporary Cultural Studies, University of Birmingham.

Chapter 5 Between women

Batsleer, Janet (1981), 'Pulp in the pink', *Spare Rib*, August, no. 109.
Cecil, Mirabel (1974), *Heroines in Love 1750-1974*, Michael Joseph, London.
Ferguson, Marjorie (1983), *Forever Feminine*, Heinemann, London.
Ho, Mary Louise (1981), 'In the tradition of the wise women', *Spare Rib*, February, no. 103.
Kent, Robin (1979), *Aunt Agony Advises*, W.H. Allen, London.
Makins, Peggy (1975), *The Evelyn Home Story*, Collins, Glasgow.
Ratcliff, Rosemary (1969), *Dear Worried Brown Eyes*, Robert Maxwell.
Sarsby, Jacqueline (1983), *Romantic Love and Society*, Penguin, Harmondsworth.

Chapter 6 *Woman's Own*: 'Britain's best read magazine'

Bryan, Beverley (1985), *The Heart of the Race*, Virago, London.
Ferguson, Marjorie (1983), *Forever Feminine*, Heinemann, London.
Harris, Martyn (1984), 'How unemployment affects people', *New Society*, 19 January, p. 88.
Oakley, Ann (1981), *Subject Women*, Martin Robertson, Oxford.
Onwurah, Chinyelu (1985), 'Sexist, racist, and above all, capitalist', *Guardian*, 3 September.
Polan, Brenda (1979), 'The toughie at the top', *Guardian*, 17 August.
Simmons, Diana (1984), *Princess Di, the National Dish*, Pluto, London.
Wilson, Amrit (1978), *Finding A Voice*, Virago, London.
Winship, Janice (1983), 'Femininity and women's magazines', Unit 6, *U221 The Changing Experience of Women*, Open University, Milton Keynes.

Chapter 7   *Cosmopolitan*: 'who could ask for more?'

Braithwaite, Brian and Barrell, Joan (1979), *The Business of Women's Magazines*, Associated Business Press, London.

Brown, Helen Gurley (1963), *Sex and the Single Girl*, Frederick Muller, London.

Brunsdon, Charlotte (1982), 'A subject for the seventies', *Screen*, vol. 23, no. 3/4.

Brunt, Rosalind (1982), '"An immense verbosity": permissive sexual advice in the 1970s', in Rosalind Brunt and Caroline Rowan (eds), *Feminism, Culture and Politics*, Lawrence & Wishart, London.

Carter, Angela (1979), *The Sadeian Woman*, Virago, London.

Coward, Rosalind (1978), '"Sexual liberation" and the family', *m/f*, no. 1.

Ehrenreich, Barbara and English, Deirdre (1979), *For Her Own Good*, Pluto, London.

Faust, Beatrice (1981), *Women, Sex and Pornography*, Penguin, Harmondsworth.

Frankl, George (1974), *The Failure of the Sexual Revolution*, Kahn & Averill, London.

Hodson, Phillip (1984), *Men . . .*, BBC, London.

Chapter 8   *Spare Rib*: 'a women's liberation magazine'

Allen, Sandra, Sanders, Lee and Wallis, Jan (eds) (1974), *Conditions of Illusion: Papers from the Women's Movement*, Feminist Books, Leeds.

Barrett, Michele and McIntosh, Mary (1982), *The Anti-Social Family*, Verso, London.

Braithwaite, Brian and Barrell, Joan (1979), *The Business of Women's Magazines*, Associated Business Press, London.

Campbell, Beatrix (1980), 'Feminist sexual politics', *Feminist Review*, no. 5.

Coote, Anna and Campbell, Beatrix (1982), *Sweet Freedom: The Struggle for Women's Liberation*, Picador, London.

Davis, Angela (1982), *Women, Race and Class*, Women's Press, London.

Fell, Alison (ed.) (1979), *Hard Feelings: Fiction & Poetry from Spare Rib*, Women's Press, London.

Feminist Anthology Collective (1981), *No Turning Back: Writings from the Women's Liberation Movement 1975-80*, Women's Press, London.

Guardian (1977), 'What do women really want?', *Guardian*, 23 June.

hooks, bell (1981), *Ain't I a Woman: Black Women and Feminism*, Pluto, London.

Kanter, Hannah, Lefanu, Sarah, Shah, Shaila and Spedding, Carole (1984), *Sweeping Statements: Writings frm the Women's Liberation Movement 1981-1983*, Women's Press, London.

Rich, Adrienne (1984), 'Compulsory heterosexuality and lesbian existence', in Ann Snitow, Christine Stansell and Sharon Thompson (eds), *Desire*, Virago, London.

Rowbotham, Sheila (1983), *Dreams and Dilemmas*, Virago, London.

Rowe, Marsha (ed.) (1982), *Spare Rib Reader*, Penguin, Harmondsworth.

'Spare Rib' (1982), *Camerawork*, March, no. 24.

Toynbee, Polly (1982), 'Lesbianism is a central issue', *Guardian*, 23 July.

Wandor, Michelene (1972), *The Body Politic: Women's Liberation in Britain 1969-72*, Stage 1, London.

Wilson, Elizabeth (1980), *Only Halfway to Paradise: Women in Postwar Britain 1945-1968*, Tavistock, London.

Chapter 9 Shifting categories: magazines in the 1980s

Ardill, Susan and O'Sullivan, Sue (1985), 'Dizzy pace in women's publishing', *New Statesman*, 25 October.

Cagan, Elizabeth (1978), 'The selling of the women's movement', *Women's Studies International Quarterly* vol. 8.

Campbell, Beatrix (1984), *Wigan Pier Revisited*, Women's Press, London.

Cartledge, Sue and Ryan, Jo (1983), *Sex and Love*, Women's Press, London.

Conran, Shirley (1977), *Superwoman*, Penguin, Harmondsworth.

Conran, Shirley (1982), *Lace*, Sidgwick & Jackson, London.

Farmer, Frank (1981), 'The effect of colour supplements on women's magazines', *Admap*, August.

Gerrard, Nicci (1986), 'Small noises, loud voices', *Guardian*, 11 March.

Hebdige, Dick (1985), 'The bottom line on Planet One', *Ten:8*, no. 19, Summer.

Karpf, Ann (1985), 'Do the glossies gloss over feminism?', *New Statesman*, 1 November.

McKay, Ron (1984a), '*Just Seventeen*: glory without the schmaltz', *Campaign*, 1 June.

McKay, Ron (1984b), 'Slaughter plans to capture the working AB woman', *Campaign*, 16 March.

Mower, Sarah (1985), 'Elle puts the faintheart out of fashion', *Guardian*, 7 October.

Oakley, Ann (1984), *Taking It Like A Woman*, Jonathan Cape, London.

O'Sullivan, Sue (1982), 'Ideological politics 1969-72', *Feminist Review*, no. 11.

Polan, Brenda (1985), 'Sally free and easy', *Guardian*, 4 April.

Rawsthorn, Alice (1985), 'IPC: is it too late to ring the changes?', *Campaign*, 22 November.

Sanders, John (1983), 'Teen magazines: reflection of the frightening eighties', *Campaign*, 25 February.

Segal, Lynne (1983), *What Is To Be Done About the Family?*, Penguin, Harmondsworth.

Wallsgrove, Ruth (1985), 'Politics is this year's colours', *New Statesman*, 15 November.

Winship, Janice (1983), '"Options – for the way you want to live now", or a magazine for superwoman', *Theory, Culture and Society*, vol. 1, no. 3.

Winship, Janice (1985), '"A girl needs to get streetwise": magazines for the 1980s', *Feminist Review*, no. 21, Winter.

Index